TEACHING ART TO CHILDREN

Boston
Allyn and Bacon, Inc.

BLANCHE JEFFERSON

Associate Professor of Education
University of Pittsburgh

Teaching art
to children

THE VALUES OF CREATIVE EXPRESSION

To my husband,
WILLIAM L. JEFFERSON,
whose suggestions and comments
were of inestimable value
in the writing of this book

N 350
J 45 t

First Printing .... September 1959
Second Printing .... September 1960
Third Printing .... May 1961

Preface

LEADING ART EDUCATORS believe that creative expression is the best basis for art education because it is the method that does the most to develop the child as an individual and as a member of a democratic society. Modern educators teach this point of view in their art education classes to both prospective and in-service teachers. There is, however, a wide discrepancy between what these leaders believe and teach and what is actually practiced with children in most elementary classrooms.

Educators and others concerned with the creative and mental development of children have often heard the term "creative expression" associated with modern art education. Much has been said and written about it. They feel that they want to be associated with a process which has received so much acclaim. I have heard teachers using the term to describe a wide variety of ways of working with children in art. The term "creative expression" in

art has become popular.   Its use is a little like the use of the word
"democracy."   Most governments say their methods of governing
and of dealing with people are the most democratic.   They believe
it — no matter how dictatorial the situation is, no matter how little
opportunity for choice the people may have.

I have visited scores of art classes in many different school
systems and have found this inconsistency in all too many of them.
In talking with the teachers and art supervisors before watching the
various classes in progress, I have been assured by them that creative expression was the method used by them in teaching art in their
classes and throughout each of the different school systems.   The
type of art experience I saw was, most frequently, not a creative
one.   In many cases it was a teacher-directed process resulting in
art work that was all alike except for some small choice the child
could make, such as: "Color it any way you wish," or "Choose any
of these three (given) designs to put on the dress," or "Make any
design you wish on the umbrella in the picture."   The teacher felt
that as long as the child had some choice, no matter how small and
insignificant, that this was creative expression.   In other situations
creative expression was taught as very limited topics assigned by
the teacher to the children.   Typical examples are: "Draw a flower
in a vase," or "Draw a picture of yourself catching a ball," or "Draw
a house."   These allow for some limited choice, but since they do
not *originate* with the child — are not *his* choices — they do not fit
under the kind of experience called creative expression.

Strongly indicated to me was the need to clarify the different
methods of teaching art and to define specifically what creative expression involves — what it is and what it is not.   This book attempts
to differentiate among the methods of art education, describing and
identifying each.

The second purpose undertaken in the writing of this book
was to present the values and implications of creative methods and
processes in such a way as to impress them deeply upon teachers and
encourage them to abandon or reject other bases for art work.

Many teachers know something about creative expression but
not enough of the deep implications in such methods to be *convinced*
that they are best for children.   If they did, they would not resort
to other processes.   In addition to the emphasis placed upon the
reasons, values, and implications of creative expression the first area

of the text also includes implications for children in other methods of teaching art.   It is not enough to describe only the *best* ways.   Educators need to know what methods are best, but they also need to know what processes are not acceptable and why, lest they use some of these methods because they know of no reason why they should not.

The third purpose of this book is to make clear the role of the teacher in creative expression and to indicate how the teacher puts creative expression into practice with children.   Teachers may be so aware of the freedom that must be given to children to do their art work in their own way and from their own ideas that they assume they do no teaching and have no part in the process.   Because of this limitation of knowledge, some teachers reject creative expression.   They are professional men and women educated to take an active role of leadership in the teaching-learning situation.   They cannot accept such a withdrawal status — and they are right.

Teachers need to teach, but there are different ways in which this can be accomplished.   The areas of creative expression have ways that are peculiar to them and entirely different from the ways skill subjects are taught.   Teachers need to know what these ways are, and how they are to operate with children in guiding the learning that accompanies the outpouring type of activity that every good art experience should be.   When specific help is not given teachers in this important matter, they tend to feel that their role is a negative one.   They have so frequently been told what not to do, and to let the child find his own way, that they are afraid to do anything.   I have heard teachers ask: "Then, must we never teach the child anything?   Just let him go ahead?" and "If the teacher is not supposed to show the child how to do something, or make suggestions, why do we pay professional people to teach art?   Why don't we just let a clerk or the janitor distribute the supplies to the children?"   Such attitudes have come from a lack of emphasis upon what the teacher does and how she does it.

Along with this it is important to know what child art is, how it differs from adult art, and what the peculiar qualities of child art are.   Many adults feel dissatisfied with children's art and are eager to have children change their drawings to conform with adult ideas because they do not understand and appreciate children's graphic expressions.   It is necessary to know not only art education methods and processes but also the creative products resulting from these practices. No matter how much a person may know of why he should function in a certain way with children, he is blocked if he cannot approve and appreciate the resulting drawings and paintings. Processes and products are interdependent.

ACKNOWLEDGMENTS

First, I want to express my appreciation to all the children with whom I have had the joy and privilege of working, for the inspiration of their enthusiasm, for their trust, and for the many things I have learned from them which have contributed to this text. I am also indebted to children for the use of their art work as illustrations for this book.

Many teachers have cooperated in providing both knowledge and illustrations. They have told me pertinent facts about the personality and background of certain individual children, which add a great deal to the value of the interpretation and explanation of these children's art work. Teachers have also helped provide illustrations for the text by making it possible for me to photograph children and teachers working on art activities.

I appreciate the cooperation of school administrators in providing the facilities of their schools and their staffs for some of the materials and illustrations for this text. I especially want to thank the children, teachers, and administrators of:

Keith School, State Teachers College, Indiana, Pennsylvania
Public Schools, Vandergrift, Pennsylvania
Public Schools, Pittsburgh, Pennsylvania
Public Schools, New Kensington, Pennsylvania
Public Schools, Aspinwall, Pennsylvania
Department of Art Education, New Zealand
Laboratory School, University of Hawaii
U.S. Government Indian Schools, Arizona and New Mexico

BLANCHE JEFFERSON

CHAPTER *I*

Methods of teaching art

THE procedures or methods used by a teacher in
teaching art to children determine how much real value the art
experience will have for the children.   There are several
methods of teaching art in practice with children.   Some have
values that contribute to the child's well-being and to his
growth; others have opposite effects.   The methods
used in teaching art are an important and vital part
of education and have far-reaching effects.   They
have an immediate and marked effect upon the child's
painting, drawing, and modeling, which, in turn, are
a result of the methods of teaching used.   They also
have a deep and lasting effect upon the attitudes,
habits, thinking, and behavior of the child.   These
habits, attitudes, and behavior patterns, formed during the most impressionable years, carry over into

adult life and become standards by which the adult functions, and therefore the art teacher needs to give attention to every method she uses with children. The effects of these methods are so important that not only teachers but everyone who deals with children should understand them.

Various teaching methods used in art education will first be described in this chapter, and then evaluated in the next two chapters so that teachers will understand why a certain practice is right for children as well as realize why other practices are harmful. It cannot be assumed that the knowledge of right procedures is enough. Other methods of teaching art must also be understood so that a teacher will not use a certain process with children simply because she knows no reason why she should *not* do so.

IDENTIFICATION OF METHODS OF TEACHING ART

Creative expression. This is a method of teaching art or a way of working with materials that gives the child:

(a) The opportunity to *choose* his own ideas or subject matter for his art.

(b) The freedom to *express* it (create or make the shape of the forms) in his own way.

(c) The right to *organize* it in his own way.

This complete freedom of the individual to choose, to express, and to organize is what creative art education means. Wherever the child is given all of these choices, creative expression is the method of teaching and working in art, and it can be readily identified because the content of each child's painting is different from that of every other. According to his own ideas one child might be painting an airplane, another a ball game, another depicting fun at the beach, while his neighbor might be doing an abstraction.

The expression is individual, with each child drawing the shape of the form in the way that seems appropriate to him for that painting. Among those children in the group who might be painting trees, every tree could be different. Then, too, any one child is free to paint a tree differently, in different compositions and for different purposes. The child chooses and decides for himself.

The putting together of the forms and the placement and arrangement of them is the organization. The organization thus shown in each child's painting is also different. The number of objects, forms, and people that he puts into his compositions is different for each child. Some paintings will be complex whereas others will be simple. The forms are put together individually to suit the taste, need, and purpose of each child. The freedom of the child to develop his own combinations of the forms he includes in his art work is another way to identify the art work as creative expression.

The group of six water color paintings (following page 6) made by first-grade children during one art work period is representative of the range of ideas expressed when children have had a creative art experience. There were 30 children in this group, and every painting was different. Emphasis was placed upon individuality and upon each doing the work his own way and according to his own ideas.

When Linda painted the beautiful picture (2)[1] of her house, she said, "This is my house in the night." By looking at the attractive colors she used in painting her house, one gets a warm, happy feeling about it. The house is not expressed in a naturalistic or visual way. It is not the way her house appeared to the eye, but rather the way she felt about it. She surrounded it with a dark color to show the night, which helps to emphasize the glow that is seen and felt as one looks at it. The brown outline represents the outside of the house; the interior looks as though she had divided it into rooms, giving an effect of the outside and inside at the same time, as children do sometimes. Children thus frequently express the emotional effect that the object they are painting has upon them and disregard the visual aspects.

Donna's picture (3) is unusual and strange in the combination of objects it contains. The old valentines that she had found at home and brought to school that day must have inspired parts of her painting, creating an extraordinary combination with the Christmas tree. Children get a great deal of pleasure from a familiar toy or possession that has been put away and then found again, and Donna was impressed by her surprise and pleasure in finding the

---

[1]The figures in parentheses refer to the illustrations.

old valentines.   The valentines probably reminded her of the fun
that she had had on Valentine's Day which, in turn, may have called
to mind the pleasant experiences associated with other holidays, and
so objects associated with these experiences and her feelings about
them appear in her painting.   Donna was remembering, selecting,
and organizing her experiences and feelings.   This is an outpouring
process that helps the child focus upon his own ideas and reactions.
Through such permissive creative art experiences, the child grows
and matures as he receives encouragement and praise for his achievements.

Mary Sara has painted herself (4) with the new red and
black plaid dress which she wore to school that day for the first
time.   She was proud of her dress and aware of it and tried to call
attention to it in indirect ways by smoothing it as she sat down and
brushing it occasionally with her hand.   The way she has placed
herself in the middle of the paper, as well as the pose and expression
in the picture, have communicated something of the pride she felt
in having such a pretty dress.   The orange part is Mary Sara, and
the red and black parts on each side are her dress.   The dress is on
her and goes down around her, so both the girl and dress can be
seen at the same time, which is Mary Sara's own way of showing
herself wearing her dress.   If children are not interfered with nor
directed during their art experience, they evolve their own ways of
expression that are meaningful to them and interesting to those who
look at and study their art.   Mary Sara's new dress was an important
and exciting thing to her that day, so she chose it for her art experience.

Jackie's lovely rich painting (5) of various stripes is bold in
the way it filled his entire page.   He has experimented with lines of
various widths, using rich and beautiful combinations of colors.   In
some cases he has kept each color separated with distinct and sharp
lines between; in other instances he has let the colors run together
and flow into each other, creating soft, almost dreamy spots.   He
was not courageous in attempting any variety in shapes, however.
He kept within the limitations of repeated straight lines.   The
personality of children is often reflected in their art work.   Jackie
is timid; new experiences upset and confuse him.   The first time
the practice fire-bell rang, although the children were warned to
expect it, he ran crying to his teacher.

Susan's two vigorous trees (6) reflect the confident quality of her personality. The trees are large, full of rich, green leaves and red fruit, and are well supported by strong trunks. They are fastened securely to the ground but go up and touch the sky. Most first-grade children draw trees in this manner, with a trunk and a round ball of leaves at the top. Susan is a friendly, outgoing child who soon became acquainted with all the children in her group. During these early weeks in the first grade, she personally greeted every visitor who came into the room. She got up from her chair, went over to him, greeted him with a smile, said "Hello," and went back to her work.

The last picture (7) in this group is an abstraction. Connie has created a sensitive, varied, and well organized painting from her own ideas and feelings. Calling attention to the features of the painting helps in understanding how Connie, through her intense concentration and emotions, has achieved such beauty. The ladder form on the right is not only different from every other form but has rich and interesting variations within itself. The composition is unified by the rich, green form on the right as it continues around the other forms. The red line also around the forms is varied as it moves from inside to outside the gray line, from wide to thin lines, and from bright to dim shades of red. Although these structural elements are important, the aesthetic experience in looking at the painting comes even more from Connie's expression of her feelings as she worked.

This small sampling from the creative expression of one group of children gives some insight into the products resulting from the creative art work. Although there are times for teaching, it is while working that the child is independent of teacher control or from influence or pressure of other children or adults. There is opportunity to choose, to express, and to organize with no interferences. The child has the power of self-determination. He has no obligation to anything except his own standards of quality. These standards are not *your* standards; they are not the standards of another more fluent or even of an "average" child in the group — they are *his own* standards.

Within the group of six paintings there is not only a range of ideas but a range of maturity as well. This range of maturity results from different intelligence levels among the children as well as from varied backgrounds of experience with art media. It is normal to find such a range existing in any group of children. Children should not be expected or encouraged to fit a certain achievement level because they are all in the same grade or are all the same age. There is great variety within every group, and this diversity should be expected. Creative expression is built upon the individuality of each child, and the individuality of each child is built through creative expression.

Assigned topics. Sometimes the teacher or the children decide upon a topic that all the children in the group use as the subject matter for their art lesson. Such a topic might be "Fun in the Snow," "What We Did on Our Summer Vacation," or "The Pilgrims and Indians Celebrating Thanksgiving Together." Every child in the group builds his art work from the ideas he finds within this chosen topic. Each is free to express and to organize the topic in his own way, not controlled by teacher direction. Assigned topics as a method of teaching art is identified by the opportunities each child has to develop in his own way a topic assigned to the group.

The group of four crayon drawings that were done on grey bogus paper (pages 7–10) illustrate the use of assigned topics as a method of teaching art. Because it was near Thanksgiving, the children in this first-grade group had been hearing stories about the Pilgrims and Indians and had discussed modern Thanksgiving customs. "The First Thanksgiving" was the topic selected. After the children had recalled some of the things they had learned, each was encouraged to choose for the subject of his drawing the phase of the topic in which he was most interested.

When Joseph's drawing (8) was completed, he talked about it to his teacher. He said: "That's in the wintertime, and here's a snake in the tree. He's climbing into his hole in the tree for winter. This is an old tree. Here's a Pilgrim shooting his gun at a turkey. Here's a flag. That's the Indian's flag. There's a rabbit's hole in the ground an a groundhog's hole near it."

It is quite obvious from looking at the picture that he was impressed by the beauty of the snow and expressed his feeling about it in the orange-centered white snowflakes against a red atmospheric background. The sky is a curving design of orange at the top of the page. Children frequently use bright colors to show emotional

1

Children apply their art knowledge to the solving of problems that arise in a variety of situations. These first-grade children are painting a stained-glass window for use in their Christmas play.

2

Sometimes a child paints in a visual manner, and at other times in an emotional way. Linda has painted her house with warm, glowing colors to suggest how it feels to her at night.

When a child is free to choose his own subjects and to make his own associations, unusual combinations of forms sometimes result, such as Donna's Christmas tree among Valentine forms.

3

Since creative expression gives to each child the opportunity to choose for his art the topic that is most meaningful to him at the moment, such diverse paintings as the two on the opposite page can result. Mary Sara's new dress excited her, and she chose it as her topic for art. Jackie experimented with abstract lines and colors to achieve his rich and bold painting.

4

5

6

Susan's two vigorous trees show a full and strong feeling for the subject. Her own happy, direct, and outgoing personality seems somehow to be reflected in her art.

7

Although children often find difficulty in verbally describing or explaining their abstract art, they create it freely and confidently if they feel their teachers accept and appreciate it as much as other forms of expression.

excitement, and Joseph may have associated excitement with snow falling in big soft flakes, or he may have felt the excitement of the presence of a snake and of the turkey about to be shot.

The part of Joseph's drawing that is aesthetically most beautiful is the snowflake and sky area.   He did not mention this part in his story about his picture because it came from his feelings, and, being an intimate thing, could not easily be put into words.

Wayne did not have anything to say about his drawing (9) as he worked or when it was completed.   He drew a very gay turkey looking around, and then put in a man about to kill it with a bright striped ax.   The sun is watching the whole proceeding.

The turkey is not naturalistic; it is a product of Wayne's imagination.   He knows what turkeys look like but simply was not concerned about naturalism at the moment.   He felt the importance of a turkey in relation to Thanksgiving, and thus drew it many times larger than the man.   Turkeys have bright colors in their feathers, and so has Wayne's; this was his expression of what interested him about Thanksgiving at that moment.

Joanne (10) said: "This is an Indian.   He likes to have lots

This illustration is the first of four that show the rich variety of art work resulting from the assigned topic of "The First Thanksgiving." Joseph thought of the Pilgrims in relation to the forces of nature in their new homeland.

9

*An assigned topic should give children broad scope for choosing
ideas for their art. Wayne associated the killing of a turkey with
the topic of "The First Thanksgiving."*

10

*Freedom for the child to shape the forms according to his own
imagination, experiences, and reactions should be a part of any art
activity. The tremendous headdress Joanne drew on the Indian
chief shows the idea that was important to her as she considered
the assigned topic of "The First Thanksgiving."*

of feathers.   Do you know why he has all those feathers?   Because he is the chief."

Joanne cared more about the Indians than about the Pilgrims or objects or activities associated with "The First Thanksgiving."   The long feathered war bonnet of the chief seemed to impress her.   And what a feathered headdress she put on the chief! It is fabulous.   It goes around and above the tree and fills the entire picture.   The Indians' tepees, in the foreground, are placed like a design across the bottom of the page.

Joanne was not concerned with factual representation.   She liked long feathered Indian bonnets, and this was her opportunity to do it her way.   She was free to do it as she chose, to stop when she wanted or to carry it as far as her imagination would go.

Donald (11) was motivated by the Pilgrims' coming ashore from the *Mayflower* in little boats.   He said: "That Pilgrim [on the right] in the boat is looking to see if it is going to rain.   There's water in the boat.   The wind is blowing and there's lightning and thunder.   The lightning set the flag on fire — mostly did.   These are the men's heads in the boats, and the oars they are using to paddle to land.   They can see the land, but it is far away."

The water is full of little boats with oars.   The sky is colored in different shades of blue, all of which are darker than the water. Together with the black clouds overhead and the lightning streaking the sky, it gives an ominous effect.   The painting of the boats and oars in black adds to the effect.   A few drops of rain are shown on the left side of the drawing.

Donald felt the uncertainty that accompanies such a venture. The people look small and powerless in the face of the new continent and the sea.   He has been successful in communicating this feeling to us.

Copy.   Activities in art which consist of reproducing the likeness of a model or an imitation of a form are copy experiences. The child undertakes to duplicate a picture, a shape, or a design as nearly as he can.   A copy activity can be done by one child or by a group of children reproducing a picture or shape, and can be recognized by the sameness of intention on the part of every individual within the group.   The resulting products are as nearly identical as the children can make them.

11

*Donald's little boats filled with Pilgrims coming ashore is another
example of the variety of art work resulting from a stimulating pupil-
teacher discussion preceding work on an assigned topic. The
sombre tone of this picture about "The First Thanksgiving" communicates the feeling Donald had about this very serious occasion.*

Directed or dictated methods.   Following a prescribed course
set by the teacher and controlled by her in a step-by-step procedure
is referred to as a directed or dictated method of teaching art.   The
teacher, standing before the group, cuts, draws, or shapes one part or
fragment of the whole drawing or composition, and all the children
in the group cut, draw, or shape the same part or fragment as nearly
as they can in the same way.   Deviations from the teacher's drawing are frequently corrected by her on the spot.   The whole class
follows the direction of the teacher and goes forward in the lesson
in the same way and at the same time.   This method of teaching not
only controls the ideas that each child must use, but also the size
and shape of these ideas as they are put into form.   In addition, the
teacher controls the placement of each form on the page.   This
means that the teacher controls the organization.   Since this method
of teaching is a step-by-step process, the teacher also controls the
speed at which the children work.   This control is one of the identifying characteristics of directed methods; identical products is another.

In some instances the teacher does not even tell the children what they are making. She does not say at the beginning of the lesson, "We are going to make a bird," or "This is going to be a boat." The children do not know what they are working on until the lesson is over and the parts are assembled. When one teacher was asked why she did not tell the children in advance what they were making, so they might more intelligently put it together, she said: "Oh, I like to see the expressions on their faces when they see what they have made." Whether or not the children know in advance the name of the object they are being directed to make does not alter or change this procedure, which is recognized as directed or dictated methods.

Patterns. As the name implies, patterns are shapes drawn or cut by another person and passed on to the children to duplicate. Most frequently the children duplicate these patterns by drawing around the outside lines. Tracing is another form of pattern work. There is sometimes a step-by-step teaching process involved in this method, too. This is usually the case when the object to be made is composed of more than one part. For instance, if the project is the making of a boat from colored paper, the teacher might give to each child a square or rectangular piece of red paper just about the right size for the hull of the boat, a piece of white in approximately the right proportions for the sail, and a strip of black for the mast. She would then provide each with the cut-out red shape of the hull to place upon his own piece of red paper, and the child would be instructed to draw around it and cut it out. After all pieces were completed in this manner, they would finally be assembled.

Prepared outlines. Coloring books and most workbooks that are available for children contain prepared outline drawings. They are lines that mark the outer limits of an object or figure. In this form they are given to the child for him to color or paint within these prescribed limitations. A teacher who uses prepared outlines in art classes frequently reproduces enough for all the children in the class from one master copy. We are all familiar with the Pilgrim men and women or the turkeys at Thanksgiving time, as well as the Easter rabbit and others.

EVALUATION OF METHODS OF TEACHING ART

As must certainly be evident to you from the description of methods of teaching art, there are two that stand out because they give to each child many opportunities for using his own ideas. These methods are *creative expression* and *assigned topics*. Both are liberal, modern methods of teaching art. The other four — copy, directed methods, patterns, and prepared outlines — give the child no opportunities to use his imagination or to depend upon himself in any way.

The next chapters deal largely with why creative expression and assigned topics are considered by educators to be the best methods of teaching art: because they do most to develop the child individually and as a responsible person. Purcell, recognizing this, differentiates the child's role from the teacher's:

> The child is always thinking, imagining, creating. It is his nature to do so. The child's world is one of self-expression. The teacher's role is to cultivate the seed of freedom, planted deep within the child, and to give him the right to think for himself.[2]

Modern methods of art education are based upon creative expression, giving the child the opportunity to accept or reject. Creative expression is based upon choices — the *child's* choices.

Assigned topics is also a liberal method of teaching art, however. There is a place for such assigned subjects in a program based upon creative expression, and they can be used to supplement creative expression by helping children to focus upon one problem to facilitate their creative art expression. Just how and when assigned topics are used will be discussed in a later chapter. Certainly, relating art to other areas of the curriculum is one of these places. Yet, within these experiences the motivation must center in the interests and purposes of each child. Lowenfeld urges that a topic, indicated by the teacher, should be personalized to each child:

> Such integration cannot take place when the teacher says: "Children, let's draw the landing of the first settlers." It can only take

---

[2]Purcell, Virginia, "Art is a personal matter," *Art Education*, Vol. 10, No. 2 (Feb. 1957), p. 2.

place when the child identifies himself with the experience. "How would *you* feel if *you* were in the group that landed; if *you* were the child of a settler, who would lower *you* from the big sailboat down into the rowboat, in a wet cold atmosphere of a dawning day?"[3]

Even though the child may not have firsthand experience with this action, he can imagine it. The teacher can bring it into his own world by helping him associate his own reactions with the situation.

In either case, whether it is creative expression or assigned topics, the child must be able to identify himself with the idea and react to it, and must be free to do it his own way. As Purcell puts it:

With enthusiasm and intense rapture ideas coming from his innermost being are expressed with complete confidence. This rapturous release of his understanding is truly an art experience.[4]

12

Working creatively with clay gives young children an opportunity to develop an interesting variety of shapes.

In the actual doing of the art work the child needs to be free, to be on his own to use his ideas and to let them flow through his emotions by way of his hands into his painting, or modeling, or some other activity. This action is an art experience. Freedom and permissiveness are essential elements of such a practice in art education.

[3]Lowenfeld, Viktor, *Creative and Mental Growth*, 3rd ed. New York: Macmillan, 1952, p. 25.
[4]Purcell, Virginia, "Art is a personal matter," *Art Education*, Vol. 10, No. 2 (Feb. 1957), p. 2.

Therefore, those methods that give to the child opportunities for making his own decisions are most beneficial to his personal growth.

Art *is* a personal matter.   It depends upon the individual expression of each child.

> Since there is nothing from which to make art except ideas, what else can art expression be?   If it is not a personalized idea, it is not art.[5]

Art is an expression of ideas — the child's own ideas, *not* the teacher's. This great distinction, between the child's way as the right way for himself and the teacher's way as the right way for the child, constitutes the broad difference between the modern methods and other less desirable practices in art education.

Art, to be creative, must be inventive.   It must be concerned with the imagination of each child.   Art brings into being something new through the exercise of the imagination.   The doing of art work involves labor and ingenuity as well as an unfolding of the child's ideas and feelings ignited by his inspiration to make this "something" that has not existed before and is not likely ever to be repeated.

Chapter III deals with the limitations and possible detrimental effects of the other methods used by some teachers in art classes.   It is important for teachers of art to know why they follow certain procedures, such as creative expression or assigned topics, in their art classes.   It is just as important to know why certain other procedures should be avoided.

Suggested activity

Visit a class in any elementary school while the art class is in progress.   Be there for the beginning of the lesson.   Try to determine for yourself what method of teaching art was used and discuss it with your classmates.

----

[5]*Ibid.*, p. 1.

CHAPTER II

Advantages of creative expression

THERE are several reasons why creative expression is considered to be the best method of teaching art. Although there is some overlapping among them, each reason will be discussed separately. It is important for a teacher to know that creative expression is the method of teaching art best suited to the needs and growth of children. It is also important for her to know *why*. Anyone studying child art or teaching art should be convinced of the values of methods of teaching art based upon the child's choices. She should also be able to convince those less familiar with modern methods of their values to children. To do this the teacher needs to be familiar with the deep implications of creative expression in solving the immediate needs of the child and in preparing him for adult life. Creative expression is a

way of life.   It is a way of expressing ideas with materials.   It is a
way of dealing with others.   Habits and attitudes are formed from
the creative processes which help the child to know himself better
and to understand and appreciate his classmates.   They help him
adjust to life about him and within him.   They give him confidence
and personal opportunity.

1. *Personally meaningful.*   Creative expression gives to every
child the *opportunity to choose the ideas or subject matter for his
art that are most meaningful to him.*   Each child in the group has
the privilege of choosing what is the most interesting to him at that
moment.   Children's ideas and interests constantly change; different days bring different interests and moods.   What seemed urgent
to a child yesterday may be dull to him today.   What excited him
and inspired him in the morning may be replaced by a newer interest in the afternoon.   In creative expression the emphasis is on
the child's choice, which lets him take advantage of his immediate
interest.   It is generally known that we are apt to be most successful in the activities in which we are most interested.   Giving the
child the choice of subjects gives him this advantage.

The topics or subjects that children choose constantly vary.
Not only does the interest of an individual child change, but also
the interests of the group vary.   During one art work period there
would probably be as many different ideas being expressed as there
are children in the room.   One child might be drawing a picture
of himself and his friends playing baseball after school, another
might be involved in expressing his experience in coming home after dark, while another does an abstract drawing.   These differences
in interests are normal and to be expected within a group.

If the child has had a disturbing scene with his mother before
coming to school, including threats of what would happen when his
father came home, he could hardly be expected to become emotionally excited by drawing "Fun with My Parents on a Picnic."   His
mood and attitude would be quite different.

By giving every child the opportunity to choose the ideas
that are most meaningful to him, creative expression provides for
individual differences in a very real and direct way.   Each child is
not only permitted but also *encouraged* to select an idea that is
uniquely his own and is as different from the work of others as he,

himself, is different.   In forming the shapes of objects according to his own ideas of how they should appear, he develops a style of expression that is just as uniquely his own as his handwriting or his physical appearance.   Creative expression encourages each child to develop the expression of his individuality in this way.   The organization of his work is developed according to his own ideas, too. The art work of some children is identified by its complex nature; that of others by its simplicity.   It is considered important in art education that each child continue to grow and develop in his own distinctive way.   By so doing, his own identity and personality become known to him.   He knows himself better.   In a situation providing so freely for the unfolding and building of individual differences the child develops a style of expression typically his own.

2. *Individually challenging.* Creative expression gives to each child the *maximum opportunity to develop his own ideas to the best of his ability.*   This opportunity also provides for individual differences.   Children within a group vary greatly in their abilities to solve problems.   Each will be able to solve a problem as far as or deeply as his ability will permit.   Some children, more gifted than others, may see and express much more complex compositions than others.   Creative expression gives each child the opportunity to do as much as he can with his idea.   It is unlikely, then, that any two children in a group will develop their ideas to exactly the same extent.   Some will stop with only a few ideas expressed in a simple way, others will see deeper meanings and relationships and be able to express them in a much more complex manner.

Ability, meaning mental ability, is not the only factor influencing the depth to which a child might go in depicting his ideas. Inspiration or motivation is a very important element.   The child's interests inspire him.   The teacher has a very real responsibility in recognizing this and in helping each child develop his ideas to the fullest.   (Her role in motivation will be discussed in a later chapter.)   An uninspired child is not apt to have the incentive or drive to carry an idea to any great extent.   This lack of incentive can block his expression and cause him to stop short of what he might have been able to do.   When the topic is not of his own choice or when he is forced to work when he does not want to the result will be lack of incentive.

Creative expression does provide every child with the op-.
portunity to choose the most meaningful and personally interesting
problems to him.   In making this provision it lets him carry the idea
as far as he can.   Such a situation not only provides enrichment for
the *gifted*, but it provides enrichment for *every* child.   Every child is
equally important and worthy of the same opportunities.   What other
method of teaching art so consistently provides the chance for each
child to carry out every one of his ideas to the best of his ability?

3. *Recognizes every child.*   Another related reason for using
creative art work is that *teachers* use such processes with children
because they *have confidence in each student as an individual who
can and wants to create.*   Confidence is the basis upon which
modern art education is built.   The child must have confidence in
the teacher and know that she will accept his every serious attempt
regardless of how it may appear or how different it is from the
others.   This is one place where the child does not need to be afraid
to be different.   His different ideas are encouraged and accepted.
Sure that the teacher will not reject his work, he feels free to create.
The teacher sets the stage for this by showing confidence in every
child and verbally saying so, as well as by showing it in other ways.
The teacher, then, has the real responsibility in establishing the
rapport necessary for such confidence.   By feeling and knowing
that every child is creative she can communicate this feeling to
children by building their confidence in themselves and so increasing their abilities in art.

Every child *is* creative.   Children are born after nine months
of a wonderfully creative process — a process that we only partially
understand.   Every child has this rich biological creativity built
into him.

Every child is *creative.*   You have only to watch a child at
play to see him constantly finding new ways, and changing, invent-
ing, and turning to new things.   You have only to listen to a child
to hear him tell fascinating tales built upon reality and upon his
imagination.   Children are so rich in imaginative powers that they
frequently cannot tell where the factual stops and the fanciful begins — nor do they care.   They make it *their* story, the way they
want it.   All this is creativity.   Every child has all this, and it is
the responsibility of the teacher to cherish and to encourage it.

If an adult feels that a child cannot create, he simply does not know children.   He makes this decision from his *lack* of knowledge of children and his own *lack* of experience with and observation of children.   If an adult feels that a child cannot create, he simply is not accepting the child's work.   Many adults do this.   Because adults are unfamiliar with the characteristics of children's art, they expect the child to draw or paint as they would.   This is impossible. A child is not an adult, and therefore does not act as an adult in many ways, including the doing of his art work.   This is a very old truth that adults, at times, disregard.   The Bible says:

> When I was a child, I spoke like a child, I thought like a child, I reasoned like a child; when I became a man, I gave up childish ways.[1]

Of course, we put away childish things when we become adults, but it is important for a teacher not to forget how it feels to be a child.

Teachers who use creative methods in their art classes are persons who have confidence in children.   They know that each child is unique and are glad to have the daily opportunity of letting him express and develop his uniqueness in art class.

They know that children *want* to create — every person does. When children are permitted to use their own ideas and are inspired to do their best work, they become excited by the art experience. Helen Parkhurst shows this in discussing art with children.   The children say:

> "You have a nice feeling when you make things with your hands."
>
> "You have a good feeling because you know it is your own."
>
> "This feeling is all over."
>
> "You feel a little excited and nervous."
>
> "When I start [the art work] I am very curious to see how it will come out.   When I do it I get all excited.   My hands get very excited and keep going.   They get a lot of energy from your head."[2]

Children, *all* children, can create.   They *want* to create.   Sensitive teachers know this and provide for such experiences in their art classes.

---

[1] *Holy Bible*, I Corinthians, 13th Chapter, 11th verse, Rev. Stand. Ed.   New York: Thomas Nelson & Sons, 1953.

[2] Parkhurst, Helen, "Creating with one's hands" (a recording).   New London, Connecticut: Alpark Records, distributed by Croft Publishing Company.

4. *Freedom to experiment.* During the creative process of working freely with materials in a personal way, children can *experiment.* When a child feels unobstructed by any feeling of being expected to do a certain thing in a certain way, he is free. He can try an idea or a procedure that comes to his mind suddenly as he works, or one that he has been considering for some time. If it results in a pleasing form or painting, it is all right; if it does not, it is also all right. He has learned something by it, and that is the purpose of education.

The establishing of the feeling of security that the child must have before he can experiment with his ideas is one of the responsibilities of the art teacher. She must, through her personality and acceptance of the serious attempt of every child, establish the type of relationship between herself and every child that makes each feel she is his friend and counselor. No longer is it acceptable in art education for the teacher to set her way as the right way and require every child to fit this limited mold. Now the teacher recognizes the child's way as the right way for him. The trying of new ideas is part of his learning process: he learns by doing; he learns that certain things work; he learns that some combinations of colors produce the effect he likes or wants, and that others do not. He learns these things best when he finds them out for himself. In addition, he learns something even more valuable: that the very act of experimenting is challenging and fun.

In out-of-school situations children are constantly testing their new and growing abilities, strengths, and awarenesses. Watch children at play: they try balancing, walking on narrow curbs or terrace walls — trying to see what they can do. This exhilarating testing, trying, and experimenting are not only fun then, but can also carry over into adult life. By trying, in art class, new uses for materials and new forms, life becomes more stimulating, exciting, and profitable. Through creative art experiences rich opportunities for experimentation are provided daily to every child.

5. *Individuality of working speeds.* Creative expression as a method of teaching art and of working in art gives every child the *opportunity to work at his own speed.* The rate of speed of working and the promptness with which people go about beginning a task are highly individual matters. Some children work fast, seeming

to be anxious to get every thought and idea into form as quickly as possible. Some work fast but slow down occasionally and then begin again. Some work slowly and deliberately from the start until they complete their work.

This variety in rate of work is determined by many factors that are individual to each child. Some children move slowly in dressing themselves, eating, and walking, and in every other aspect of their behavior. Art work is another aspect of a child's behavior, and he may be expected to function in this as he does in everything else. The same pattern applies to the child who is excitable and jumps into everything; this child gets an idea quickly and pursues it immediately. It does not mean that one speed of working is better than another. It simply means that each child's own speed of working is best for him. Interfering with or trying to control the various speeds of work within one group during an art work period confuses children.

Control of working speed might also interfere with ideas. One child, working quickly, might be expressing only the large shapes at first, returning to complete them when he has exhausted his fast flow of ideas or inspiration. Another might plod slowly, having only a little completed while others are much farther along. Slowing of the first child could cause him to lose some of the ideas that come so fast. Insisting upon speed from the second child could discourage his ability to work at all.

Children approach their work or start to make the first form at different speeds, too. Just looking at a blank sheet of paper or a chunk of clay causes some people to hesitate in starting; others are anxious to get something started and go on from there. This is not only a child's problem; artists of every age work this way. Some artists apply a flat color over their canvas just to get over the hurdle of beginning. There are no other educational experiences except the creative ones in which the child begins as wholly from nothing. Only his experiences and his thoughts guide him; there is no form to follow, no logical step-by-step pattern; each child is on his own. This very feeling at the beginning causes children to work at different speeds.

Then, too, some children have more trouble with motor control than others. Manipulation of materials is a problem. This causes different rates of speed within a group.

Differences in working speeds are normal and to be expected within a group of children. A few will do two paintings during an art work period while one might say, "I didn't have time to finish mine." Because a daily program of varied school activities must be administered by the teacher, sometimes children are unable to complete their art work in a given amount of time. When this happens, additional time should be provided, either during the next art class or in the child's free time.

6. *Child-determined task.* The child enjoys the privilege and responsibility of *setting the task for himself.* It is not always easy to decide what to do and to determine the amount of time and effort to spend on a job. It takes thought and planning to determine what task is important enough to undertake. To decide what things to omit and what to include in his art work takes judgment on the part of the child doing the work, and is a measure of their value to him. It is a privilege to make these decisions and to set the task for himself. A confident student will *want* to do it. Not to want to set the task for himself is evidence of too much dependence upon the teacher. Such a child needs self-confidence. He needs to feel that his ideas are right for him and that he *can do* it.

Setting the task for oneself implies responsibility for the outcome of the job. Children like responsibility. It makes them feel grown up. Children will enjoy this responsibility unless it becomes burdensome or unpleasant by standards that are set too high by too much being expected, or by too much pushing. When this occurs, the child tries to avoid such responsibilities. This escape from obligation deprives him of the opportunity to develop judgments and assume obligations, which are qualities of character just as important in childhood as in adulthood.

Setting the task and working it through to completion should be a pleasant experience for every child. If a teacher is negative in her criticism of the way a child works or of what he does, it is discouraging to him, and accepting the responsibility for its outcome then becomes unpleasant. A child profits from the opportunity that creative methods in art education provide for him to set the task for himself.

Learning to set the task for himself helps the child learn his capacity for achieving certain goals. He knows, by trying, whether or not one job might be too difficult for him, or whether only a difficult and complicated task challenges him.   This knowledge helps him estimate other tasks in relation to what he has learned about himself. He also discovers how long he can remain interested in any one job. Some children, by the nature of their personalities or their abilities, cannot work through a long undertaking, whereas others prefer it.

7. *Emotionally personal.*   Creative expression *helps each student to face his own thoughts and feelings.*   We do not always face what our own feelings really are.   We rationalize.   We try to hide our real feelings, especially those that we suspect may meet with disapproval or ridicule.   We try to hide our disappointments and fears.   Children do this, too.   They care so deeply about what their parents, teachers, and friends think of them that they try to conform to what they think they are expected to do or feel.   If they sense disapproval in, for example, being afraid in the dark, they might say that they are not afraid and make some other excuse for their fears.   It is not always easy to face true feelings.   Children need help to do it.   The teacher needs to help the child focus upon what his real feelings are and to help him identify them.

In one instance when the children in a group were talking about ideas and activities that they might use in their paintings, one child whose name was Joe said: "I ran all the way home from Jimmie's house last night.   I was afraid to come home after it got dark. All the way home I thought there was something behind me in the night — something big.   I couldn't tell what it was, but I felt it was going to get me."   Before Joe had quite finished this statement, many of his classmates laughed and some of them said:

"Ah, I'm not afraid at night."

"What are you scared of?"

"You shouldn't be scared when you are big enough to be in third grade."

Joe said: "I wasn't just afraid of the dark.   I was afraid I might be late getting home.   My mother would be mad."

He changed his story from the first statement of what he really felt and was afraid of to what he thought would be a more acceptable reason for his fear.   He chose the second reason because his classmates and friends would understand how his parents would react if he did not get home on time.   This is a common experience and one that children share and talk about — something that they are not ashamed of, or have not been made to feel ashamed of.

The teacher, being sensitive to Joe's need to face his real feelings, said: "It's all right to be afraid. Sometimes we are all afraid, but not all afraid of the same things. I have things I'm afraid of. Your parents have fears, too. All adults have them, only we call them 'worries.' Most of the things we adults worry about never happen. Joe is afraid of something outside in the dark. We are all afraid at times. Maybe some of the rest of you are, too. Maybe your fears are different from Joe's."

Such a brief discussion helps children to bring their feelings into focus, to realize that their feelings are shared by others, and that there is no reason to be ashamed of them.

Learning to face his fears and his other feelings helps a child focus more keenly and understandingly upon his emotions. His art work profits as a result:

> If it is the function of a painting to arouse feelings of excitement, tenseness and perhaps anger, then every square inch of that canvas, every vivid brush stroke of the artist, is governed by this function: each color, shape, texture, or line strives to fulfill this end.[3]

It is important to face our emotions, to talk about them, to organize them, and put them into form. This is good for the child's art. It is also good for the child's mental health. Once the child's real feelings and emotions are out in the open and he feels no reason to be ashamed of them, he can think about them constructively, put them into organized form, and express them. This process is one way the child can deal with his emotions. Creative art experiences provide this opportunity by giving the child the freedom to choose *what* he does and *how* he does it.

The process of organizing one's thoughts and feelings requires concentration and self-appraisal. The child, in doing so, turns his attention to himself to examine and find out what he thinks and how he feels. When this has been determined, he usually decides to put the most important part of his idea into his drawing first and place the other related things in other areas of the drawing. The expression of a feeling or emotion in organized form not only helps

---

[3]Faulkner, Ray, Ziegfeld, Edwin, Hill, Gerald, *Art Today,* revised edition. New York: Henry Holt & Co., 1949, p. 160.

the child face his feelings, but also helps him relate them to personal situations and to his environment.

8. *Complex undertaking.* In creating art work the child *learns how to deal with a complex situation.* Few situations we encounter or few tasks we set about to do are simple, one-operation affairs. There are usually several facets of an operation to which we must give attention at the same time, and more than one decision that must be made at a time.

In creative painting, for example, the child is not only faced with the decision of which, among the many ideas that come to him, is the one he will choose to paint, but he must also decide what object to put into the composition first. At the same time that he is dealing with this problem he is faced with choosing the color he wants, judging the right amount of paint to put on his brush, and making sure the paint is of the consistency to flow freely and give the intensity of color he wants. The motor control of his hands is involved, and he tries not to drip the paint onto his desk or other areas of the paper.

After the first figure or shape is painted, the next object is placed in relationship to it. Every object added to the composition increases the complexity of decisions for the child. The size and shape of each subsequent form are determined by the shapes already painted as well as by the size and shape of the free space around them. While this is in progress, unity among the forms must be solved and, at the same time, variety of shapes and colors must be considered and decided upon. The outcome of each object or area as it is painted affects the child's emotions, too. If the first few are successful, he is encouraged and in high spirits to continue. If they are not, he must deal with his discouragement and disappointment as he works, trying to resolve them. At the same time, he may even be considering the possible effect of what he is creating upon those who will see his work.

Painting is a complex task, but so are most life situations both in and out of school. For example, there are many things to do and to keep in mind while eating a meal: choice and amount of foods, speed of eating, chewing of food, table manners, the choice of appropriate conversation, and helping others as well as ourselves. Driving a car is also a complex situation. Creative art expression provides opportunities for children to deal with complex situations. This practice helps them adjust to life within themselves and around them.

9. *Develops self-evaluation.* The child *learns how to evaluate* his work as it progresses as well as to evaluate the finished art product. A child begins his art work in high hopes that it will be successful and that he will be proud of it. He is excited and inspired to begin to put his ideas into form. But it is not always as easy as it may seem for a child to put his ideas into organized form. He is not always able to shape the form in just the way he imagined it should be. Then, sometimes, his anticipation gives the idea such an emotional glow that seeing it expressed in form is disappointing: "It doesn't always come out as right as I want it to," said Jane in discussing her painting.[4]

The child decides to what extent he has been successful in every shape or form he creates. He evaluates it. In doing so he measures its worth and the degree of its excellence. He determines to what extent he is satisfied with it. Every form or part he adds to his composition affects the total undertaking and causes him to reappraise. Evaluation is a continuous process, becoming more involved as the composition grows. The decisions the child makes as a result of this evaluation guide him in deciding what to do next, what changes to make, what needs to be added, and how he can improve his work. It also tells him when his work is completed. Other persons may feel that perhaps he has omitted parts which, to them, are important, or that he could do more with the idea than he has done. These persons are looking at the child's work through *their* eyes, putting *their* values upon his work. It is difficult at times for other people *not* to do the evaluating for the child.

An adult may think a child cannot evaluate; he can. Naturally, the child cannot evaluate a piece of art work as an adult would do it, any more than he is able to do many other things on an adult level. When he is six, he will evaluate his work as a child. When he is sixteen, he will look at it as an adolescent. Only when

---

[4]Jefferson, Blanche W., *Art Experiences in the Primary Grades: A Presentation through Color Transparencies with Accompanying Script.* Project, Ed.D., Teachers College, Columbia University, 1954, p. 241.

he becomes an adult will he be able to see and evaluate his art work as an adult. Teachers need to keep this obvious fact in mind when dealing with children and their art.

Each child has his own values or measurements of quality that he applies to his work. Adults and other children need to be careful not to interfere with the child's opportunities to estimate the degree of his own successes. Self-evaluation means constant growth and improvement for each child, permitting each to grow and develop at his own speed. This provides, in some measure, additional opportunities for the gifted child, whose greater mental ability makes it possible for him to do more and to see more deeply into causes of success or failure. He can discern more speedily what needs to be done. It provides just as well for the slow learners who will evaluate their work according to their own less involved purposes and simpler intentions. It provides for *every* child to learn how to recognize his own achievements and appreciate them. Each child learns to judge his less successful attempts or areas of a composition and to correct them or to discover the reasons for the failure. He does this for himself and by doing so learns to depend upon himself. When creative activities are provided in art education, each child develops a valuable ability that carries over to other situations in which he is called upon to make decisions and determine action.

Just as the child learns to evaluate his work as it progresses, he also learns to evaluate the finished product. When he feels satisfied that he has expressed what he had in mind and how he felt about it, he looks at the work, appraising the results. He may feel satisfied with the task, as a whole, but feel dissatisfied with some part of it. He needs to learn to see and to estimate the *whole* work and not continue to look at only the less important spot that may not have turned out as well as he hoped.

When the child sees his art work hung or exhibited, he evaluates it again. He privately studies its strengths and weaknesses. He also studies it in relation to his classmates' work. Studying his work in this manner is a real learning situation for the child and he should not be deprived of it either by having all of the evaluating done for him or by having his own or some other children's work omitted from the showing. Each child needs to see every other child's work. Nor should the art work be hung in any order of preference, such as hanging the "best" first. When the teacher does this, it deprives the child of the opportunity to make his own comparisons and decisions. To study the art work from the teacher's preferential hanging would only confuse him and may discourage him as well. An important role of the teacher is to discuss the children's work with them. This discussion helps them learn. (Just *how* the teacher does this will be discussed in a later chapter.)

10. *Develops aesthetic awareness.* There is no method of teaching art that provides the rich opportunities for the child to make as many *aesthetic judgments* as does creative expression. Judgment is the very essence of art. Beauty, pleasing proportions, and harmonious relationships between objects or colors are basic to the purposes of art. Since we are teaching art to children, it is imperative that they learn how to make aesthetic judgments; and they can be made by the children in their daily art classes in association with their own art work and that of others.

The expression of his ideas and feelings in organized form makes the creating of art a personal experience for each child. The actual performing of the art activity as well as the finished art work is also peculiarly different for each person. Since this is so, judgments of art can be made only with the purposes of the creator in mind. If, for instance, a child, in painting a picture of the sea, is attempting to express a feeling of fear of the big waves, the colors and shapes he puts into his painting would probably be very different from those of the child whose purpose was to paint "Fun at the Beach." The same subject was chosen but the purpose of each child was quite different. It is necessary for a teacher to project herself into the creative activity of the child before she can determine what his purposes are. (This is necessary if we are to understand *any* work of art.) The choices the child makes as he works are determined by his purposes or intentions. The child concentrates upon his ideas and constantly searches for shapes and colors to state them. As his selections are made by and motivated by the same reasons, the resulting art work is harmonious with his purposes. This concentration unifies his thinking and makes the activity easier for him to do and more related in color and form.

Harmony in art means that forms and colors relate to the purposes of the art and that the forms and colors within the work are in relationship to each other.   Each provides something that adds to the effect of the other forms or colors.   When colors or shapes are harmonious or related, each individually supplies a quality that adds unity among them and gives the whole work a feeling of "oneness" or "rightness" or "wholeness," which we call the *aesthetic quality*.

Illustration 13 is an example of a work of art that shows how a fifth-grade child has expressed her ideas and feelings about the sea.   Her expression has resulted in a harmonious and related piece of art work.   In this painting Jane, who is ten years old, has shown very clearly her fear of the big wave.   The wave is large and over-powering, it is very close to her and threatens her, and is dark and ominous in color.   She is alone, it is getting dark, and there is no one to help her.   The figure of the girl and the big wave stand out sharply against the light color of the beach.   Every form and item in the composition adds to the feeling that the child concentrated upon as she worked.   The resulting finished art product is truly a work of art.   It has aesthetic quality.   If some people feel that they do not like the painting, they are probably reacting to the danger and the fear.   Certainly, we react strongly to these things, and we react in this way to Jane's painting because she has been so earnest

13

By concentrating on the expression of an emotion associated with an exciting personal experience, a child can create an aesthetic art product, as Jane has done in this example.

in expressing this feeling.   She was motivated by a strong purpose, she concentrated on it as she worked, and she was successful in expressing it.   These factors bring about an aesthetic work of art. Persons looking at it need to be aware of the child's purposes and see how she has related the forms and colors to her purposes and to each other.

Making aesthetic judgments indicates that the finished art product is viewed in terms of the qualities of the forms as they relate to the purposes of the piece of art work.   It also implies that quality between the forms and colors should be considered.   Practice in making aesthetic judgments comes most abundantly in creative art expression in which each piece of art work is different, each having qualities peculiar to it that must be judged independently of every other piece of work.   Practice in making aesthetic judgments, richly provided in creative art education, builds within children a responsiveness to quality in art.

Personal reactions, alone, without being founded upon art knowledge, are inadequate as bases for quality judgments of the art. Whether a person likes or dislikes a work of art is such an individual matter, dependent upon knowledge and background, that it gives no substantial basis for the guidance of children's aesthetic judgments.

There are sounder reasons for making art judgments than one's likes and dislikes, which depend, very largely, upon the experience and background of the person making the judgment.   "We like what we know" is a frequently used statement.   If we have seen only naturalistic scenes or likenesses of objects and people, we will understand them best and like them best.   The more abstract art would be disliked and meaningless because we do not understand or know it.   Teachers and children need to become acquainted with a variety of kinds of art expressions and experiences and to try to understand them.   The appropriateness of the shapes of the forms, the way they are put together, and the way each enhances the other are bases for judgments.   Art products should be studied and discussed by the teacher and children.   This process of education leads to broader and deeper understanding of the values that are inherent in art products.

Children learn best how to make aesthetic judgments under the guidance of a teacher who knows how to make such judgments

herself.   Developing aesthetic judgments is a process of education
— a matter of understanding and appreciation.   Practice and guidance are needed to develop this ability, just as they are needed to
develop most other competences.

The children and the teacher study together the forms in
nature and in art works, discussing qualities that bring about harmonious relationships.   Displaying the child's art work and that of
other artists provides additional opportunities to make and to develop aesthetic judgments.

Discriminating judgment of art is an essential and frequent
responsibility of daily living.   Too often the idea of what art is
includes only painting and sculpture.   This is, indeed, a very limited
concept.   In our modern life nearly everything we use and wear
has been designed by an artist and, therefore, is an art product.
Some of the commercial products are of poor design, and so are poor
art products, whereas others are excellent.   There are so many different shapes and sizes of each item competing for attention that
discriminating judgments are needed if the items we choose are to
be both efficient and satisfying in appearance.   There are many
styles, shapes, and colors of automobiles, cooking utensils, flower
holders, dinnerware, can openers, furniture, window curtains, and
many other objects that we use daily, in addition to the clothing we
wear.   Within the variety of designs found in any one thing, such
as drinking cups, for example, the aesthetic quality also differs.
Some objects are beautiful to look at whereas others are not.   The
eye appeal of a cup is not the only criterion for selection: the ef-
ficiency of the object is really the first virtue to be considered.   After
all, the purpose of the utensil is to hold a liquid so that one may
drink it.   We want it to do its job efficiently and to serve well.
Beauty and function are related.

Learning how to make aesthetic judgments brings with it the
ability to choose not only more beautiful objects but also more useful ones.   Making aesthetic judgments is a necessary part of daily
living.   We use it every day in grooming and in dressing ourselves,
as well as in purchasing and arranging furniture and other objects.
Because it is so frequently used and because it is such a necessary
part of an art education, the making of aesthetic judgments should
be a part of every art experience.

The child's ability to make aesthetic judgments grows under

the guidance of an art teacher who knows how to make such judgments herself and knows how to guide children in understanding *how* such beauty is achieved and *why* it is considered beautiful. It is an excellent way to provide knowledge and information that lead to better art judgments. This ability leads, also, to better art expression, deeper appreciation of art, and more qualitative selection of art products.

Learning how to make aesthetic judgments is such a vital aim of art education and so necessary a part of daily art work and selections that it might well have been placed first among the reasons why creative expression is the best method of teaching art. After all, this is *art* education. We are educating children through *art*.

11. *Self-knowledge gained.* As well as requiring abilities to evaluate and make aesthetic judgments, *the child learns to know himself better* through creative expression in art. Constantly during the process of expressing his ideas the child must focus attention upon himself. The art work must represent *his* ideas guided by *his* choices. In working through creative processes the child gains interesting and valuable knowledge that guides his future action. The necessity of choosing his own ideas helps the child to realize what his own ideas are and to see which ideas are most important to him. He might begin to see a pattern of thoughts and choices that could reveal a trend. The outgrowths of new knowledge are numerous, as you can well imagine. The child might find a hobby, or might be led into his vocation, or find a topic for investigation in other areas of the curriculum leading to broader understandings.

Instead of a pattern of interest in one area evolving from his choices, the child might discover that he has many interests and that he is aware of and affected by the ever-changing life and activities around him. This knowledge helps him know what kind of personality he has. When he knows even this much about himself, he can function more effectively and plan his activities to develop himself according to this enlightenment.

The character and shape of the symbols or forms that the child makes and his own particular choice of colors constitute his expression of his ideas in art. The way he shapes the forms and the way he colors them reveal to himself, as well as to others, knowledge about his uniqueness. The *kind* of forms and colors

he chooses, imaginative or realistic, are determined by his background of experiences and by his individuality.[5]

Through evaluation, which is one of the processes in creative
expression, the child determines what his areas of strengths and weaknesses are, which also tell him about himself.   He learns whether he
works better in a group or alone.   This one particular bit of information in itself can be very helpful in choosing a profession.   He
learns whether he works better entirely on his own resources or
within a suggested topic, whether he has enough drive to carry a
task to completion, or whether he functions better with occasional
re-motivation.   Such information about himself guides the child in
many important decisions.

12. *Rivalry discouraged.*   Creative art experiences bring with
them a *freedom from competition.*   Since the art work of each child
is accepted and respected for its own quality, no comparisons are
possible or desirable.   Comparisons imply a common basis for
judgments.   Creative expression implies the opposite.   In creative
expression a premium is put upon differences, individuality, and
personal expression.   For children imposed competition and creative expression are incompatible.

The individual must feel free to create.   Freedom to express
his ideas in art implies freedom from teacher dictation, freedom from
adult standards, and freedom from the *fear of failure.*   Each person
concentrates on his own ideas in his own way, with independence
and freedom built on *confidence* in one's self.   To achieve this atmosphere for self-expression each child must receive recognition on
his own particular merits.

Each person feels within himself an urge to excel in some
way, which is natural and should be encouraged.   Each child has a
right to such personal recognition; this is consistent with the purposes of modern art education.   Comparisons, made by the teacher
or by another person, in the work of one child with that of another
defeat the purposes of creative expression.   Comparison depends
upon a quality in one work against which another can be measured.
Comparing of art work makes each child feel apprehensive.   The

---

[5]Jefferson, Blanche W., *Art Experiences in the Primary Grades: A Presentation through
Color Transparencies with Accompanying Script.*   Project, Ed.D., Teachers College,
Columbia University, 1954, pp. 54–81.

feeling of confidence is gone, and confidence is a strong asset to success in art. The embarrassment of an unfavorable comparison can damage further desire to create. A child may think after such an experience that he "can't do that" or that he "won't try that way again."

Competition is rivalry for the purpose of gaining some advantage over another person. When this atmosphere prevails, the child is aware of what the others are doing and how they are doing it. He must keep in mind that he will be measured against their ideas and ways, which confuses him. The quality of his art work lessens because concentration is lost. His art work ceases to be purely his idea and becomes mixed up with the impression that the work of others is making upon him. Individual personal involvement is lost. The resultant art product is less dynamic, is less aesthetic, and has less *art* quality. Only that which comes from the strong personal inspiration of its creator is art. Competition destroys art as it destroys the child's self-confidence. The processes of teaching creative expression free the child from competition. (In a later chapter dealing with contests and competitions fuller consideration will be given to competitions.)

13. *Builds self-confidence.* Modern creative art education *builds the child's self-confidence through acceptance.* This aspect of the creative operation has previously been referred to as it relates to other reasons of why such art activities are best for children. Many of the other outcomes of creativity depend upon the confidence that the child feels as he works.

Self-confidence is an important asset in the success of those who possess it. Most of us have been in situations where we have failed to make a contribution because we feared it might be met with criticism or not be accepted. Even though we felt the contribution might be worth considering, we failed; not because we did not have an idea, but because we did not have the self-confidence to express it. Certainly we make mistakes — we all do — but the fear of such a possibility should not overcome our desire and need to make our contribution. Self-confidence does not mean boldness, or a boasting or swaggering pretense; it is rather simply a feeling of assurance in one's own judgment, ability, and power.

It is not necessary to prove the importance and value of con-

fidence.   We know it from our own experience.   It does seem both
necessary and desirable to point out the strong contribution that
creative methods of teaching art make to its establishment.   The
teacher and other adults working with children need to be aware
of how they deal with the child and his art.   Their attitude toward
his work and their acceptance of it is valuable in building his confidence.   Encouragement and praise are the tools to help the child
grow and express his ideas.   Too strong and exaggerated praise can
also be damaging.   There is pressure in praise — pressure to go on
or to try something else.   Too much pressure can be felt as a burden
to the child.   He can begin to feel that he cannot live up to such
extreme expectations.   He may also sense the disproportion in the
praise and feel aversion to its falseness.

The child needs genuine help in seeing and recognizing his
achievements.   This task requires an adult who *knows* how to make
such choices and how to help the child grow on his successes.

Every child, including the timid or emotionally blocked, can
be helped to more confidence through acceptance of what he tries
to do.

14. *Responsibilities accepted.*   Another valuable contribution that creative art methods make to the self-development of each
child is that they help him *accept the responsibility for his own
choices.*   Since the child is faced with the necessity of making his
own choices in art, the responsibility for the outcome of those
choices can only be placed upon the child.   Accepting the responsibility for our choices and actions is a desirable character trait.
The more obligation the child feels toward making these choices the
greater responsibility he is accepting.   He matures as he accepts
responsibility.

It does not necessarily follow that because it is better for the
child to make his own choices that he wants to do it.   It is easier to
have someone else do our thinking and make our choices; it takes
thought and energy to do our own.   The child likes to depend upon
someone else — but he cannot always remain a child; he must learn
to depend upon himself.   Art work helps him do it.   Once a child
has learned the feeling of personal satisfaction that comes with self-
reliance, he will not want to give it up.

Others, however, never seem to have learned to accept the

responsibility for their own actions and choices. They try to evade
"blame," but are eager to accept "praise." They do not want to
face the unsuccessful attempts or the less perfect areas of their
work. Perhaps this is because too much emphasis has been put
upon the finished art product. The child should feel free to experiment. If his work turns out badly, he has learned what not to
do and that his idea does not work in that way. He has made this
decision himself. The teacher accepts this for what the child intended it to be (an experiment) and for what he has found the outcome to be. She accepts his failure, which helps him avoid the
feeling of shame that so many people associate with the absence of
success. It is a part of trying, a part of learning.

15. *Socially unifying.* During the processes involved in creative art expression, *the child learns how to get along with and to
appreciate other people.* Such art work gives each child many
chances to study, to understand, and to appreciate the work of his
classmates. People are important, what they do is important, and
how we get along with them is important. Whether or not we learn
to get along with other people who are different and have different
ideas and ways can mean the difference between war or peace.

The way each child works is different. Each child chooses

14

*Joe felt an unidentifiable fear of going home alone at night.
He expressed it by giving it form and organization.*

*Children often fear what they do not understand.   Emily said,
"I was afraid of my grandmother after she died."   The child
was able to give expression to her fears through art activity.*

15

and expresses his ideas differently.   The teacher accepts the work
of each child by setting up an atmosphere in the classroom so that
each feels free to try any idea in art in any way.   These and other
processes, procedures, or methods used in modern art education
should be accompanied by an appreciative attitude toward every
piece of art work produced.   This is necessary if individual expression is to survive.   When the work of one or a few children is reacted to negatively or is passed by without comment during the
discussion period, the incentive to experiment or to try one's ideas
often ceases to exist.   Children, like all people, want to receive
favorable attention.   When they fail to receive it, they abandon
their own ideas and are influenced by the work of those children who
receive the favorable attention.   This not only destroys creativity,
but it sets up a feeling of personal inadequacy that destroys self-
confidence.   It also sets up feelings of envy and jealousy, which can
lead some children actually to dislike other children.   Such feelings
of hostility can be avoided if the individually different work of each
is appreciated for its uniqueness — if the *differences* can be enjoyed.
    A part of teaching creative art expression is to see something
of beauty or value in *every* child's work.   *Every* child is important;
the way he feels about himself is important, the way he feels about

others is important, and the art work that he has decided to do is also important or he would not be doing it. Since it is important to him, it should be important to his teacher and to his parents.

The child has made the selections of ideas, forms, and colors that make up his art work. His thoughts are in it. What he considers most valuable and urgent to him at the time determines his selections. His feelings are projected into the work as he develops it. There is much of his personal self in it and revealed by it. Therefore, he is very sensitive to it and to the reactions that others have to it.

Any favorable comment made about his art work is in effect an acceptance of the child's own personality — of himself. Any unfavorable comment, or the absence of a favorable comment when others receive it, appears to be a rejection of the child. The teacher should, of course, make comments to every child about his work, and these comments should be positive and helpful in the effect that they have upon the child; they should *never* be critical or negative. Rather than "correcting" children's art expressions, the teacher should try to understand the psychological reasoning behind the interesting and unusual forms that children create. Teachers can do this by learning as much as possible about the personality and interest of each child rather than by asking him to tell about his art.

When the teacher, in guiding discussion of art, helps the children interpret and understand the creative art of each child, she is helping them understand each other. In this way the child begins to know what his classmates think is important, what they like and dislike, and how they react to different things. In pointing out the achievements that each has made, the child learns to focus upon the good qualities in his classmates' art. He sees the *good* in the ideas and intentions of others. Each child, of course, intends to make some achievement. This is his purpose in doing the art work. To have his achievements recognized gives him confidence in himself and in his peers, whom he can regard as persons to be trusted — persons who will not hurt him. After many such experiences he learns to regard favorably those who also regard him favorably through his art.

Building attitudes and habits of looking for, recognizing, and appreciating the achievements of every person helps the child learn how to get along with other people. Such behavior patterns are conducive to peaceful and happy relations among those who share them.   There are few areas of activity in the school curriculum that provide such rich opportunities for the child to learn to understand and appreciate the individuality of others as does creative expression. Here is concrete evidence of the contributions that each can and does make.   Here is something that we can see, feel, manipulate, and display — something we can appreciate and understand.

Because each child is different his art is different.   In these practices of sharing of appreciation the child learns to *look for* differences in the art work of others.   In creative expression, a premium is put upon these differences, which become the marks of personal distinction.   Because the child's art is so closely tied up with his personality, he learns to look for and to appreciate the differences in people themselves.

Appreciation of others is the basis for the sound, lasting relationships of getting along together.   This is an important asset not only in childhood, but in adulthood as well.

Appreciation comes through respect.   *Tolerating* differences is inadequate; it indicates that the differences are distasteful and that we put up with them.   Acceptance is little better.   Appreciation is a deeper, more positive, and more outgoing quality.   It can be developed.   When it is developed in the classroom, it carries into community life.   Such attitudes, deeply impressed upon people, will greatly aid the cause of world peace.   Creative art education provides almost unlimited opportunities for children to learn how to get along with and to appreciate others.   Herbert Read speaks of the importance of creative activity in relation to war and feelings of hostility:

> For when the individual has been deprived of his creative functions, he is ready to take part in collective destruction.   And then, if he can't have the real thing, which is war, he will indulge in fantasies of cruelty and mass murder, mass produced for one and all.[6]

Much can be learned about art through looking for and understanding the achievements of others.   The discussions shared by the teacher and children help the child to see *what* makes the quality

---

[6]Read, Herbert, "Education through art — A revolutionary policy," *Art Education*, Vol. 8, No. 8 (Nov. 1955), p. 5.

of the art worthy of mention and *how* this was accomplished.

As the child matures, he wants to know how he can improve the less successful areas of his composition. Pointing out and discussing these areas of his art should be privately done between the teacher and the child when the teacher is sure that such comments are sought by the child. It is embarrassing to have the personality of the child identified with poor work. It might be done in some general way if the teacher feels certain that no child would associate the art work with the creator. Such disassociation is difficult in group teaching. In the elementary school it is best to concentrate upon the *achievements* of each child.

> *Bill is creating with paper, constructing supports to hold his figures erect. He said, "This is a man talking to a bird and there is a snake coming. They are going to have a conversation."*

16

16. *Prepares for American culture.* There is no method of teaching art that prepares the child for *life in our culture* so well as does creative expression. All of the ways in which creative expression best develops the individual have already been discussed. Whatever prepares the child to be a better person also better prepares him for life in our culture. However, there are some specific ways in which this practice of teaching art directly contributes to the preparation of children for life in present-day America.

The original purpose of the early settlers was to provide for themselves a government in which each would have a voice. Our government is structured on the right of choice for its citizens. The continuation of a democracy depends on the quality of the choices its citizens make. There are few areas in education that provide such a wide range of individual choices as art does. The tangible results of these choices can be looked at, handled, and evaluated. This tangible evidence of his choices helps the child to see the value of depending upon himself. The constant evaluation associated with art education helps the child improve the quality of his choices. The better the art choice, the better the art product. The better the civic choices, the better the government.

We also put a premium on individuality in our American way of life just as we do in art education. Each person can develop his life as he sees fit and find his own unique place. We are all familiar

17

Every child wants to and can create. All children have a deep creative urge that develops as they work under the guidance of a sensitive teacher.

with the success stories of people who have done this, some having attained high positions from meager beginnings. In art the child learns how to express his own individuality and to organize his ideas in an acceptable form. This is, perhaps, not as easy as other ways of working in art, but the child learns that self-development requires effort.   It is not something that someone else can determine for us or direct us in doing.   The child learns in art that he can carry an idea far and develop it from every facet or he can stop with merely what is expected of him.   He learns how much drive and additional effort are required to go beyond a "satisfactory" job and to do a "superlative" one.   He also learns the additional satisfactions that come with it.   It is the teacher's responsibility to see that he enjoys such satisfactions.

Our American system of private enterprise needs persons who have ideas, who can think creatively, and who can not only present new ideas but improve existing ones.   Private industry and businesses of almost all types look for such qualities when employing personnel.

Creative expression provides children with the kind of art experiences that develop these needed qualities.   In an art activity the child is faced with the raw materials with which he is challenged to make some acceptable article.   A blank sheet of paper and paints, a ball of clay, various craft materials, and other materials provide the basis for some of his art.   The way the teacher inspires and guides the work determines the opportunities for creativity.   The child takes the raw materials and his inspiration, and by adding his ideas and knowledge creates something entirely new.

It is a demanding experience for any person to see the various materials spread out in front of him and to think of some way to make them into a pleasing object.   When such activities are among those provided daily, children develop habits of resourcefulness. They become more inventive in the ways they use and combine materials.   Ingenuity is a characteristic on which our private enterprise system depends, because our creativity has brought us a very high standard of living.

Along with these qualities our American democracy has a deep regard for the intrinsic value and worth of every human being. We believe in the rights and privileges of every individual.   This quality is developed when children learn to expect their classmates to work differently from them and to appreciate their individually different work.

America is accepting a position of world leadership, our people mix with people from all over the world, and we become involved

in the affairs of other people.   We are learning to work with, to
understand, and to appreciate them.   Creative art experiences with
all the variety of processes and products help prepare a child for
the variety of people and ways he will find everywhere.   He will
learn also that others respond as he does to praise and encouragement and that they share his hopes, fears, and ambitions.

   17. *Balances classroom activities.*   Children need varied
daily activities to *give a balance to classroom activities.*   Many areas
of education, especially in the elementary grades, are skill subjects
that stress the learning of facts.   Of necessity this must be so.   The
word "house" means a building where people live or work.   Words
in reading must mean the same to all readers or we could not communicate with each other.   In spelling the child must not only have
all the correct letters but also have them arranged in the correct
sequence.   In arithmetic he learns that 2 and 2 are 4, and that he
had better not be very creative about it!

   The child comes to school from a home where he is usually
the only one of his age and the only one with his particular needs
and interests.   He is unique and is accustomed to having his uniqueness recognized and provided for.   In school he finds about thirty
other children of the same age with approximately the same needs,
about the same size, and trying to play the same games and study
the same lessons.   The child is apt to get lost in the sameness.
Children find their own ways of gaining recognition for their individuality.   Some of these means are acceptable, others are not.
Creative art experiences are excellent ways of providing for the
unique personal expression of each child.

   There are facts and concepts to be learned accurately in so
many areas of education that creative art activities become a necessary balance between such general learnings and a more highly individualized education.

Suggested activity

   *Compile a list of materials that could be used for the creative
art experiences of children in the elementary grades.*
   *Make another list of combinations of media that would be
interesting, stimulating, and appropriate for children in kindergarten
and through grade six.*

CHAPTER *III*

Evaluation of other methods

of teaching art

ALTHOUGH creative expression is the method of teaching art to children that has the deepest and most meaningful values for them, other methods of teaching art need to be dealt with and evaluated, so that teachers can study them in relation to their benefits to children. The deep educative benefits that can be derived from creative art experiences need to be kept in mind as other processes of teaching art are discussed. The satisfying enjoyment that comes to children from solving their own problems through art expressions that are individual and unique can be shared by a teacher who understands *why* such activities are beneficial and *how* other methods fall short in these values. The term "creative expression" is popularly used to describe a wide variety of ways of teaching art regardless of how broad or how limited the children's opportunities for making choices may be. An evaluation of *all* methods of teaching art will help establish a more specific idea of what it is and what it is not.

ASSIGNED TOPICS

Assigned topics is a liberal method of teaching art. It is not as wholly determined by the child as creative expression, but when the topic is broad enough to give each child many opportunities to make his own choices, it has definite values.

The one big difference between creative expression and assigned topics is that in creative expression the child determines for himself the topic that he will use as the subject matter for his art. He is free to select the one that at the moment is the most interesting to him. In the method of teaching art called assigned topics all the children in the group use one topic for their art lesson, which is either chosen by the teacher or decided on by the children. Such a topic might be inspired by a field trip, "Our Trip to the Zoo," or another experience common to all, "A Rainy Day." The topic chosen must be one with which every child is familiar. Each child must have a background of information, experiences, and emotions about it before he can work with the topic. However, even when the children in a group are working within the scope of one theme, provision should be made for any child who urgently wants to express some idea other than the one decided on by the group.

To stimulate originality and to help the child express his ideas the teacher must be careful to see that each child has a background in the subject from which he can contribute ideas. Child-centered topics are selected, and subject-centered topics avoided.

Within the limitations of an assigned or suggested topic each child may develop it in any way he chooses. He is free to choose any phase of the topic, to select from among the many ideas it suggests, and to reject what he finds irrelevant to his purposes at that moment. It is evident that this is a liberal method of teaching art. Since the value of an art experience depends upon the opportunities the child has for making and evaluating choices, this method of teaching art presents many such chances for making choices. It is, of course, more limiting than creative expression.

In a wholly creative art situation the child chooses:

(a) The *topic* for his art work
(b) The way he will express it
(c) The organization of it

The last two, expression and organization, are still entirely his to determine in assigned topics. Exciting as the selected or suggested topic may be to the child, he is still deprived of making that choice himself. He should not always be deprived of this challenging responsibility. If it is the only method of teaching art used with children, assigned topics does not present the broadest possible opportunity for the individual development of each child.

The broader the topic assigned to children, the more value it has for them. "Fun in the Snow," for example, gives the child many more choices from all kinds of snow activities than does the topic "Putting on My Skates." He may think of helping to build a snow fort, snowballing, skating, sliding on slippery sidewalks, rolling in the snow, catching the flakes, sledding, skiing, jumping in deep snow, or many other activities. He can choose any phase of any snow activity. He can picture a few people or many. He can put them in various kinds of positions and activities. He can select many kinds of interesting objects to put into his composition. He is free to organize these objects into groupings according to his own ideas.

The assigned topic can also influence the emotion he will try to express if the topic is a limited one. "Fun in the Snow" indicates humorous or enjoyable activity. If, perchance, the child or his family were involved in an automobile skidding mishap the evening before, such a frightening event may be uppermost in his mind the next day in art class. As the topic "Fun in the Snow" is discussed and developed he will usually suppress his own more urgent emotion and comply. A broader topic, "What Happens in the Snow," is more inclusive. It would include this child's experience and maybe that of others. It would still, however, not include the child who may want to draw about his puppy or about playing with his train, or any of a multitude of ideas that may be especially important to some of the children that day. It is true that the assigned topic does include the experiences of every child and is meaningful to each, but it is also true that it is not *the most per-*

sonally important idea that some of them may have.   Since, to be art, the process must be highly individual to its creator, it is evident then that assigned topics, broad as they may be, are lacking in a basic personal quality.   The quality of *personal choice of subject matter* is denied the child.

Unfortunately, in some cases the subject of the assigned topic is limited in scope, such as "My Mother Combing My Hair" or "Walking to My Desk in School."   They are experiences common to every child in the group.   There is no question about the background each has from which to work, but there is little opportunity for originality.   What possiblity is there for the imagination?   How can the child learn to be inventive within such a limited subject?

The narrow scope of the topic strongly suggests only one or two persons and a very limited organization of these persons.   There is little or no suggestion of emotion.   It is such a commonplace occurrence that it fails to stimulate much excitement on the part of the children.   It is difficult to imagine a child choosing such a topic from among the many exciting, new, and fascinating events in the daily lives of children.   It seems that such narrow topics would be used with only a few children who have specific needs.   The teacher might try to help a child overcome a particular problem by encouraging him to focus upon one limited area in this way.   (Just how the teacher might do this will be discussed more fully in a later chapter.)

Children have a broad opportunity for aesthetic, personal, and social growth when the topics assigned to the group are centered in *co-operation*.   Presentation and stimulation of topics that suggest co-operation give the child many variations for the organization of the forms in the composition.   Co-operation suggests working or playing together.   Grouping of figures, which makes for more unified art, is almost mandatory when depicting co-operation.   Learning how to group figures in an interesting way adds to the child's aesthetic knowledge, and to his knowledge about art.

Co-operation-centered topics help the child in his social growth.   By thinking about himself in relationship to others, he concentrates upon functioning *together*.   He not only *thinks* about co-operating with others, but *works it out* in his art expression.   This helps him understand his role in group activities.   Young children are more self-centered than older ones.   A child in the kindergarten or primary grades will frequently draw himself first in his

composition and quite often will draw the form of himself larger
and in more detail than that of his friends.   In the picture that Jane
has drawn of herself playing with her friends in winter (18), she
has drawn herself very large in proportion to the other children and
to the house.   She does it because at the age of seven she is still
quite self-centered — perhaps especially so at the moment when
she drew this picture.

   Not every child of this age will use such proportion, nor will
the same child repeat it in every drawing.   The second drawing
(19) was made by Tony, six years of age, who is playing in a circle
with his friends.   The sizes of the children in the group vary greatly
because they were changed to fit the shape of the drawing paper.
This is Tony's own choice of a subject that he drew within the as-

*Children often draw objects in proportion to their feelings about
them. Jane, being most interested in herself, as are many children
at her age, has drawn herself larger than the other children.*

signed topic of "Playing with Others."   He decided upon the game
he would illustrate, he determined the organization, and expressed
the shapes of the forms in his own way.   He fitted the children into
a circle and shaped it to fit the rectangular paper.

   Only broad topics have art value for children; narrow subjects deprive children of choices and decisions that are basic to their
art education.

All children enjoy the companionship of co-operation in play-ing with other children. They want and need to be with other per-sons as well as with their parents. Co-operation is essential to their happiness and normal to their daily lives. It becomes, therefore, natural to include other people and the child's associations with them in his art. When topics are assigned to a group for their art work and when these topics are centered in co-operation, the child has many opportunities for aesthetic, personal, and social growth.

In an art program based upon creative expression some as-signed topics are desirable. (This will be discussed more in detail later. Chapter VII will show how to determine when assigned topics might be used.) There are specific ways in which such art activities help a child face and solve his problems.

19

Children will develop their own solutions to problems, as Tony has done in arranging the children in a circle game.

Children occasionally need the feeling of security that comes with working on the same general topic as the others in the group. They sometimes want to feel the closeness of association that comes when all the children are dealing with the same topic. Their right to their own individual interpretation must be protected. Some-times this can be used as a challenge to see how differently each deals with the subject. When this happens, individual differences are being recognized and provided for, and originality is being developed.

Sometimes assigned topics can broaden a child's scope of expression and may open up a new area of interest and thinking to him. This in itself is a valuable use of assigned topics.

CREATIVE EXPRESSION CONTRASTED WITH ASSIGNED TOPICS

However useful assigned topics are, creative expression provides advantages for the child's development that assigned topics lack. In reviewing the reasons why creative expression is the best method of teaching art we can see many differences between the two:

Assigned topics deprive the child of the opportunity to *choose the ideas or subject matter for his art that are most meaningful to him.* This is the basic difference. When the child may no longer choose his own ideas, he learns to depend upon someone else. The self-confidence that comes with the independence of motive and of making one's own decisions has little ground for growth.

The child has just as much chance to *develop his ideas to the best of his ability* within the scope of an assigned topic as he has in creative expression, assuming that the topic is a broad one. He may not, however, be as deeply interested in a topic suggested for the group as he could be in one of his own choice. The lesser interest would create weaker motivation. He may not have the incentive or drive to carry it as far.

Teachers who use creative expression with children *have confidence in each student as an individual who can and wants to create.* The fact that the teacher uses assigned topics as the basis for her method of teaching art indicates that she lacks a certain confidence in the child's ability to find or even to have an interesting idea. People who work creatively with children realize that they have many wonderful ideas. It seems obvious that a group of 30 children would be able to present a great many more ideas than one person could think of. Children have ideas, and some adults need to realize this and feel confident that children can solve their own art problems. Often the feeling of lack of confidence in children results from the adult's desire to have them produce work of adult standard.   Such adult standards in art are no more appropriate for the child than adult standards are in other areas of his behavior.

The freedom of the child to *experiment* is considerably limited in assigning a topic to him.   He may want to see what happens by simply making different shapes in clay, and be unconcerned with any topic; or the fast-moving creativity in finger paint may fascinate him to such a degree that he creates one form, erases it with a broad sweep, and creates another.   The process of *creating* is the important thing.   In many cases the last finger-paint composition he does on the paper may not be at all the most aesthetic or interesting one. If the child had been assigned a topic, the depicting of that subject would have been impressed upon him, discouraging such free experimentation.   Even though all topics are not assigned in the mandatory sense of the word, the fact that one is suggested and discussed in the motivation deeply impresses the child.

Assigned topics give to each child just as great a privilege to *work at his own speed* as creative expression does, providing the topic is broad and the opportunity for personal choices great. Children work at different rates of speed determined to a great extent by personality patterns.   Interest, or the lack of it, also affects speed.

To a great extent the child is denied the privilege of *setting the task for himself* when the topic is assigned.   The self-determination of what he will do is a challenging privilege that is missing when the topic is not of the child's own choosing.   Within a broad topic each has the choice of deciding how much he will do with the subject and how far he will carry it.   This is a matter of degree in carrying out a task and not in setting the task for oneself.

Creative expression *helps the child face his own thoughts and feelings.*   To what extent can he do this with an assigned topic? There is some opportunity if the subject happens to involve an emotion that he has recently experienced, such as "Afraid in the Dark" or "Fun with My Friends."   However, it is difficult to find one topic that will suit the individually different emotional feelings within a group of children at any one time.   If a child has just had an embarrassing episode with his peers and is assigned either of the topics just mentioned, he may have some difficulty concentrating upon the emotional aspect or summoning enough interest at that moment to do the quality of work of which he is capable.   He has not been given the opportunity to face the thoughts and feelings that are disturbing him and are pressing for recognition and release. In facing and dealing with his most urgent emotions he has an opportunity to give expression to them and to present them in organized form. Thus, the child learns to face his own emotions, whatever they may be, and to deal with them in an organized and rational way.

In both methods of teaching art the child *learns how to deal with a complex situation*. Only when a topic is extremely limited, such as "My House" or a "Fall Tree," would the child be deprived of dealing with a complex situation. This would be true whether the subject were self-chosen or assigned.

The child can learn a great deal about *how to evaluate his work*, whether it is based on assigned topics or creative expression. With the guidance of a sensitive and sympathetic teacher, the child learns to see and to appreciate his achievements. By listening to the teacher and to other children as they point out the strong points in each of the pieces of art work, he realizes what he has accomplished and senses what achievements might be possible for him. Handled in this way each child can see and understand his own strengths and weaknesses and decide for himself how he will profit by his new knowledge. There is no embarrassment to the child and thus no discouragement. Each feels an urge to build on his own successes.

The wider the scope of subjects within a group of art work being discussed, the broader *the opportunity for making aesthetic judgments*. When all children in a group work on the same topic, aesthetic judgments can be made, of course; but when each chooses his own subject, there is a much broader variety of work that can be studied and more possibilities are presented for developing aesthetic judgments. The variety of choices of subjects made by the children provide a more interesting investigation of the completed art work. Children tire more easily of looking at a display of 30 or so examples of the same subject in art, no matter how variously it has been handled. It is even possible that comparisons might be made of the finished art works. When this happens, recognition and appreciation of the individual merit of each piece becomes more difficult and the purposes of art education weakened. Assigned topics have some merit, but as a continuous method of teaching art, they deprive the child of certain advantages inherent in creative expression. The educational value of an assigned or general topic does not lie in its daily use but rather in its use in an occasional, particular instance to focus the attention of the children upon a needed knowledge or skill.   After this experience, the group should return to creative expression.

Every piece of art work is judged on its own merits.   It is difficult to find a set of rules of composition or a principle in art that would hold true for every art product.   One painting might be strong or interesting because it has been expressed or organized in a certain way, whereas some of the same qualities added to a different painting would destroy it.   Learning to make aesthetic judgments is a process of education resulting from an attempt to understand the varied work of many persons.

In an assigned topic the children can learn a great deal about *how to get along with and how to appreciate other people.*   They can see how their classmates have expressed in a different way their own reactions to and ideas about the subject and can learn to see and to expect such individuality.   In learning this, children can adjust to the individuality of others and so learn to get along with them better.   Art based upon assigned topics does not, however, provide them with the dramatically different reactions and ideas that are the outcomes of creative expression.   In looking at the results of creative art work the child looks at an abstract painting hanging beside a picture of a group of children playing and then a composition of trees or airplanes.   The deep and pointed interests of each person are keenly expressed.   It is so with the emotional reactions as well. One child may express a feeling of fear in his creative composition whereas a child near him may be portraying fun and excitement.   In such an atmosphere there is rich opportunity for the child to see and to appreciate the differences in other people and in the art.   This is an important step in learning how better to get along with other people.   Assigned topics do not reveal the personality differences that are revealed by creative expression.   Assigned topics are limiting and should be used only for specific reasons that contribute to a child's facility in creative art.

The extent to which *the child learns things about himself* through developing in his own way ideas originated by someone else is limited by the extent to which he can inject his own personality and ideas into the subject selected by another person.   He is deprived of the search among his own thoughts for an idea important and meaningful to him. When assigned topics, as a daily method of teaching art, prevails with children, they are not challenged to find out which ideas are really most important to them, but learn to lean upon the teacher for that first big decision, "What shall I draw?" They do not even have to try to learn which among their own ideas are most important at the moment, which are most stimulating, and which are dull.

A child can learn something about his own reactions to the ideas of others through assigned topics. He can learn whether or not he expresses his ideas in art in a simple or complex way. He can learn something about himself by studying his art, if a pattern of reactions to the teacher's ideas appear. He can learn something further about his own personality as shown in his own individual expression or interpretation of the common subject, *but* he *cannot* learn what his own ideas and interests are. Although he can learn many things about himself when assigned topics is the method of teaching art, creative expression provides broader opportunities.

Whether or not the classroom atmosphere is *free from competition* does not depend upon either of these methods of teaching art but rather upon the attitude of the teacher and school administration toward the desirability of such experiences in art for school children. When all the children in a group are dealing with the same topic, comparisons between the children's work can be much more easily made than when each has expressed his own topic. Each child's work should be regarded according to its own merits and in relationship to the personality and background of the child who created it as well as to the materials he uses. Since this is the case, removal of a basis for such comparisons is just as important as the removal of an attitude favorable to it. Assigned topics lead more easily to comparisons than does creative expression.

Creative art education *builds the child's self-confidence through acceptance.* The atmosphere for the acceptance and appreciation of each child's creative art work is set by the teacher. Acceptance and appreciation of the ideas of each child means the acceptance and appreciation of his personality. When the child feels that the teacher likes what he does (likes him), he is more sure of himself the next time he attempts to express an idea. The teacher's manner of discussing and of dealing with each child's work in art establishes the atmosphere in which self-confidence is built.

How can the child learn much about accepting the responsibility for his own choices when someone else makes the first and often the most important choice for him?   One indication of growing up is the willingness to accept the outcomes of our own decisions. In order to do this decisions and choices must be made by the person who is to be responsible for them.   In adulthood each person is expected to know how to appraise a situation and then make an intelligent decision about it.   Preparation for this responsibility can be started early in school experiences by permitting the child to make his own decisions, evaluate the results of them, and learn how to accept the responsibility for them.   He learns how to accept and appreciate his successes and how to face his less successful attempts. He studies his work to see how he might improve it the next time. Assigned topics give many opportunities for choices, but within a more limited range than creative expression.

Since life in our culture is based upon the right of the individual to make choices, the more we restrict the opportunity for making choices, the more we restrict *the child's ability to adapt to life in our culture.*   The very maintenance of our American way of life depends upon the quality of choices we make.   A high premium is placed upon creativity by our economic and industrial society. Persons who have ideas are in demand.   How can we develop this ability fully if the teacher deprives the children of searching for and deciding upon a good idea?

Classroom activities are, to a great extent, based upon a teaching-learning situation in which every child is being taught the same thing at the same time.   When all or most of the art experiences are assigned topics, there is still a great deal of sameness.   Children need a balance to classroom activities.   In the child's out-of-school life his individuality is constantly being provided for.   Special attention is given to him and to every family member because each is different in many ways from all the others.   In school, in art class, such personal development can best be provided in creative expression.

As a method of teaching art, assigned topics is liberal, giving the child many opportunities for developing an idea in his own way. The broader the topic, the more opportunity for giving expression to the individual differences among children.   Assigned topics do not do as much for self-expression of the child as creative expression does, but, at times, are desirable art experiences and have definite educational value.

Although assigned topics have certain limiting features when used as the basis of the art program, there are times when such experiences are desirable and helpful to children. (To be discussed in a later chapter are ways in which subjects common to the group can be used to develop the child's facility in creative expression.) In addition, a child sometimes needs the security of working on the same general topic as his classmates. Children are more alike than they are different. If left to his own resources every day, the child begins to feel in need of a fresh start, new ideas, new inspiration. By a skillfully motivated topic the teacher can open up new interest areas.

Assigned activities may seem easier for some children, because they have learned to feel more secure when the teacher sets up an atmosphere of approving work done on a topic that she has selected. Children are sensitive and try to please. They are also very adaptable and soon fit into whatever pattern of art activity the teacher establishes. The teacher is extremely important in art education. Her influence determines the kind of art education the children receive and the establishing of value standards. Under the teacher's influence the child soon learns to what extent it is important to follow topics suggested by the teacher or whether it is important for him to express his own ideas in his own way.

OTHER METHODS OF TEACHING ART

Among the art experiences that have been identified earlier are copy, directed methods, patterns, and prepared outlines. Such activities have little or no art value at all for a child. They give the child no opportunity to make choices, nor do they provide him with any expression for his imagination or emotions. Without the inclusion of the child's ideas and feelings such activities are questionable as art education.

In copy experiences the child's purpose is to reproduce the form given to him. His ideas, his background, his experiences, his reactions to them cannot possibly be included. There is no place for the inclusion of his personal relationship to his art, his thoughts, feelings, or ideas about it. Copying is simply a mechanical process, with the success of this work depending upon each child's ability to make his work resemble the original. The products are all alike. Any differences among them depend more upon the child's *lack* of ability to reproduce exactly someone else's ideas, expression, and organization than upon his own ability to have and to express ideas.

Sometimes a teacher will place before the class a vase of flowers and have each child in the group draw or paint it. When the resultant products show differences in size, variations in the shape of the leaves or flowers or colors, some teachers explain these differences as representing the individual expressions of the children. The children did not mean to have these differences in their work. Each was attempting to eliminate such differences and make an exact reproduction of the model, as was expected of him. Therefore, when such differences arise, they happen in spite of the children's efforts to make their work as much like the model as possible, and have no relationship to individualized expression. The child can scarcely, then, be credited with achieving them. The variations within the finished work appear because the child could not or would not conform.

The directed or dictated method of teaching art, as the name implies, is a lock-step process of having each child follow in a step-by-step manner the directions of the teacher. She has worked out in detail the idea ahead of time and the class participates in mass-producing her idea. Such an activity can take place in any art medium, such as clay, cut paper, paint, etc. It is the *process* or the *way* or the *method* that the teacher uses in her dealing with children in art that determines the value of the experience to them. Directed methods are teacher-centered. The teacher thought of the idea, she decided upon the shapes of the forms, and she put it together in organized form. She, or whoever originally developed the idea, is the only one who profits by the thought-provoking challenge of creating. When the teacher directs the children in making the same object that has already been developed, she is not providing them with activities necessary to growth in art ability. They do develop habits of following directions, of doing exactly what everyone else does at the same time and in the same way, and of doing exactly what the leader directs, but these things hold little value in preparing children for life in a democracy. In fact they do a good job of setting habits and establishing attitudes that suggest totalitarianism. Children learn to rely upon the leader (the teacher) and feel secure only when doing so.

Some people may think that copy experiences and directed activities provide a child with a vocabulary of forms that he can draw upon later for his creative art work. They lack confidence in the child. They fail to realize that each child *can* and *wants* to create. Neither do they recognize the qualities in the characteristics of child art. By such controlled ways of teaching art they continually discourage and prevent the child from using any of his ideas. He loses confidence in his ideas and in himself. Then when faced with the necessity of actually creating from his own ideas, he finds he has trouble. He does not know what to draw, and when he does draw, the work is often stiff and limited in its organization and complexity. Directed methods do little or nothing to prepare a child for later creative activities.

The art work done by John shown in the accompanying group (20–25) illustrates this point. During the first three grades John attended a school where directed methods were used with children. Illustrations 20–23 show his work done under direction. One rainy day the first-grade teacher, in trying to relate the art to life situations, directed the children in making a drawing of an umbrella like the one in Illustration 20. Under her step-by-step direction, everyone drew the big curve for the top, then the smaller curves below, and then the handle. The *child's relations* to the umbrella and to a rainy day were completely omitted. Children like to stamp in puddles or see reflections in them. They have different reactions to rain experiences, such as getting caught in the rain, falling in the mud, or playing in the water that runs along the curb. These activities and the children's reactions to them make interesting pictures for children to make and for others to see.

In the first grade at Hallowe'en time every child in John's group was directed in the making of a pumpkin face, like John's example in Illustration 21. The mouths and other features varied in size, but the children tried to make them all resemble the teacher's drawing; the smiling expressions on all the drawings were as identical as the children could make them. When they were displayed around the room, one quick look was enough to see them all. They were all alike and so required little individual inspection.

In the second grade the composition of three cherries and the word *Washington* (22) was decided upon by the teacher in recognition of Washington's birthday. In view of the many exciting events and adventures in Washington's life, this group of cherries seems trite. A child probably would not have chosen this subject. If the child had been free to decide what he would do, his drawing would have been full of activity and the exciting things that Washington did.

If you have difficulty trying to determine the subject of Illustration 23, you are not alone. Few people who see it know what it is. Difficult to recognize though it is, the teacher has placed a star on it indicating that it was among those that turned out best. It is the head of a girl wearing a green scarf in recognition of St. Patrick's Day. It looks grotesque because John was only following directions without any other purpose in mind while developing this project. He was not interested in the subject. What active third-grade boy would think of such an idea for his art? It is an adult's choice, and a dull one.

The star on this piece of John's art shows that the teacher's motive was to have the children imitate her own model as nearly as possible, under her direction. Those who, in her judgment, accomplished this purpose were rewarded by the star; the recognition of receiving a star was withheld from the others, regardless of the sincerity of their efforts. Such discriminatory practices have no place in art. They discourage those who fail to receive them and cause these children to lose interest in art. It is difficult for a child to understand why he did not receive recognition. Children become confused by such practices, trying to gain the satisfaction of receiving the star rather than for doing a satisfying job. The premium is placed upon following directions, mass-producing the teacher's idea, complete acceptance of the ideas and expressions of the leader. No wonder children are confused and bored by such "art" activities. They are in opposition to life in our culture, to the interests and choices of children, and to a respect for individual differences.

After John's third year in this school, his family moved to another town and he was enrolled in a school where creative expression was the method of teaching and working in art. For a while John was disturbed in art class. He seemed not to have any ideas.

20

21

WASHINGTON

These first four examples of John's work, made during his three years in the primary grades, are the results of teacher-controlled experiences with art materials.

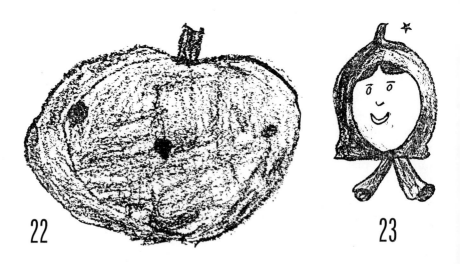

22

23

24

In the fourth grade, where John made these two drawings, his art was based on creative expression.   These
examples of his work show the influences of his earlier
experiences with art materials.

25

He was ill at ease and lacked self-confidence.   During the first part
of the art work period, following a lively teacher-pupil motivational
discussion of the topic, the other children went right to work, but
John just sat and looked around.   He seemed to have difficulty deciding for himself what to do and how to do it.   When he finally
decided upon an idea and got started, he drew one object and quit.
One object on a page had been his background of art experiences for
three years, and he had a difficult adjustment to make.

For the first few weeks the teacher thought that he was
troubled by the usual adjustment problems a child has to face in a
new town, in a new school, and in making new friends.   When she
noticed he was adjusting faster in other subjects and still having
trouble in art, she discussed it with his parents.   Fortunately, his
mother had saved his art work, of which Illustrations 20–23 are
examples.   This revealed to his teacher a deeper problem for John
than just adjustment to a new school.   The teacher realized that
building John's confidence in himself and in his own art ideas was
the first task and encouraging him toward more complex relationships in the work he did was another.   He was helped to learn to do
it his way.

Illustration 24 shows how he tried to draw a group of seated
men.   Because for the first three years his own ideas of how to draw
were continually interfered with by the teacher's imposing her ideas
upon him, he was confused about how to draw people.   He was not
prepared for creative art and his drawing of these people seems
grotesque.   But you can see his successful achievements, which the
new teacher readily pointed out to him.   He shaped the people to
fit the chairs and formed the figures into a group facing the center.
He was working on his own and organizing his ideas, which was a
step forward for John.

More and more he discovered the excitement of using his own
ideas as he wished.   He became intrigued with designs and put
them on everything, even all over a train as Illustration 25 shows.
John became interested in art and was just as full of good ideas and
just as eager to express them as were his other fourth-grade classmates (Illustrations 26–27).

Some people believe that there is value for children in the use
of prepared outline drawings because they impress upon them the
"right" idea of how Pilgrims were dressed or how an Indian looked.

If John had been taught art through creative methods, he would
no doubt have been able to produce work as interesting as that of
other children of his age. Mac's fire picture shows excitement, while
Nola expressed the soaking feeling of being caught in the rain.

There is value in this knowledge which can be gained without having children fill in the prepared outlines of a form with color. Art for children should be centered more in the *child's* ideas, imagination, and emotions.

Another reason sometimes given for the use of prepared outlines is that they teach motor control. The child learns to stay within the lines when he colors — but he would be much more interested in coloring inside the lines of a form that he made than one already drawn according to an adult's idea. The child takes more pride in what *he* does. Therefore, it seems logical that he would take more pride in coloring within the lines of his own picture *if staying inside the lines is what he feels would express his ideas best.* There are times when the effect is more satisfying if he does not stay within the lines. He will learn this and other skills better in relationship to his own work than by applying an isolated operation to a prepared outline.

Teachers have a grave responsibility in choosing the methods of teaching art because children trust their judgments. This trust and confidence causes children to become impressed with the teacher's choices and decisions and to feel that they are "right." The art experiences chosen for children should be those that do the most for them educationally.

Suggested activity

Have each of several students bring to class a set of art work made by children in any of the elementary grades. If possible these should represent different grade levels and different school districts. Each set should contain all the art products made in the group during any one art work period. Study the products with these objectives in mind:

(a) Determine the possibilities for the growth of the individual in each.

(b) See how you might improve the teaching that led to these products.

CHAPTER IV

Role of the teacher in art class

THE teacher plays active and very important roles in creative art education. Her responsibilities are varied. It is important for a teacher, or anyone involved with children and their art, to know what she is expected to do, what leadership she must assume, and what leadership and responsibilities she must inspire in each child. In short, as an art educator, the teacher needs to know specifically what to do and what not to do. During every minute of the art class the teacher is needed by the children. It is not a time when the teacher can put the children to work on an art problem, provide them with materials, and withdraw to correct workbooks from a previous session or to put some work on the chalkboard. Creative expression provides the richest opportunities for individual expression and growth. The child must be free of teacher control and direction in order to accomplish this at all. Since teachers may not show children how to draw, direct progress of the art class, or provide the children with examples to copy, it may seem to some that there is little the teacher *can* do. There is, however, much that the teacher *can* and *should* do. The teacher is extremely important in art education. Much of the responsibility for the success of the art experience depends on the teacher. She has a job to do at every step of the way. Her roles change several times during each art class. Since art is such a personal and individual thing for each child, teaching it is challenging.

The responsibilities of the teacher during the art class are clear and specific. They include:

(a) Motivation   (c) Evaluation
(b) Guidance   (d) Exhibition

Of these, motivation is the teacher's most important work. It is a separate function in itself, and it is a part of every other action during the art class. Each of these four functions overlaps; each becomes a part of the other. Learning is the outcome of each and of the combined four. The child will have learned something through his own efforts to choose, to express, and to organize his own ideas in his own way; but he needs to learn not only through his own efforts but by way of the teacher as well. The teacher needs to teach, to educate, to impart new knowledge, and to open new insights. Just how she does this and yet does not interfere with or direct the child from his own intention will be described.

MOTIVATION

When a person is prompted to do something, he is motivated to do it by having some incentive for the action he undertakes. A motive is an inner urge that causes the person to act in one way or another. An art activity, to be a truly creative one, should come from the child. Within a group the art work will be as different as the children are different because motivation has a different effect upon each, inspiring each to his own ideas and ways of working.

At times a child will not need to be motivated in art by another person.   The child frequently paints or draws simply because he wants to.   Children at home will, without urging, get their paints or clay and create.   This happens in school, too.   Sometimes a child will want to paint or draw in an activity period or when he first comes into school before classes begin.   This is a matter of individual self-motivation.   People working alone can work in this way whenever they choose and for as long as they choose, but groups of children in school cannot.

Because we have group teaching, a program of education must be administered that will provide learning opportunities for every child in every subject.   Therefore, art activities are scheduled for a specific hour and a specific length of time every day.   Although each child wants to create, this set time may not be the moment when he is most inspired.   If the children have been deeply involved in the lesson just preceding the art class or if a new process in arithmetic is still occupying their minds, other interests may be crowded out.   Children enjoy art and want to create.   They are anxious to express their ideas and proud of the independence they develop through creative art.   Art is only one of many interesting areas of education that demand the child's attention.   It seems highly unlikely that there could ever be one selected time when every child would feel his most intense urge to create.   Therefore, the teacher, from her education and experience with children, selects the time she feels would be best for the art class.

Every artist of every age needs to be inspired before he creates.   It is not easy to create.   There is perhaps no other area of learning where the child begins so wholly from nothing as he does in creative work.   In art he has a blank paper or chunk of clay and maybe a few tools, and that is all.   He must get his own idea and when he runs into difficulty, he must work out his problems.   Since creating is a difficult task, the child needs to be strongly motivated to begin and to carry it through.   To take the lead in helping the child become inspired by his own ideas is the teacher's responsibility.

The teacher needs to learn how to induce action, to rouse the child enough to work hard in his own best manner.   She should continue the motivation until she senses that every child is excited to begin.   With questions directed toward their interests she stirs up the feelings of every child until each is eager to go to work with whatever materials he has.

It is plain from this explanation of motivation that it is closely allied to the child's emotions. Emotion causes motion. The more intense the emotion, the more intense the expression; the stronger the emotion, the stronger the will to produce the ideas associated with it. Through the emotions, art comes from deep within us; the clearer the focus upon the emotion, the freer the product will be from confusion. There will be a definite purpose and a strong inspiration that will keep the child's mind centered on his one idea.

To accomplish this strength of motivation the teacher cannot function in a matter-of-fact, dull, dispirited, or lifeless manner. To arouse children successfully, to excite them, to make them *want* to create and to make them *eager* to do it, the teacher must be lively and alert. Discussion, to be motivating, should be encouraging and enlivening. The teacher takes her cues in the motivation discussion from the children. She receives their suggestions with enthusiasm, and she responds warmly and approvingly to each contribution, no matter how brief her responses. Some teachers can do it with only a quick gesture that indicates and communicates admiration. Every child needs to feel this radiation of the teacher's respect, regard, confidence, approval, and pleasure in their ideas. Such a position taken by the teacher inspires children and makes them *want* to create.

Dramatize a little. Children love it. They catch the spirit quickly and soon feel the glory and the excitement. They are ready to create because they have been motivated.

Teachers can learn to motivate in the specific way that creative activities require. Become the inspirer and be enthusiastic enough to make every child forget his troubles and problems and become fired with drive to put his thoughts and feelings into organized form. See what wonders it will do for your own enthusiasm for art as well. You have good qualities if you are matter-of-fact, unimaginative, or logical in your approach to life and to teaching, but realize that there *is* a place for the emotional and the imaginative and learn it from your children. When they tell an imaginative story, try telling one yourself. When they draw in a fresh, spontaneous way, appreciate the drawing or the parts of the drawing that are not realistic. You should encourage emotional and imaginative qualities and also develop them in yourself.

In motivating children for art, the teacher begins a discussion by asking a question phrased to draw individually different ideas from the children. The co-operative discussion between teacher and children continues until a high point of anticipation is reached, *not* until the topic is exhausted. If the discussion is carried too far, the children will tire of it because they feel that they have worked it out pretty well verbally — then there is no need to work it out graphically. It takes only a little practice for a teacher to learn how to judge the high point of anticipation. Be alert to the indication of eagerness on the part of the group, feel satisfied that the children are ready, and then know that the motivation is over and the children are ready for their most important role — to create independently.

Only those ideas that the children know about and that are a part of their life and experiences are suitable for art. As has already been said, the child decides upon his own topic for the art experience by choosing what is most meaningful and most important to him at that time. During the discussion the teacher may add suggestions of how the subject may be broadened or of something else the child can do with it, but these are to be merely other thoughts thrown into the melting pot of class discussion. The child should feel free to associate the suggestions with his idea, reject them, or ignore them. When children feel obligated to incorporate into their work ideas presented in the discussion by the teacher, then it is no longer a situation in which each child determines his course. When many examples of the completed art work show the teacher's suggestions, the teacher's influence is too strong. At all times during motivation the teacher should depend almost entirely upon the children for ideas. The teacher's contributions should be her skill in interrogation as well as her enthusiasm in reacting to the children's suggestions.

It is difficult to say just what amount of time is required for a motivational discussion. In a 45-minute art period it is difficult to determine just how many of those minutes are needed for the focus of attention upon creativity and the stimulation of sufficient emotional drive to begin and to carry through a complex task.

If the art project is a long-range one, the time required for motivation will likely be much longer than a problem lasting for just one day. A long-range project requires a combination of introduction, motivation, explanation, and development of the idea with the children. The teacher needs to build a co-operative discussion with the children and continue it until each child has an over-all view of the whole job. Each child should understand the whole problem and have a mental picture of it in his own mind before he begins any part of it. With children in the upper elementary grades it may take at least one entire class period to accomplish this type of motivation. Then additional separate stimulations will be needed for each step in the process. The motivation for each step can be brief and to the point as required.

Some art experiences that are quickly done still require a motivation that may consume as much time as the actual work if an explanation of some procedures is included, as in finger painting. Since finger painting and clay work are considered "messy" media, some procedures for cleaning up of the work areas and the children themselves need to precede the actual motivation. This additional explanation requires time, but time so spent pays in orderly organization of work. Time so spent also aids the motivation because the children are already considering what ideas they might choose.

Some motivations can be quite brief, consisting of just enough to focus attention. Pete's drawing of Hallowe'en figures (29, on the opposite page) shows what exciting work a child can do because of the combined motivation of a recent first-hand experience plus enthusiastic teacher-pupil discussion. The day following their school Hallowe'en party, there was still a great deal of excitement. The personal attention each had received for his costume plus the informal fun of the party carried over into their thoughts and feelings the next day.

At the beginning of the art class, the teacher briefly discussed the party with them, helping the children focus upon their expression of it with art materials. The children worked enthusiastically on it, and Pete's frightening and amusing figures are one example of the achievement they made.

Some educators feel that actual first-hand experience is the best kind of motivation for creative art work. It is true that first-hand experience gives the child a good background from which to create, but it is sometimes not enough in itself to start him painting or modeling. Lawrence McVittey made an experimental study with fifth-grade children on various methods in art motivation, to determine the effectiveness of each. As methods of motivation he used:

28

The teacher guides each child individually with his problems
as they arise. When each child is working on an individual
basis, the problems of each are different.

29

When recent experiences and feelings associated with the fun
and fright of Hallowe'en are followed by lively discussion,
children can then create exciting art work.

30

Children's art work often reflects the teacher's stimulation
or the lack of it. The first example of Donald's drawing
(above) resulted from a lack of discussion when the topic,
"The First Thanksgiving," was assigned to the second-grade
group. The second piece of his work (below) shows the influence of a stimulating and enriching pupil-teacher discussion.

31

32

Debby's Christmas tree ornaments (above) resulted when her kinder-garten teacher simply said: "Draw something about Christmas." The second drawing (below) resulted from an exciting exchange of ideas.

33

34

Teacher and children listen as one child comments on the strengths of one of her classmate's paintings.

35

Children profit from and enjoy seeing their art work exhibited. Whether it is individual work or a group project, the original work of every child should be shown.

(a) Verbal stimuli
(b) Emphasis on hearing
(c) Reading
(d) Visual stimuli
(e) Active participation in an event
(f) Informal unplanned activity, extrinsic stimuli which causes the child to be moved or accelerated toward expressing himself spontaneously

McVittey concluded:

> The motivations which included the "Personal Factor" of student-teacher participation resulted in the greatest degree of creative growth. . . . Motivations which do not include student-teacher participations should be carefully considered before they are used. Mere participation by the student alone does not guarantee learning.[1]

The effect of lively discussion-type motivation between teacher and children is shown in the accompanying samples of two children's art work (30–33). The first example in each case was drawn with little or no verbal exchange before the drawing began. The second was a result of stimulating discussion between teacher and children.

The first two drawings were made by Donald, a second grader. The lesson was an assigned topic. Since Thanksgiving was near and since the class had been studying about the Pilgrims and Indians, the teacher selected this subject as an appropriate one. The introduction to and motivation of the art work period consisted of the teacher's saying: "We have been studying about the Pilgrims and the first Thanksgiving. Draw whatever you want to about the first Thanksgiving."

The first drawing Donald made (30) resulted from his serious attempt to comply with the teacher's assignment. He drew whatever ideas came to him in association with the subject. He drew two Pilgrims and, from their appearance, it is evident that he has achieved an understanding of their character. The Pilgrims are plainly dressed, wearing the straight hats we so frequently see in other pictures of them. Color is noticeably lacking in the picture.

---

[1]McVittey, Lawrence, *An Experimental Study on Various Methods in Art Motivation at the Fifth Grade Level.* Doctoral dissertation, Pennsylvania State University, 1954, pp. 91–92.

Donald knew that the Pilgrims cooked outdoors over a fire, so he has drawn a piece of food on a spit held by two forked sticks.

A few days later the teacher repeated the topic of the first Thanksgiving with her second-grade art class. Instead of merely assigning the topic, she engaged in a lively discussion of *many* things that the children had learned about the Pilgrims and their celebration of the first Thanksgiving. They recalled many facts that they already knew that served to remind the children of the many interesting things from which they could choose or could include in their compositions.

Not only were facts recalled, but emotions were discussed. The children, through the questions of the teacher, tried to imagine themselves as among the Pilgrims. They tried to project in their imaginations the ways that the Pilgrims might have felt under the various new and sometimes frightening situations in which they found themselves. The exchange of ideas continued until many aspects of the first Thanksgiving were discussed. During this time the children were reviewing what they knew and were thinking about it from a different viewpoint — as a subject for their art.

Donald's second drawing (31) is much more interesting than his first. The Pilgrims are seated at the table. Donald has shown people on both sides of the table. He has included a log cabin with a roof colored to suggest a primitive one made of leaves, sods, and branches, as some of the Pilgrims' early homes may have had. Donald has drawn three trees without leaves to indicate that he knew it was late fall and the leaves were gone. As in the first picture, Donald shows food being cooked outdoors over an open fire.

Donald probably knew all these things when he drew the first picture, but these facts were not predominant. He needed to be reminded *again* of what he had learned and to think about what he would select for his drawing and how he would arrange his picture. It is the responsibility of the teacher to help children to recall and to excite, stimulate, and encourage them to think and to draw. Motivation is a powerful force in art that gives to children the responsibilities of selection and organization. Children can reach new heights of achievement with teachers who inspire them, and the results are as gratifying to the teacher as to the children.

An example of the power of an intensive motivation is shown in the work of Debby, a kindergarten child, 5 years and 1 month of age.   Her two drawings are the result of the assigned topic of Christmas.   The first drawing (32) was made without a discussion-type motivation.   The second (33) is the result of a dramatic, warm, and exciting motivation.

Before the first drawing was begun, the teacher gave to each child a large sheet of gray paper and crayons, saying: "Since Christmas is coming, I thought you might like to draw something about Christmas.   Go right ahead and draw and color anything you like about Christmas."

Debby drew simple shapes on her paper and colored each with a bright color.   She worked the entire time on the forms shown in the first example of her work.   When her work was finished she said: "These are the shiny balls you hang on your Christmas tree." This certainly is an idea associated with Christmas, and Debby remembered the loops for hanging some of the balls.

Several days later the teacher decided to use the same topic of Christmas for the art lesson but with much more emphasis upon her role as the guide in a stimulating discussion before the actual art work began.   The children talked about the many things that they think about when Christmas is mentioned.   In many instances the teacher asked questions that caused deeper thinking about some of the people and objects named and discussed by the children.   She inquired about details of appearance and relationship of ideas that might encourage the children to group or to associate some of the people and objects when they put them into their pictures.   Never at any time did the teacher tell them what to draw or even suggest how they should draw it; this would have been directed teaching.

Children of any age learn through their own efforts to express themselves in their own way considerably more easily when they have a clear mental picture of what they want to do.   Through the discussion, the child's general thoughts crystallize, become more lucid, plainer, and thus easier to put into form.   It is the responsibility of the teacher to guide the discussion in such a way that every child will experience sharper focus of thoughts and feelings.   By motivation the teacher helps the children to become conscious of their own ideas and experiences and relate them to the problem at hand.

When it seemed evident to the teacher that their remarks and behavior indicated that the children were ready to begin, she quickly drew the verbal expression to a close to give the children an opportunity to put their enthusiasm into art form.

As a result of such a motivation, Debby drew a much more complex, detailed, and interesting Christmas picture (33). Instead of just the shiny balls for the Christmas tree that she had drawn in the first picture, Debby drew a Christmas tree decorated with balls and lights of different sizes and colors. The discussion helped her to associate the two. Before Debby came to art class she knew from her first-hand experiences with Christmas trees that the balls were placed on the branches, but she did not bring this knowledge into active thinking. With the help of recall and stimulation she was able to think of many ideas associated with looking at her Christmas tree and presents on Christmas morning.

In the first example, without such stimulation, Debby made no such associations, nor did she show much evidence of the excitement and pleasure she felt in connection with Christmas. The gaily decorated tree and the bright red dress that she is wearing in the second picture communicate her feeling as well as her ideas. Without being helped, through motivation, to remember her thoughts and feelings, she participated in the art experience in the same simple, barren way that the teacher had participated in the motivation. She drew only one isolated idea because the teacher had said ". . . draw something about Christmas." Debby was impoverished by such limitations and her art work showed it.

Children need the suggestions that they gain from their classmates' statements as well as the stimulation of their own thinking through the teacher's questions. Each child takes, from what he hears, those suggestions that apply to the broadening of his own idea. As each child talks, the others are thinking about and responding emotionally to their own *different* ideas and planning what they will draw or model.

Debby drew herself in the second picture. The form at the top of the page is Debby. She colored her dress bright red with stripes. Red is an exciting color. Most children enjoy using it. In this composition she has associated herself with the color. She was stirred by the motivation and remembered how excited she was on Christmas morning. The stimulating discussion helped arouse her excitement. Debby transferred this feeling to her art. In drawing herself she included her blonde hair and strong arms and legs along with facial details. She was thinking deeply. When her picture was completed, Debby said: "This is me. I am looking at my tree on Christmas in the morning when I first get up. I got a dolly that walks and some other presents." The doll is in the picture, too, and so are some other presents in boxes decorated for Christmas. She included two of the same shaped tree decorations that entirely filled her first picture. Debby started to draw another form in her picture, but did not complete it, which children sometimes do for various reasons. One of these reasons might be a lack of time to complete the work. Debby worked hard during the art class, accomplishing a great deal and doing it well.

Debby must have felt quite a lot of satisfaction with this example of her art work. Every child in the group profited by the motivation. The completed crayon pictures showed it. When the teacher projects her enthusiasm for and confidence in the children through her reactions to their contributions during the motivation, the children catch the feeling. This feeling stirs thinking and promotes richer, more meaningful art.

An assigned topic was chosen for the example that illustrates the effect of motivation on the art work of children. The change that took place is clearly shown when both examples have been drawn from the same topic. Whether the topic is an assigned one or whether the children are free to choose their own topics, a stimulating motivational discussion helps children to have a deeper, fuller art experience.

The way a teacher works to stimulate, to excite, to provoke, to incite, and to motivate children to express their own ideas in their personally unique way is an extremely important part of the art lesson and has a deep influence upon the children. Leading the motivation in art is a very important role of the teacher. The teacher *leads* the motivation. The children and teacher together *create* the motivation through the presentation of and response to the ideas presented orally before the drawing begins. Each child, to be sure of himself and of his ideas before the work begins, needs to feel the warmth and personal interest of the teacher in his ideas — in himself.

Encouragement and praise are the keys to successful art expression. Appreciation for the child and for his efforts and achievements are essential. This viewpoint should saturate every phase

of the teacher's operation with children. Not only is it basic to the
motivation of art work, but it is the foundation from which she helps
the children to solve their problems through guidance.

GUIDANCE

When the children have reached a point of excitement and
seem to have ideas for their art, the teacher ends the discussion.
She gives the children the opportunity to put into form the feelings
and ideas that are the driving force behind this impatience for action. Children want to *do* art. The teacher then assumes a different role and becomes less the leader as she puts every child in
the position of leadership, each determining his own task, facing and
solving his own problems. During this period of the children's
concentration upon their expression of ideas, the teacher quietly
studies what each child is doing and observes his working habits.
This is a period of intense concentration on the part of the children.
Each is giving close application of attention to the ideas stimulating
him. There is a complexity of tasks to be undertaken by each child:
each needs to keep in mind the idea and feeling behind his work,
the control of the medium, the attaining of satisfactory shapes in
the composition, and the management of his own partially developed
abilities. Every form or shape already included in the art work
regulates, to some extent, the shapes that follow it. As the art work
progresses, less and less space or materials remain, creating a problem in the placement and size of other things that the child may
want to add. Although art work is challenging, fascinating, and
personally satisfying, it is not easy. While children are intent upon
their purposes of expressing their flood of ideas and feelings, the
teacher protects them from interferences and interruptions. As
long as the children continue to work on the expression of their ideas,
they should be permitted to do so undisturbed. The teacher lends
support by standing by while the children are working. Her
presence makes them feel confident. The stimulation from the discussion during the motivation carries the children through this intense concentration and work.

As a child continues to develop his art, problems sometimes
arise that he finds difficult to solve. A child needs help and guid-

ance. If he does not receive it, he may become discouraged or even abandon his work. By helping children as their problems arise, the teacher performs her guidance responsibilities.

Guidance in art is an indirect action. Through guidance the teacher leads the child toward:

(a) Definition of his problem
(b) Consideration of possible solutions
(c) Information that aids in a solution
(d) Incentive to develop his art work to the extent of his ability

Throughout the motivation the teacher worked with the children as a group. Even though she talked with them one at a time, many of the things that she said were directed toward the group. During

36

The teacher should always be ready to give help and guidance as it is needed.

the guidance period, which follows the motivation, the teacher does most of her work on an individual basis. There are times, of course, when the group, or a large part of it, needs direction or re-direction, but most of her attention, at this stage of the children's work, is given to each on a personal basis as individual problems arise. Since each child is working on a different basis from every

other, his problems will likely differ from those of the others.   Therefore, guidance will be most helpful when approached individually.
Although the teacher discusses his own work with each, it does not
follow that only this child is helped by the teacher's assistance.
Everyone who hears what is said learns something.   The amount
that each child learns is in ratio to the importance to *him* of the
knowledge given at that time.   It may be that the guidance and
help being given to one child will be related to the difficulty another
is having.   As the teacher instructs or helps the first child to focus
upon his problem, the other child listens, applying what he hears to
his own work.   If the child is interested in the guidance being given,
if it has meaning for him at that time, he listens and learns.   If it
has no significance, he disregards it.   Nevertheless, he does hear
it and when it is presented again it will be somewhat familiar to him.

Because the teacher gives help and guidance to children as
they work in art, it is not to be assumed that she tells them what to
do or shows them how to do it.   This would be an infringement
upon the child's right to choose, to express, and to organize.
Neither does the teacher give the children pictures to copy because
they say they cannot draw a certain thing.   This work interferes
with and damages the child's own creative concepts of a form.   Children *want* to do their own work.   They want and need the teacher's help but not her interference.

Some teachers feel that when a child needs help, their job is
to take the child's work into their own hands and solve the problem
for the child, explaining as they proceed what they are doing and
why.   Erroneously, they reason that this type of help given at that
moment will carry over into other similar problems that the child
may later encounter.   What happens is that the child loses the
personal feeling or the identity with his work.   It is no longer *his*.
He no longer wants it, and he has lost interest and pride in it.   How
can he, then, learn much by it?   The child may form a distaste for
his art work.   If a child knows or suspects that a teacher functions
in this manner, he may refrain from soliciting her help or even re-
vealing that he needs help.   He wants to protect his work against
such an encroachment; he wants his work to be true and honest —
to be *his*.   Even though others may think the addition of the teacher's work improves it, *the child does not*.   He does not feel "right"
about it any more.

The teacher's role in guidance during the art work period is one of helping the learner toward understanding. She does this as she explains. Through talking, through questioning and discussing, she helps the child develop his ability to put his ideas into art form. In the first place, a problem arises because the child does *not know*. He cannot analyze. He has no clear or certain idea or plan of what he wants to do or how he might do it. Sometimes he does not even know the nature of his problem. He may sense that something is wrong or incomplete about his art and not even be able to indicate the reason for this feeling of dissatisfaction. He needs someone to lead the way. Since he is immature, he has only partially developed skills, a limited background of experiences, and needs and wants the leadership and advice of someone mature, skilled, and experienced. When given, the advice should be consistent with the child's age, mental ability, and purposes.

Children in the elementary grades need the teacher's guidance during the working period while their work is still incomplete, and they should receive it within a short time after encountering the difficulty. Children are not as patient as adults. If left to cope with a problem too long, they can lose the inspiration that keeps them working, or they might change the course of their art work, abandoning the challenge and substituting in its place a form or idea they can do or have successfully done before. This limits learning. It is of little help to a child to be exposed to guidance influences after his work is complete, as it tends only to create a feeling of dissatisfaction with his work. To a child of this age, confidence in his completed work is important. The child needs to feel that his work is accepted and his achievements appreciated. After the art is finished, the teacher leads the discussion of it on another basis, for another purpose.

There are many reasons why children need guidance as they work. The reasons vary with the children and with the problems. In modern art education based upon creative expression, every child's work is different from every other, and every individual's work varies from day to day. Each medium presents its special problems as well. Therefore, the teacher should bring an open mind to every problem, expecting it to be somewhat unusual. From conversation with children during the motivation and from observation during the working period, the teacher brings to the guidance knowledge of their feelings, ideas, and purposes. Although it is true that no two problems are identical, there are some common ones.

Helping a child to define his problem is one of the general areas of guidance with which a teacher deals. As was mentioned earlier, sometimes a child has a feeling of dissatisfaction about his work without being able to identify the reason. He may say: "I don't like it" or "Something's the matter with mine" or "I can't make it look right." If the teacher asks a question like, "What don't you like about it?" or "Why doesn't it look right to you?" sometimes a child may simply name a part of the art work in order to give an answer, which may not be the problem bothering him at all. Or he may answer in much the same way as he first spoke: "I don't know. It just isn't right" or "I didn't do it right." This state of discontent with a vague cause is frustrating and discouraging. The child needs to be led to see what his problem is. Such guidance is the first step in showing the child the way. The teacher might ask the child to put his art work a greater distance from himself and to look at it, or she might have him look at it in a mirror to give him a fresh view. Sometimes, then, he sees the trouble for himself. If not, the teacher can point out the area of success and ask him if any area is not as well worked out. From her knowledge of art, the teacher would recognize the difficulty. The easiest course would be simply to tell the child, but he has more to gain by learning how to discover it for himself. The teacher might also ask the child questions that will help him focus upon one aspect of the work at a time. She might ask: "Do you have a variety of widths in those spaces or are they a great deal alike?" or "Is there any part not unified with the rest? Does any part seem left out or by itself?" or "If the wind is blowing the waves like that, would it be blowing anything else?" Frequently as the child defines his problem, solutions come to mind. When this is the case, the child should continue with his art unaided. He *knows* what has been troubling him and what to do about it. His incentive to continue has been rekindled by this additional insight and purpose.

A child who has been led to recognize his problem may still not know what to do about it. Through further questioning and discussion of what he knows about art and about his subject, the teacher guides the child to determine his own course. The teacher seeks suggestions from the child as to what he might do. If there is a class atmosphere of friendliness, she may involve other children in the discussion or in suggesting ideas. The use of this procedure depends on how the child might react to it. The better the teacher knows her students, the better she can help them. The first suggestion may be the solution the child is looking for, or several may be considered before he decides. The teacher may, from her more mature viewpoint and with her rich background of education, see solutions that are quite different from those suggested by the child; she keeps in mind that hers are right as adult suggestions and the child's are right for his level of maturity.

In addition to helping the child to define his problems and to consider and decide upon possible solutions, the teacher guides the child toward information that aids in a solution. He may know what his problem is and how he wants to organize and continue with his work, but his lack of some technical skill may block his way. In this case, the teacher simply teaches the skill to him and to other children who may be interested in learning or watching. The child may want to form a particular animal and realize as he works that he does not know enough about it to produce a satisfying shape. Questioning him about the animal will draw out what he does know and point to what he needs to learn. The teacher refers the child to pictures of the animal. After he has studied them for a while, she helps him by calling his attention to points that are characteristic of the animal. In a giraffe, for example, she would point out the shape of the head, how the head and neck join, how the body slants, and the differences in the front and back legs. Knowing a few of the typical features would help the child form his own mental concept of a giraffe that would facilitate his art expression. He has *knowledge* to drawn upon. From his own ideas, he creates, imagines, and designs as he works.

There are other resources to which a teacher may lead a child in helping him add to his knowledge. Knowledge is one of the bases for creative art work — knowledge about objects, operations, or art principles. Knowledge, imagination, and emotion are the sources of and driving forces behind a child's art. In her guidance role the teacher encourages the children to use pictorial and textual material.

A great deal of the teacher's guidance work is in remotivating children to continue. In spite of a strong desire to put ideas into form, a child may stop working simply because his enthusiasm runs low.   To rekindle it, the teacher herself should be warm and zealous as she talks to the child about what he has accomplished and what other related ideas he might consider.   The teacher questions and draws out; the child thinks and develops.   Sometimes the whole group needs to be remotivated, but often it is an individual matter.

As the teacher moves among the children while they work, she gives some word of encouragement or assistance to each child. Children are aware of their teacher's presence and want some bit of personal attention from her.   Teachers are never neutral influences; what they say affects children.   The fact that the teacher passes a child by without making some comment about his work, or offering some incentive for him to go forward, affects the child.   He may think that she sees nothing worthy of mention in his art or he may feel left out.   Each child is important.   Each deserves some personal comment.   Ruth Strang indicates how the teacher functions with students in the role of guidance in the art class:

> In no other classroom, perhaps, is there more opportunity for skillful, unobtrusive guidance than in the art room.   There the teacher works almost exclusively with individuals.   He brings out the student's ideas, waits for him to discover his difficulty, makes suggestions that enable him to complete his work successfully.   Pleased by the teacher's praise and helped by his tactful hints, students work with increased effort and interest.   The teacher can usually find something of promise in any piece of work and is resourceful in making suggestions for improvement: a shift in line, the addition of another color, a detail added for balance.   Under skillful, unobtrusive guidance, students grow in creative ability and in personality.[2]

A teacher can judge when the art work is completed by the attitude of the children.   When they seem to have developed their work to the extent of their interest and ability and are satisfied with it, the teacher should accept it.   Her role changes again as she discusses the work with the children.   She deals with the whole group again as she helps the children to evaluate the completed work.

---

[2]Strang, Ruth, *The Role of the Teacher in Personnel Work*.   New York: Columbia University, Teachers College, 1946, p. 162.

EVALUATION

Evaluation, a vital process in elementary-school art education, is a measure of the quality of the art — a search for value within each piece of art work. Quality is measured:

    (a) By the child as he works on his art
    (b) By the teacher as the child works on his art
    (c) In pupil-teacher discussion of the completed art work
    (d) In study of the exhibited art work

Evaluation has deeper implications than grading, which may or may not be an outcome of evaluation. Since grading of art is in opposition to the purposes of creative expression, evaluation will be considered as a learning situation.

Evaluation by the child as he works. The child's evaluation begins as he begins to consider an idea for his art. Many ideas come to him and he chooses the one that he considers important enough to concentrate upon and that he judges to be valuable enough to absorb his attention. He gives consideration to each idea, evaluating its interest to him and its appropriateness to the materials with which he is working. Thus, before the child actually begins dealing with materials, he begins to evaluate. He continues to make judgments of his art work from that point until the work is completed and during the time it is exhibited. As a child works in art, he forms an opinion of every shape he creates, deciding whether they measure up to the standard he expects of himself. Before he proceeds, he also appraises the form he has created in relation to the dimensions of the background or the space around it. Every form and area he structures is evaluated in this way. As each form or area is added, the whole composition is also re-evaluated. The more skilled the child is in making evaluations, the more proficient he can be in developing and improving his work. The child learns from making his own judgments. He learns many things by working them out himself, especially if his own experiences are supplemented by the help of a teacher who points out ways of making deeper or more appreciative evaluations of art work.

Evaluation by the teacher as the child works. In order to make the guidance period more significant, the teacher evaluates,

Teacher and children together evaluate some aspects of a group embroidery project before the work is completed.

37

38

Teacher and children evaluate completed art work as they discuss the strong points of each child's work.

appraises, and measures the child's achievements and problems by studying the child's art as he works. The children evaluate their own work as it moves forward, and so the teacher does also. The child's purpose in this constant appraisal is to create the best piece of art of which he is capable; the teacher's purpose is to help the child grow in his ability to express his ideas in art and to learn how to appreciate the work of others. Evaluation is an important tool in furthering both purposes.

Pupil-teacher discussion. After the art work is completed, further education takes place as this work is evaluated and discussed. As the discussion begins, the role of the teacher changes. Again she works with the group as a whole instead of with the children on an individual basis. Children have much to learn by hearing what is said of the strengths of their classmates' work. They see and hear an explanation of what each child has done and how he has worked it out. The teacher's role is to establish a point of view toward evaluation and to guide the evaluation discussion of the completed art work.

Study of exhibited art work. As long as the art work remains on display and within view of the children, each child forms his own private opinion of the success of the project and of the relative quality of each child's work. Regardless of what was said of it during the discussion, a child is free to make his evaluation in terms of his own values, experiences, and emotional responses. Independently of the viewpoints of others, he admires certain works and studies them more closely. With no intention to copy the successes of others, he is further inspired toward his own achievements. Such evaluation can lead to improvement of his own art and to the development of a unique style. His personal preference is frequently for the work of those children who express their ideas as he does. Then he explores the challengingly different ones. He learns and is inspired as he studies the exhibition.

Purposes of evaluation. Evaluation in art is a discipline through which the child:

(a) Learns how to make or to improve his judgments
(b) Gains more art knowledge
(c) Adds to his general knowledge

(d) Understands the work of others
(e) Learns what to look for in observing works of art
(f) Learns how to talk about art products
(g) Improves his own art expressions

These advantages are the result of the child's evaluation both as he works on the expression of his ideas and feelings and after the art work is completed.   Both the children and teacher have responsibilities for the appraisal of the finished work and for the discussion that can accompany it.

Evaluation constitutes the making of judgments.   Children develop the ability to form opinions, to appraise, and to judge.   The children's skill in estimating and selecting of quality grows as the teacher guides and supplements their evaluations.

Through the pupil-teacher discussion of the completed art work, children gain more *art* knowledge.   They look at each piece of work to see how they react to it, what particular element makes it interesting.   Then they study it further to try to find out why they react to it as they do or why they find it interesting.   They look for a spot or for an area that they consider more successfully worked out than some others and attempt to ascertain *why*.   Not every child will be able to do all of these things and should not be expected to.   Neither should every child in the group be expected to come to the same conclusions.   Evaluation should include an approach to the study of art.   By evaluating, the child learns that art is something worthy of study.   He discovers the rewards of such evaluative procedures and feels the satisfactions that come from closer association with a variety of types of art work.   Quite often after closer study and more searching evaluation, the child discovers art qualities that previously he failed to notice or to understand.

As the child discovers what particular quality of the art expression causes his reaction, he associates this element with the emotion he feels.   Therefore, he builds knowledge about additional ways of expressing and communicating feelings through art.   Sensitivities are developed through every attempt to associate one's own feeling with that of the artist by the responses that must be alerted.   This deliberate quickening of the senses helps the child become more responsive to art and to the reactions and feelings that the artist has expressed through his forms, colors, and organization.

Many of the disciplines of art are learned through the evalua-tion of works of art. As the children and teacher jointly discuss how a certain thing has been accomplished, they sometimes refer to structural principles of art. They may talk about how colors have been mixed to bring about particular shades and tints, and what qualities of these colors create a pleasant relationship among the group of which they are a part. They are probing deep in order to learn why these certain colors are pleasing.

When an evaluation has shown that organization is a strong point in a composition, together the teacher and children discuss how this organization has been achieved. They want to see what there is about this particular arrangement of forms that makes for an organized grouping and how it is structured to give the impres-

39

The teacher discusses with children the work of mature artists.

sion of belonging together. Since every piece of art is different and every organization different, many such evaluation experiences help children to form criteria for making judgments about art.

As the child evaluates art work, he finds out about forms, ideas, and meanings unfamiliar to him. Other children have had experiences that may be unknown to him, or they may have reactions that differ from his. As these are expressed and discussed, the child adds to his general knowledge.

Through this new knowledge, the child also becomes more familiar with his classmates. He observes their work and listens to their comments during the evaluation discussion. As children discuss their own work and that of mature artists, they learn to appreciate the work of others and understand and enjoy a much broader range of expressions in art.

When evaluation of art work becomes a regular part of the art program, children learn what to look for as they view art. Since art is basically a visual subject, knowing what to look for helps people to enjoy it. They have criteria that help them to analyze the work. A viewpoint of evaluation based upon a search for achievement builds a positive attitude toward the approach to art. Children need to learn what to look for in a wide variety of art products. It is helpful in everyday living if they learn how to evaluate textile designs, appropriate and harmonious dress, and the products of industry such as utensils and furniture.

As the child learns what to look for in art by helping to point it out and hearing it discussed, he will grow in his ability to talk about art. He will have developed an art vocabulary and will have learned how to use it. He will have learned phrases that can be used to describe certain relationships in art, as well as how to describe the novel, fresh approaches to art with which he will, no doubt, come in contact.

One of the most important outcomes of evaluation is the improvement of the child's own art expression. From all the information that he gains as a result of his participation in evaluation study and discussion, the child is most deeply impressed by that which interests him most. He also learns many things that will be most helpful to any subsequent art experience.

It is unnecessary to conduct an evaluation discussion of everything that children produce in art. This is a valuable although time-consuming procedure. Children in the elementary grades want to *do* art. They will enjoy the evaluation if it is not done so frequently or so extensively that they begin to feel deprived of working with materials. Sometimes, however, an evaluation can be quickly done. Small groups of children may hold their art work up as the teacher and children simply make one brief value statement of each or a general favorable statement can be made of the group of art work shown. The same is true when all the art is exhibited.

One brief comment may suffice. Indeed, there are times when the work can be hung, looked at, enjoyed, appreciated, and evaluated by all who see it — without an accompanying discussion. Children may become somewhat apprehensive if they feel that *everything* they do will be discussed.

Some teachers may feel that an evaluation is not complete without adding to the positive comments a discussion of the areas that need improvement and suggestions of how the child could have improved his work. They feel that suggestions of this type will help the child solve similar future problems. Such reasoning seems logical to adults. The mature teacher may feel that *she* would gain more if an evaluation of *her* work were handled this way. Such reasoning is based upon adult thinking, purposing, and reacting. Children are not yet ready for such mature ways. Having one's shortcomings pointed out by his teacher and classmates in front of his peers and friends is a difficult situation and an embarrassing experience for a child. Something may be gained by it, but there is also much to lose. Feelings of confidence could easily be lost and pleasure in art may suffer. With the pointing out of the shortcomings of their work, children become ill at ease and fearful of what may be said. Art is an experience to be enjoyed, not endured. Indirectly, by having areas of success recognized, children realize that other spots in their work are not as well developed. As they continue the evaluation, children think about these parts as well as about their strongest points. Education is a gradual process, but children will learn rapidly with teachers who care about them and provide rich learning opportunities.

EXHIBITION

A final rewarding part of creative art work is the showing of the completed art product. The opportunity to share his ideas and thoughts with others is important to the child. Therefore, some type of display of every child's work should be planned as a part of the art project. To have each work shown is just as important to one child as it is to another. Therefore, *every* child's work should be shown. To have all the work displayed without any indication of favor or disapproval of any individual child's work is also important. Hangings based upon the preference for one child's work or for a selected few children's work would be contradictory to the viewpoint stressed throughout this book. Every child is as important as every other. Every child's work is important to him. Therefore, every piece of art work produced by a group of children is important. Whatever is significant to the child should be of consequence to his teacher.

Limited display space. The display space in some classrooms is, unfortunately, so limited as to make it impossible to hang every piece of work at once. In this case, the children should have their work hung indiscriminately and in turn, with no child's work being displayed twice until everyone's work has been shown once. There are many ways to deal with such a space limitation. As examples, the teacher might display the work of children who sit in groups together; or the boys, then the girls; or one portion of the class on Monday, another portion on Tuesday, and so forth.

When inadequate display space exists, the teacher should occasionally provide some opportunity for all the children's work to be hung together even though the exhibition is hung outside the classroom. The school hall is a fine place and frequently looks more colorful with children's art work filling up the empty walls. Children need a chance to study their own work in relation to that of their classmates.

Suggested bases for display. Although a display hung according to someone's ideas of "quality" is difficult for children to accept, they approve of exhibits arranged on other bases if they understand how the selections are made. They can agree with exhibitions arranged on some basis that makes a more aesthetic appearance. Then, too, art exhibitions are more attractive and interesting when the arrangement of the exhibit has been so chosen. A few bases for more pleasing displays might be: pieces light in color shown alternately with those dark in color; or complex pieces beside those containing few large forms; or pieces of a certain size or shape arranged together; or pieces that seem related in subject matter or form shown together.

When children see an aesthetic exhibition of their art work and understand the principle determining the placements, they are adding to their art experiences and art knowledge.

There are times when a child may not want to have his art work included in the exhibition. He may have come to this conclusion because an experiment with the media, color, or form may not have worked out as well as he had anticipated. He tried it but it did not work; he should therefore be free to dispose of the result if *he* so chooses. The initiation of the idea to withhold his work from the group display should come from the child (without the teacher's suggestions, subtle or otherwise) and should be respected by the teacher. If, however, such withdrawal becomes a habit, there is a different kind of problem.

Exhibitions outside the school. An exhibition of children's art held outside the school is stimulating to children and gives them a sense of pride. It also creates public interest in children's art. Store windows are fine for art exhibitions, and so are the public library and empty store rooms. The exhibition should be hung in spots easily accessible to the public. A little imagination in considering the community resources may lead to some excellent locations. Keep the exhibition simple. Do not undertake too much or let it become burdensome so that the pleasure is gone and the initiative to do it again dulled.

Mounting and backgrounds. Mounting the art work appropriately adds to the beauty and effectiveness of each piece. Displaying it against a background that brings out its unique qualities adds interest to a piece of art work. A light directed at the three-dimensional art pieces is simple to install and can be so placed as to cast shadows in any direction or to elongate them. The shadows, cast against a background, add interest to the art work and become a part of the exhibition. Children find such a simple device fascinating. Mounts for flat work should be selected to bring out the unique quality of the art work; they can vary in color, or can be all white, gray, black, or any neutral shade suitable to the work.

The background area for the display can be changed to emphasize the various types of work exhibited. Textured material such as corrugated paper, wire, string stretched in a pattern, or strips of colored paper are a few suggestions. Children will have other ideas to offer. Appreciate their suggestions. Let them work some of them out and hang the display. When participating, children feel more responsible for and more personally involved in the exhibition and in its relation to the whole classroom appearance. Often, children's art work needs nothing more than to be displayed. Although mounting it or arranging special backgrounds enhances it and adds to the appearance, neither is necessary. Child art is attractive just as it is.

Change of exhibitions. As soon as a new exhibition of their art work has been arranged, children study it intently. With each succeeding day their interest in it wanes. The younger the child, the more quickly he has exhausted the potentials of the exhibition. His attention span is shorter than that of older children, and he has not yet acquired the background of knowledge necessary for deeper study. Then, too, the art of young children is less complex than that of the older child, containing less material for study. After two or three days children in the primary grades have lost interest in an exhibition. Children in the upper elementary grades do not lose interest as quickly, but after a week, at least a part of the display of upper-grade art should change. Large projects upon which the group has spent possibly several weeks can be more permanently shown.

There are four specific and important roles that the teacher of art plays. They include:

(a) Motivation of the children to do art work
(b) Guidance of the children during the art work period
(c) Evaluation during the work period and leadership during the evaluative discussion of the completed art work
(d) Arranging for exhibition of every child's art

Although each of the four major roles of the teacher is treated separately in this chapter, they overlap and extend into each other.

From the beginning of an art project until the end, the teacher is active. She has a vital responsibility for the art education of the children. The teacher is always an influential force. Therefore, it is important for her constantly to keep in mind that encouragement and praise are keys to help children grow in art.

Suggested activity

Begin to collect pictures that could be used as examples for children to study. These pictures should be large enough to use with a group. Children might use these pictures as resources for particular information, or they could be used by the teacher in introducing a new project or new use of materials. Assemble the pictures around central themes, such as mask designs, abstract painting, modern sculpture, mobiles, or animal forms.

CHAPTER *V*

Teaching creative art expression

THERE is a certain definite series of actions that constitute the role of the teacher as she motivates, guides, evaluates, and exhibits the work of the children in her group. In order to free the children to create, the teacher needs to proceed in such a way as to inspire each child's confidence in his own ideas and ways as best for him. So as not to interfere with the individually different intentions and purposes of each child, the teacher works in a general way with the group and on an individual basis with each child.

The art processes that the children use and the teaching processes that the teacher uses are interdependent. If the teacher wants the children to work in a free and independent way she must be permissive in letting them choose their own ideas, improvising and creating as they go. They need to feel this continuous operation of her inspirational influence, her confidence in them, and her appreciation of their work.   The children take their cue from the teacher; she takes hers from them.

The example of how a teacher functions with children in creative expression constitutes the major part of this chapter.   This is a method that teachers may use with children without in any way interfering with the child or directing him in his work.   It is a method designed to free the child, to stimulate him, and to give him confidence.   It gives help where help is needed as well as instruction and information at the time least likely to influence a particular art product and most likely to contribute to the child's general knowledge and creative ability.   It is a procedure that each teacher can adapt to her own personal way of teaching.   In creative art expression, there are individual ways of teaching just as there are individual ways of working in art.

The entire process of teaching creative art to children can best be shown through an illustration of the way one teacher functioned with the children in her third-grade group.   The same procedure is applicable to children of any age.   Because of the individual differences among teachers, no two would conduct the motivation, guidance, and evaluation in exactly the same manner. Each would ask questions with different phrasing and content.   The example in this chapter, however, is not intended as a pattern that teachers should copy verbatim.

Creative art requires creative teaching.   To present a pattern of teaching to be copied would bring results as barren and limiting as expecting all children to copy the same picture.

The inclusion here of a specific example of the teaching of modern creative art serves as a basis for a better understanding of how this teaching method is put into operation with children. Teachers need to have some idea of *how* to teach it, and *what* to say and *when* to say it.   Reading and thinking through one example of an art lesson can serve as a guide to inspire teachers to think of other approaches, other ways, *their own* phrasing, and *their own* responses and questions.   Each teacher knows her own group of children better than any other person does.   She is aware of the personality of the group and of each child within the group.   The example that follows is a presentation of the actions and conversations that took place in one situation.   The example and its accompanying comments, however, represent the method that serves to draw from each child the expressions of his unique thinking. Such a process of teaching inspires children, helps them recall events, motivates imagination, and excites and challenges them without interfering with their intentions.

MATERIALS AND PREPARATION

Preparing and making available the materials is a part of the pupil-teacher work that precedes the discussion. In addition, procedures for obtaining paper, paints, and other necessary materials are determined by the children and teacher together. The children should know where to put their completed paintings to dry, how to clean up after their work, and what to do in case they finish before the others. Such preplanning before the motivation discussion begins frees the child to concentrate upon his ideas and to create. An example of the way one group of children decided to handle the problem of tempera paint gives a basis for considering other desirable ways of procuring and sharing paint and facilities.

Before any discussion began the tempera paint was mixed and stirred and placed on a large table on one side of the room. A brush was put into each jar so that the children would not carry color from one jar to another by using the same brush for each nor dilute the paint by cleaning the brush between each color.

All the jars of paint of different colors necessary to complete a painting would require a great deal of space. For that reason, the children decided to get one or two jars of paint from the table just as they needed it, then return it so that the others might use it. This procedure gives the child an opportunity to move around. The physical freedom contributes to freedom of thought. The children have already put their names on their papers and have accomplished all other details ahead of time so that they are ready to begin to put their thoughts and feelings into form as soon as the discussion is over.

One child may already have an idea and seem ready to begin but since he is such a quick thinker, he would contribute to the discussion. Participation in the thinking session will likely broaden his ideas as well as enrich and stimulate some of the other children.

If some children begin to work before the discussion is over, it distracts those who have not yet chosen an idea or have not become emotionally stimulated enough to begin. The latter group may feel pressured by the fact that some of their classmates are getting ahead of them and, consequently, they may start to work before they have had time to think about painting or to decide upon what they would like to do. Conversely, the continued discussion may disturb those who have begun to paint, so it is better for all the children if everyone participates in the entire discussion.

Some people feel that to be wholly creative, the child must not only be permitted to choose the subject matter for his art, but should also have the choice of any medium he wants. This idea of each person choosing whatever materials he wants is fine for people working alone or with groups of people mature enough to make a choice and to stick to it. There are, however, many reasons why the free choice of a variety of materials during one art class does not function well for elementary-school children.

In the first place, the length of time for art activities in the elementary grades is usually shorter than with older children. If a variety of materials needed to be distributed according to individual needs, it would consume a disproportionate amount of the time allotted for art.

Then too, children of this age change their minds. They think they want a certain material until they see a classmate have something else. If the teacher helps these children make the change, more time is taken. If there is an arbitrary rule that a first choice must be the final one, some children will be unhappy because they are unable to change their first selection for another; this unhappiness is not conducive to creative art work.

If children are to have free choice of any materials for the work period, all materials must be prepared and placed in a convenient location for easy accessibility. There must be quantities of each in readiness, for it would be difficult to predict how many children will want to paint or work with clay. If the clay is not all used, it dries and hardens. Other materials that have been prepared and placed in an available location for the children require handling. All this varied preparation uses teacher and student energy in an amount disproportionate to the value of such a procedure.

In the elementary school, working habits and procedures

*Children enjoy participating in the preparation and distribution of
art materials and supplies.   Such activities help build habits of responsibility and give each child an opportunity to contribute to the
group activity.*

40

41

*Children need a variety of experiences with different materials to
enrich their education through art.   These sixth-grade boys are using
wire, paper, cardboard, string, and papier-mâché; other material
will be added as the sculptural forms develop.*

are being established, and with various materials and under different circumstances, this takes time and effort. Until such habits are built, constant reminders need to be given and supervision provided. Children need to know how to get clay, where to put the finished clay piece, and how to clean up. When this is well in mind, children are free to give thought to their work. It takes many repetitions of this procedure to establish the habit. Children in the elementary grades have not yet mastered the various procedures with different materials. They still forget and need to be reminded.

Therefore, it works more satisfactorily for a group of children to use the same material at the same time. This in no way interferes with their right to choose their own ideas and work them out as they desire. If the child who wants to paint today knows it is coming tomorrow, he will be satisfied. A variety of materials presented, each at different times, develops flexibility and ingenuity with children and is good for the creative and personality development of the child.

MOTIVATION

The teacher might begin by saying: "Some of you already have some good ideas for your painting. What would you like to paint? What is one idea you might use for a painting?"

Alice: "I'm going to paint about our summer camp where we go for our vacation. There is a lake there and we go swimming. I'm going to paint us in swimming. Our dog, too. He goes."

Teacher: "Is your summer camp in the woods or near the lake? What is the place like?"

Alice: "It is right by the lake. The shore is right by our cabin. But there is a kind of woods there, too. There are some trees. No other cabin is very near ours."

Teacher: "How does it make you feel to be there? Are you glad or how *do* you feel?"

Alice: "Well, it makes me feel glad. I like to go there. I get excited when my mother tells me we are going to go. Then I can hardly wait. We have fun, Mary and me.

[Mary is her sister.]   We can just play and don't have to
watch out for cars or anything.   It is kind of cool feeling
by the trees and in the cabin.   But the sun is good, too."

By asking the location of the camp, the teacher encouraged Alice
and the rest of the children in the group to think about the other
objects associated with the topic.   The question was pointed to
Alice, but many others would realize that it would make their picture fuller, more interesting, and more informative if they thought
about the landscape and the objects and people near or associated
with their ideas.   The question was a cue to the children to think
about emotional responses to the subject each had chosen.   We all
react to every experience we have.   This reaction is a part of the
experience.   Recalling the reaction is part of the motivation for art.
The experiences (real or imaginary) that children have plus their
reactions to the experiences determine their art.   It is not necessary
for the teacher to question each child specifically about his feelings
because the answers of one or two children will serve to remind the
others.

Teacher: "Who has a *different* idea for a painting?"

Joe: "My Dad took us to the airport.   We watched the planes
go up and land.   Some were refueled.   The gasoline
trucks went right out beside the planes.   There were big
planes came in while we were there, and people got off."

Teacher: "You have lots of interesting things to put into your painting, Joe.   Exciting things happen at the airport and to
planes while they are flying."

Although the teacher did not question Joe about his emotional reaction to his visit to the airport, she sensed his feeling of excitement
from the way he told about it.   From this cue she said: "Exciting
things happen at the airport and to planes while they are flying."
The second part of the sentence, ". . . and to planes while they are
flying," broadened the topic and may have inspired Joe further or
set other children thinking about exciting things.

Teacher: "We don't always have to paint or draw about things that
are exciting or amusing.   Other kinds of things happen
to us, too, sometimes.   What might be one of them?"

Helen: "Getting scared.   Sometimes at night I get bad dreams

and get scared. But I'm not going to paint about this
for my art. I already have my idea."

Teacher: "You can paint about anything you want to. Can anyone think of *another* feeling that we sometimes have besides fear and being happy?"

Harold: "I get afraid sometimes when I have to go home after it
gets dark."

Since this was a different experience, but the same emotional reaction, the teacher did not comment on Harold's contribution. She
simply accepted it with a nod of her head.

Teacher: "Can anyone think of *another* feeling we sometimes get?"

Doris: "When I have to practice my piano lesson, I get mad.
I don't want to do it. It's always when I have started to
do something important or something."

Teacher: "Yes, we all feel that way at times. You could paint
about how you feel, or you could paint about some idea
you have — a real or an imaginary idea. You don't have
to choose any particular thing."

42

*Sometimes the expression of an emotional reaction motivates a
child's art. Margaret said of her work, "I was sled-riding down a
hill last night. It was snowing all around, and the wind was blowing so hard I just screamed."*

By making such a statement, the teacher was trying to free the children from any obligation of being expected to paint about a feeling or emotion, specifically as such, just because attention was focused upon it briefly. It is the responsibility of the teacher to help children to think broadly about many aspects of their ideas for art. She added the suggestion that they could paint an imaginary composition: "a real or an imaginary idea." At the same time, it is also her job to help them keep in mind that the choices are *theirs*, that there is nothing in particular that she expects of them, and nothing that she will be looking for as a result of their discussion.

Teacher: "Who has a *different idea* for his painting?"
Jack: "Baseball."
Teacher: "What about baseball, Jack? What will you put into your painting?"

The other two children who had presented their ideas seemed to have not only a subject in mind but also an experience associated with the subject. They mentioned action, people, and environmental objects associated with their idea. Jack's contribution to the discussion lacked such broad associations.

Jack: "Me, hitting the ball."
Teacher: "What other players were in it, too?"
Jack: "The pitcher."
Teacher: "Anyone else?"
Jack: "The guy catching."
Teacher: "Anyone watching you?"
Jack: "Yes. There were some other kids."
Teacher: "Where were you playing, Jack, in the street or in a field?"
Jack: "Behind Fred's house in his yard."
Teacher: "How would I know this when I look at your picture?"
Jack: "I could put in the house."

It is clear that Jack is not very vocal and thinks about his idea in only one step at a time. There is much more that the teacher could have developed with Jack. She could have brought into the discussion other children who would have other ideas, and often this is a good practice. The teacher would not always wish to function in the same way with Jack nor with the other children in the group. Although Jack knew all the things that the teacher talked to him about, they were not in his active thinking at that moment.   He needed help in making association and in thinking through his idea about baseball.   He also needed practice in vocal as well as graphic expression.

The teacher's more detailed discussion with Jack served several purposes:

(a) To help Jack broaden his concept into a whole composition that included more than just one person holding a bat.   Although simply one person holding a baseball bat could make a strong and vigorous picture, the teacher, knowing Jack, realized that one of his personality characteristics was to draw just one thing or say just one or two words.   She felt he needed this developmental process of learning how to think deeper and of making more associations.

(b) Jack has a tendency to think only about himself.   This interrogation pointed toward the inclusion of others, especially those who co-operated in helping him play ball.   Because Jack is shy, the teacher included the question "Anyone watching you?" to suggest to him that he was a person worth watching.   In so doing, the teacher developed the personality of the child as she developed ideas with him that would develop and improve his art.   Both took place at the same time.

(c) The teacher's probing of more and more ideas that Jack might include in his art makes other children think more deeply about their own ideas or else concentrate on Jack's whole idea from *their* viewpoint.   This is a learning situation in which *every* child benefits directly or indirectly.

At *no* time did the teacher make any suggestions to Jack of what he might include in his painting.   She was, in her questions, sensitive to him, taking her cues from what he said and from what she felt he needed as a person.

Teacher: "You have lots of interesting things to put into your painting, Jack."

Jack: "Yes, and trees were there in the yard.   I could put a tree in."

Jack was stimulated to the point of thinking independently about objects and ideas associated with baseball.

Teacher: "Who has a *different* idea?"

Janice: "Could I paint about last summer?"

Teacher: "Of course, Janice. What do you think you might paint about last summer?"

Janice: "About the baby pigs. Last summer at my grandma's farm their pig had baby pigs — lots of them. I could make them in my picture."

The teacher nodded approvingly at Janice, who indicated by the tone of her voice a feeling of emotional excitement about the little pigs. It was not necessary for the teacher to stimulate Janice further; her own emotions did that.

The teacher makes the children feel at ease during the discussion by talking with them on their own level, omitting academic or professional phrasing but at the same time being grammatical.

She also helps put them at ease by accepting *every* idea presented without either a hint of criticism or a suggestion that certain contributions might be more important, more imaginative, or better in any way than others. These two ways of dealing with children are keys in encouraging participation in discussion.

Teacher: "Who else has a different idea?"

By this time in the questioning several children raised their hands, indicating that they had an idea for art that they wanted to tell about. Just because some children, however, do not volunteer to talk about their ideas before they begin to paint does not mean that they have no ideas. They may have been thinking in terms of form and color and about the painting of *their own* ideas. They are not interested, at this point, in discussing them orally. Children are different in this respect; they function, as all artists do, according to their personality demands.

Mike: "I'm going to paint an abstract."

Teacher: "All right, Mike. What are some of the things we have discussed that help to make abstract paintings more interesting?"

Mike: "Not to make everything alike."

Teacher: "Yes. What else?"

Rachael: "Make some large things and some small — all kinds of things."

Sam:	"Just make it up as you go. You can tell what to make next when you look at what you have already done. But don't make it like the one you've seen or like one you already made before."
Teresa:	"Make your picture all over your paper."
Andrew:	"When we were looking at those pictures painted by real artists, we saw that the colors were put in different places in their paintings. They didn't put all the red in one place. They distributed it around."
Mike:	"They used light and dark colors, too."
Teacher:	"Can anyone think of anything *else* you could paint — a different idea from those we have talked about?"
Dominick:	[excitedly and with lots of gestures] "I'm going to paint airplanes — fighting and getting shot at by the soldiers and with people watching them."
Jerry:	"I'm going to paint a war picture with airplanes fighting."
Teacher:	"That's Dominick's idea, Jerry. What other exciting things do airplanes do?"

Creative expression gives every child the opportunity to choose *his own* ideas for art. It may seem at first as though Jerry were avoiding the responsibility that freedom of choice places upon people. It is often easier for a child to take the idea suggested by another than it is to concentrate upon selecting an idea meaningful to himself. Because a certain way is easier does not mean that it is better. In this situation, the teacher has several points to consider: (a) this is Dominick's idea, and he has a right to it without having someone copy it, (b) Jerry's apparent dependence, (c) the possibility that Dominick's suggestion may have precipitated a feeling for which Jerry was trying to find form. Since it is difficult to know the intention of the child from this brief conversation, the teacher should avoid a statement based upon a quick conclusion which might embarrass or discourage one of the children. The teacher said gently, "That is Dominick's idea, Jerry." Her tone indicated no reproach; it was just a reminder that someone else had thought of the idea first. Her next question, "What other exciting things do airplanes do?" was intended to help Jerry think about a little different type of activity that he might deal with in this exciting topic.

The teacher did not embarrass Jerry, for embarrassment

causes a child to become self-conscious and sometimes emotionally confused. Such procedure would not have been conducive to his further and more independent thinking. Neither did she insist upon an immediate answer to her question, "What other exciting things do airplanes do?" Some children may have a ready answer, and others might require a little time to reflect upon it. She did not tell him that he could not paint an airplane war. She merely tried to encourage him toward more independence.

Since creative expression gives every child the right to make his own decisions and to use his own ideas, it also implies, to a great extent, the right of a child to the protection against having his ideas used or copied by another. The teacher stepped in immediately when Jerry repeated Dominick's idea to communicate this thought to both children. She wanted Dominick to know that she *knew* that it was his idea in the first place. He would realize with satisfaction that even if someone else used the idea, the teacher credited him with originating it. She wanted Jerry and the other children to remember this, too.

In the few seconds required for these two questions the teacher did a great deal of teaching. She was not only talking to the two boys about this practice of using the idea of another, she was also teaching fairness to all of the children, which would help in character development. Every child in the group heard and was reminded that each is privileged in creative art expression to express his own individual personality, that each should think for himself, and that each idea is accepted and is important.

Although it seemed to the teacher that enough discussion had taken place to motivate every child, she decided to ask one more question so that the last impression of the motivation would not be the situation of two boys with the same idea. Throughout the discussion the emphasis of the teacher had been upon the *different* ideas that children think of. Consider how many times she used the word "different" and the emphasis she placed upon it every time. Creative expression in art richly provides for individual differences, and the teacher stressed this during the motivation.

Teacher: "Does anyone else want to talk about what he thought of to paint?"

Patricia: "I was thinking I might paint mine about the Indians.

> How they lived before the white people came here.   You
> know, what we have been learning about."

Teacher: "Yes, you could make a painting about Indians.   Stories
we read give us lots of ideas for art."

Janice: "I could paint about Bill and Jean going for a ride in the
train.   Our reading story is all about the train ride."

Children get many ideas for art from the vicarious experiences in
the stories that they hear and read, and also watch on screens.   The
most meaningful and exciting correlation of art with another school
subject is that which comes from the suggestion of the child himself.
Patricia, apparently, had been interested in Indians as her group
studied about early American life.   She thought about it and was
still emotionally involved in the subject when art class came so
chose that subject for her art idea.

Patricia's discussion of her idea plus the added assurance of
the teacher that other stories might also provide subject matter for
art gave Janice the inspiration to paint a picture based upon a story
that the children had been reading together.

During the discussion, as often happens in a class, Janice
presented two different ideas for painting.   Some children are more
imaginative than others, and some are more vocal.   Some may express two or three ideas while, at the same time, there are other
children who will not enter into the discussion at all.

Even though a child may talk about an idea, he may paint
something entirely different from what he describes.   Children have
wonderful imaginations when encouraged to use them.

By the time that Janice volunteered her last comment, it was
evident to the teacher that the group as a whole was motivated to
begin to paint.

Teacher: "All of you seem to have lots of good ideas.   Why don't
you go right ahead and paint them without discussing
them any more?"

THE WORK PERIOD

After such a stimulating motivation, the third-grade group
of children were eager to begin to paint.   With this last suggestion
from the teacher the children began the wonderful *outpouring* of

creative expression that is the very core of art work. The teacher took the lead during the motivation; now each child takes the lead for himself. For the next several minutes the children work intently. The teacher steps aside, but does not withdraw from the group. During this first beginning period of intense personal expression the children work in a concentrated manner, usually quietly, trying to get all their ideas into organized form.

Because there is no active work for the teacher to do at this time, she may be tempted to fill in the time by doing some other work such as reports, correcting workbooks, or preparing work for another class. When she does, she withdraws from the art activity. There are few other situations in school where the child feels so much on his own as he does at this time. The child needs to know that he has the support of his teacher while he is working so hard. The teacher should be in a position where the children can see her and where she can give an encouraging smile and nod of her head to anyone who looks to her for some little indication of her support. Her role, although an inactive one, is important to the children.

This period of outpouring is the basic, vital core of the art lesson as far as the child is concerned. The child depends upon the teacher to protect him from interruptions. Any break in the child's concentration could mean a discontinuance of and lack of contact with his creative art activity. An interruption, even a temporary one, can displace, with another emotion, the feeling he has already associated with his art. Such interruptions can change the course of his work or disturb the child so that he finds it difficult if not impossible to continue the intense outpouring at this stage of his work.

GUIDANCE

After the initial stage of expression, children work more slowly and less intently but just as seriously. They were pressured by their desire to put feelings and ideas into form. This, when partly accomplished, often results in a slower pace of work. The child is mentally active in probing deeper into his subject and into his feelings for material to complete the expression of his ideas. Re-

lationships between what has been done and what else he decides
to do must be established.   Not only are ideas associated with his
original subject included and put into a meaningful relationship
or organization, but what the picture needs from an aesthetic standpoint also receives consideration.   The child may decide to put a
tree in a certain spot simply because it would make the picture look
better or he may decide to omit something about the subject that
he recalls.   He may think, "I could put all the bases and the fielders
in this picture of myself batting a baseball, but if I do they would
all be too small and my picture wouldn't show up well."   He may
consider one possibility after another before deciding what to do.
He may be influenced in his thinking by color.   He may think, "In
this picture of Larue and me taking a walk in the woods I could put
some more trees over in this corner, but it might make too many
trees the same.   I could just color it green for grass, but the trees
are green.   I might have too much green.   I could put in a house
or a stream of water or rocks."

This evaluation is best done by the child without adult or any
other interference as long as the child can carry it alone.   His decisions will be based on previous learnings.

During the first intense outpouring of creative expression the
child feels alone.   He is concentrating deeply upon his work, which
is unlike any other.   After the first flood of expression is over, his
first reaction may be to re-establish contact with his group.   Children approach this differently.   Sometimes a child looks around at
his neighbors just because he has felt alone for a while and likes to
see that they are still working at their art, too.   Another child might
want to show his work to his neighbor for a bit of approval as encouragement to go on.   Another may hold it up for the teacher to
see.

Now is the time when the teacher becomes more active.   She
moves among the children doing little more than looking at their
work and giving a smile to some, a pat on the shoulder to another.
During this period of self-evaluation and decision, children need
the teacher's support.   Although the teacher may plainly see room
for improvement in much of their work, she should refrain from
offering suggestions based on her adult judgment.   As a teacher, she
should project her thinking into every child's different problem and
try to see and to understand what each is doing.   Children want to

solve their own problems; they also want to know that their teacher is right there to support and to help them over a difficult spot.

As children exhaust their own resources, some may still feel dissatisfaction with their work and may be unable to continue alone. Now is the time for the teacher actively to give whatever help and guidance children need.   During the time the children have been making decisions and working from their self-evaluations, the teacher has been studying their work, trying to understand each child's purpose.   This familiarity helps her respond more helpfully to their questions.   Children become ready for guidance at different times; some may want none of it, having solved their problems to their own satisfaction.   All children need stimulation and encouragement, but the teacher can sense which children are self-sufficient on that day from the manner in which they work and otherwise conduct themselves.   (The same children who work in such a confident manner today may need more teacher help at another time.)

As the third-grade teacher works among the children, she meets some of the problems in this way:

Teacher: "I am interested in this blue area you have here, Mike."

Mike: "This is my abstract painting, and the blue I just put in there."

The blue was a strong dominant spot on one side of Mike's painting that seemed to overbalance the pale colors on the other side.

Teacher: "Put your painting up on the chalk tray and let's look at it from here.   Sometimes we see our picture from a little different point of view if we look at it from a distance." [Mike put his painting on the chalk tray, walked back, and stood beside the teacher.]

Teacher: "The blue does look well, doesn't it, Mike?   It shows up very well."

Mike: "Maybe I should make some more blue in it."

Mike felt proud that the teacher had made such a favorable comment about his successes and so he wanted to build more onto what his teacher admired.

Teacher: "Where could you put it?"

Mike: "In between those places on the other side between the white and the pink."

The teacher tries to understand what a child is attempting before commenting on his work. Kenny colored over his picture to show night and for no other reason.

43

Teacher: "That's a good idea. It usually helps to use a color in more than one place."

Mike could see that repeating of the blue would add strength to the other side of his composition. As a final remark the teacher had stated a general art principle that applied to Mike's problem. Mike thus learned that repeating or balancing or distributing color is a good way to make a painting look better. He would remember this principle, because it had applied directly to his own work. Mike had learned something that would help him better express his ideas in art, would give him more satisfaction in his finished art product.

Probably some other children in the group were interested in looking at Mike's painting on the chalk tray and hearing the conversation about it. They, too, would learn something about color distribution, but probably would not remember it as well as Mike did because at that moment it was not their personal problem.

The teacher led Mike toward seeing for himself what he needed to do. Through pointing out his achievement to Mike she helped him focus upon the strong point in his painting. Although the teacher could plainly see that his painting was out of balance, she did not approach her discussion with Mike from this adult and negative viewpoint. She spoke to him of the strongest point in his work. Because he knew that the bright blue area was a strength, he realized that another area of his work needed more strength. So Mike suggested that he put some blue on the other side. There are more mature ways in which this problem could be solved. There are many more solutions that the teacher could think of. Perhaps Mike's suggestion was not what the teacher had in mind as she considered his painting, but she was quick to grasp and to approve Mike's solution.

We cannot expect an eight-year-old boy to solve his problems as a mature adult would. We cannot expect a graduate of the second grade to solve a problem as a college graduate would. We cannot expect *any* other person to solve his problems as we would. The teacher is the one who should reach out to the child. She should adapt her thinking to his and not expect him to try to fit her pattern of thinking.

Mike did not carry the solution of his problem very far as he and his teacher looked at his art together, but he did make one step in learning. He made a suggestion as to how he might bring the other part of his painting into somewhat the same strength as the blue area. This is enough to expect from a child in one art class. Even though the teacher and perhaps other children in the group could see areas that they would change, the suggestion of such "help" could make a child feel that he had not accomplished very much and that it was not satisfactory. A child needs to feel that he has succeeded and that he has built and can build upon his successes.

Jack's hand was urgently signalling to the teacher, and she went immediately to the distress area. As she approached him, Jack said: "I can't draw it."

Teacher: "What can't you draw?"

Jack: "Me hitting a ball. I can't draw it."

Teacher: "You want to make a picture of yourself hitting a ball and you can't draw the arms. Isn't that it? [Jack shook his head to indicate "Yes."] I can see that you have drawn yourself very well but I can also see that you have been trying to draw yourself holding the bat."

Jack: "I don't know how to draw the arms."

Teacher: "You know how to bat a ball though."

Jack: "Yes, I know."

Teacher: "Take this yardstick and show me how you do it."

Jack knew very well how to bat a ball.   He had done it many times, but now when he came to draw a picture of the action, he had difficulty.   As he held the bat in a ball game, he had concentrated upon the action and less upon the actual visual appearance of his arms while holding the bat.   The teacher asked Jack to hold a bat this time so he could focus upon the position and action of his arms.

Teacher: "Look at your arms.   How do they bend?"

Jack: "They bend up."

Teacher: "Do they go straight up from your shoulders?"

Jack: "No, they go down then bend up."

Teacher: "One crosses over your body.   Do you see where it crosses over in front of you?   Do you see which hand is the upper one on the bat?   Is your right arm close to your body or far away?"

Jack: "The arm halfway down is close, then it goes out to the bat."

Teacher: "Now let Kenneth hold the bat, so you can see how it looks when someone else does it.   Do both arms bend alike?"

Jack: "No, the one that goes across his body is wider.   Now I know how to do it."   [He successfully continued his drawing.]

Jack was led, through the guidance of the teacher, to a deeper knowledge of the way his arms and hands function and look in holding a bat.   The more a child knows, the more intelligently he can express his ideas.   One of the keys to better creative art expression is knowledge about objects, people, activity, and the general principles of art.

The art education program evolves around the child and his ideas, imagination, and problems.   Teaching develops as an outgrowth of these problems.   As the problems confront the child, he is ready for the learnings that facilitate the solution of the problem. Knowledge gained at the time of most intense interest or need is remembered longer.   Children not personally involved with the problem would gain little if required to give their attention to it and would only lose interest in and contact with their own art activity.

Not every child is ready to learn the same thing at the same time. The guidance procedures that accompany creative art experiences provide in a very real way for individual differences. Every teacher knows that she cannot explain a thing once and have every child learn it because only those who are ready to learn will remember. The teacher will doubtless be called on by another child at a later time for help with just such a problem as Jack had in drawing himself holding a baseball bat. The problem may be that of someone holding a broom, or a little girl holding her doll, with essentially the same arm positions. By helping another child toward more specific knowledge the teacher will be repeating her teaching. Some who may not have paid much attention to the first explanation may listen and learn. Some who remembered the first explanation to Jack will profit by the repetition. To the child who asked the question the answer will have a familiar sound and be more easily remembered. Everyone hears but those most personally involved learn most.

Teacher: "You're getting along fine, Maxine. Keep right on going."

Maxine looked up and smiled in response to her teacher's remark. She was having no difficulty at the time and seemed to be self-sufficient. The fact that the teacher recognized this and seemed pleased by it was encouraging to the child. Maxine received a challenge toward further achievement or broader development of her idea when the teacher said, "Keep right on going." Every child needs help. Every child needs encouragement. Every child needs a challenge to stimulate him to the extent of his ability. The gifted and the independent can become indolent if not challenged.

Just because she seemed not to be faced with a difficult problem at that moment was no reason why the teacher should pass Maxine by. Certainly it is important for the teacher to help those children who are having difficulty, but it is important for the teacher to help the others as well. *Every* child is important. Since we provide for individual differences in American education, we provide for the capable as well as the less able. We provide for the self-sufficient as well as the more dependent ones so that each can be helped toward fuller development of his abilities. The range of maturity within a group broadens with every new experience.

Judy had stopped working on her painting and was still looking at it and apparently thinking about her work when the teacher
approached her.   In the center of her page, Judy had painted a
picture of a girl jumping rope and had added nothing more.   Judy
had held the paper in a position that gave it much more width than
height, so there was considerable amount of empty space on each
side of the girl skipping rope (see Illustration 47).   Judy had
thought about one person doing one thing and not about any other
people who might have been involved in the activity or about any
environmental relationships.

Teacher: "You did a good job of painting this girl jumping rope,
Judy.   The rope is swinging over her head, her arms are
out to the sides, and she is holding the rope with both
hands.   Where is the girl, Judy, in the town or in the
country?"

Judy: "In the town, on our sidewalk."

Teacher: "How would I know this when I look at your picture?"

Judy: "I could put in the sidewalk."

Teacher: "Yes, you could.   What else could you add that would
tell more about where she is jumping?"

Judy: "I am jumping rope by my house, so I could put my house
in."

Remotivation is a part of guidance — perhaps the most important
part.   The teacher realized that Judy had concentrated on her
painting and on representing herself doing what she liked to do, and
that she needed to think more deeply about related ideas.   This is
not true of every child who paints one figure in her picture and stops.
Sometimes the one figure so fills the area or is formed in such a way
that it satisfies the feeling being expressed and nothing else needs
to be added.   Such a judgment has to be made by the teacher before
she comments.   The teacher makes this judgment from the depth
and maturity of her experience with art.   She probably decides
that the page looks empty, that the figure is not in relationship to
the size of the space on which it is drawn, or that one figure alone
on the page would have been better related to the space if the paper
had been held the other way.   However, the teacher does not say
these things to the child.   In the elementary school the child is concerned with his own purposes.   He has yet to learn much art

knowledge that will help him see further possibilities in the development of his own work, so the teacher refrains from imposing her own judgments upon him. Rather, through comments and questions about his intention and ideas related to it, she guides him toward deeper and broader thinking about his ideas. The teacher studies the child's work from the child's viewpoint, trying to understand his purposes. She then communicates with him in terms of his own understandings that are consistent with his purposes. That is why the teacher questioned Judy about where she was and included a need for environmental relationships. Such a question as "Where is the girl, Judy, in the town or in the country?" seemed logical to Judy. The question was an easy one for her and the answer was quite obvious. She sensed immediately the need to tell more, to think more deeply, and to relate her idea to other objects. Such insights help the child to better understand how to express his ideas. Through his own attempts and through understanding of the relationships as they apply to his own work, the child learns some valuable things about color, composition, and expression. The terms used are within the vocabulary of the child and are consistent with his purposes on that day for that problem. The teaching has been personalized to him during the guidance.

When the teacher first began to talk to Judy about her art, she referred to the figure in the picture as "the girl." The last statement made by Judy revealed that her real intention was to draw a picture of herself jumping rope: "I am jumping rope by my house." Children frequently put themselves into their pictures. They are more interested in their own activities than in the activities of others, so it is natural for them to choose for their art the subject in which they are most interested. In an oral discussion the child does not always reveal this intimate involvement. He is sensitive to the intimacy and is afraid of exposure and possibly being hurt by the reactions of others to his ideas and the way he has expressed them. Therefore, he often discusses his art in the third person. It was only after friendly teacher interest was established in this particular picture that Judy felt sure that no embarrassment or hurt would come to her. She felt confident in her trust of her teacher. This trust carries over to some extent to the next dealings that Judy has with her teacher but may not entirely replace her caution about identifying herself with ideas and feelings that she feels are per-

sonal or intimate.   A new situation is faced by Judy every time she
undertakes a new art problem.   Trust in her teacher and in her
classmates is built slowly and can quickly be destroyed.   We all
learn this as we grow up.   Judy, like all of us, is cautious.

Teacher: "Are any other people with you or near you?"
Judy: "No, I was by myself."

The teacher, feeling that Judy had gained something by individual
attention, moved on to another child.

Teacher: "Are you finished, Harold?   [Harold shook his head af-
              firmatively in reply.]   Do you want to get another sheet
              of paper and paint some more?"

Harold did not answer.   He liked to paint, so he immediately put
his completed painting in a safe place to dry and got another sheet
of paper.   There was, he felt, no need for conversation on this
point.   It seemed as though he was just waiting for his bit of attention from the teacher.   He also wanted further assurance that
he could paint some more and that there was time to do it.   Not all
children work at the same speed, of course.   Some will complete two
paintings while others are still working on their first, as mentioned
earlier.   Then, too, some children attempt a more difficult subject
or carry their idea farther than others do.   Through guidance, provision is made for problems arising from individual differences as
they occur.

The teacher noticed that several of the children were using
the same paint brush with different colors.   The outcome was that
colors were beginning to be mixed in the large jars of paint.   When
the class had started, there was a brush put into each jar of paint in
order to keep each color in its original hue.   Provision was made
for mixing paint by making available the small water pans used in
water-color painting.   The child could mix paints as he chose.
Several of the children were using more than one jar of paint, and,
instead of using the brush found in each different paint jar, were
using one in the red for a while, then putting the same brush into
the white, and then into the yellow.   As a result the white was
turning pink and the yellow becoming more orange.   Since several
children were involved, the whole group needed guidance at this
point.

Teacher: "Children, I think many of you are forgetting about keeping each brush in its own color. Some of our colors are
getting mixed and are more difficult to use. Some of
you who are putting the same paint brush into different
colors really don't want to mix colors. You are just forgetting to change brushes. [The teacher went over to
the table where the paints were. Picking up one jar,
she said:] See, this was plain green when we started and
someone has put a brush with black paint into it. [Show-
ing the paint to the class, she said:] If anyone were looking for green, he wouldn't want to use this jar. Try to
remember to use the brush that is already in the paint in
order to keep the paint a clean color for yourself and for
others."

This procedure is group guidance. The teacher is not telling the
children what to paint or how to paint it. She is helping with the
use of materials. It is the responsibility of the teacher to give guidance and help to children in ways that will help them express their
ideas more freely and more to their satisfaction.

Virginia: "I can't find any blue."

Teacher: "Does anyone have any blue paint that he isn't using at
the moment? Virginia needs some."

Jerry: "I have some here, but I'll need it again in a minute."

Teacher: "Will you need to use it for very long, Virginia?"

Virginia: "I just want to paint the sky. Then I'll bring it right
back to you, Jerry."

The teacher should help the children learn how to share, as she did
with Jerry. She should also suggest that a child not take advantage
of this sharing and generosity by saying, as she did to Virginia, "Will
you need to use it for very long, Virginia?"

Jimmie: "See, I painted a boat in a big storm."

Teacher: "Yes, you did. You made it a very frightening storm,
too. The lightning is all around the boat. Is your painting finished?"

Jimmie: "Not yet."

Although this was simply a picture of one object in the center of the
page as Judy's painting of a girl jumping rope had been, the effect

was quite different, and the way the teacher functions with the children would also be different. Judy's composition looked as though it needed related objects to make the expression more meaningful, so the teacher in her guidance role remotivated the child in this direction. Jimmie's picture of a boat seemed most effective alone on the big sea with the lightning flashing all around it. The very loneliness of the boat made it seem more helpless and more acutely affected by the storm and big wave caused by the wind. The teacher, realizing this as she looked at Jimmie's painting, commented upon his achievement, simply leaving him to complete his painting in his own way. The teacher then approached Stephen's work as he was beginning to paint all over the picture of a locomotive engine that he had just completed. Stephen was starting at one corner of his paper and covering everything he had painted as well as the spaces in between the forms with yellow paint. (See Illustration 44.) As she approached Stephen, the teacher saw the painting of the engine with the smokestack, the engineer at the cab window, and such details as the connections between the wheels. The picture that Stephen had made was an interesting one. The engine was large, strong, and boldly painted and looked as though it had been painted by a person who knew something about the subject. The teacher regretted to see him begin to cover the entire paper with one color of paint, but she did not interfere with his right to do it. She could have stopped the boy from destroying his painting and thus would have saved his art product, but she realized that he had a compulsion to obliterate his work quickly so that others could not see it. The teacher also knew the reason for this behavior.

Stephen was having difficulty in other subjects as well as in his art and in his social adjustments. He almost never smiled in school. He was withdrawn and never volunteered a contribution to the class nor addressed the teacher or a classmate first. The teacher could remember no time when Stephen had approached her. When he recited in class, he gave a brief minimum answer and sat down. Although he was a quiet child and gave the teacher no trouble, she knew that such behavior was abnormal for an eight-year-old.

The economic level of Stephen's family was above average. His father was so busy with his business that he gave little time to his two children. His mother was ambitious and demanding.

The first example of Stephen's work (above) reflects the emotional problem he experienced in the third grade. The second example (below), done by Stephen in the fifth grade, shows his work when the emotional problem had been resolved. Teachers need to have faith in children and employ teaching procedures centered around kindness, patience, and concern for the child's welfare.

Stephen found it almost impossible to meet the high standards his mother expected of him. She constantly found fault with his behavior — what he did or what he did not do. When he showed her something that he had made, a typical remark from his mother might be: "Oh, that's all right, but you'll do much better the next time." In effect, she was indicating that it really was not quite up to her standards. She destroyed the value of Stephen's work and discouraged him. He had worked hard on a piece of art work, for example, and felt a satisfaction in the doing of it and a pride in the finished product. He took his achievement to the person he loved best, his mother, and she was dissatisfied with it — with him. She destroyed his pride in it, his feeling of accomplishment. Since his art work, as well as his behavior, represented his ideas, his work, his choices, and since his mother always criticized and never accepted whatever he did, Stephen began to feel that his mother rejected him, too, and was disappointed in him. Because of fear of criticism or rejection, Stephen became afraid to approach people, afraid to expose himself and his ideas. So he began covering his painting all over with one or more layers of solid color. Sometimes the paper would feel weighty from the layers of paint. He did this for two reasons: (a) He wanted to shield his ideas against those who would neither understand nor appreciate; (b) since his mother expressed no confidence in him, he lost confidence in himself. He wanted to show that he, too, knew it was not good. He wanted to show that he at least knew this. Hurting himself was somehow more acceptable than being hurt by someone he loved.

All this the teacher knew as she approached Stephen. She realized that he must regain confidence in himself and in his ideas before he would be ready to lay himself open, by showing his work, to possible hurts again. She knew that building of trust and confidence in his teacher and in all of his many classmates would take time. Stephen's next step was to learn to know that *whatever* he did was acceptable.

In this case the teacher knew that the child's general learning could not develop as it should with such an emotional block. Her guidance was based upon this knowledge of his individual need. The teacher's responsibility is to provide for these individual differences and problems of all types.

Teacher: "Stephen, that is an excellent painting of an engine, and
              I see the engineer. I have noticed your paintings of
              trains before, and you do them very well. You must
              know a lot about trains to draw and paint them so well."

This was richer praise than she had given any of the others. Stephen
needed it more, because his self-confidence needed to be bolstered.
The teacher made her remarks with enthusiasm and so all could
hear, but it was only one of many steps toward helping the child.
The teacher knew that it would take many repetitions of favorable
acceptance for Stephen even to begin to gain self-confidence. She
knew also that there would be growth and possible relapses because
overcoming of such an emotional block is slow. She did not pick
up his paper and show it to the class because that would come a
little later. At this point it was enough for Stephen to feel her approval. Involvement of the other children could also wait. The
teacher would help Stephen by building upon one step at a time.
She neither pressured nor forced him by overpraise or intimation of
what he should or should not be doing. When the teacher walked
away, Stephen continued to paint all over his picture with the yellow
paint.

*Judith was inspired to paint this bold fire truck from her many
associations with the fire truck that was housed across the
street from her home.*

46

Judith: "This is the fire truck. It has just been shined. The firemen keep it in the place across the street from our house, and I often watch them working and fixing it, and once they gave me a ride. I was away up on the high seat, and I was afraid at first, but it was good. This is the fire truck (46)."

Teacher: "What are you going to do now that your painting is finished?"

Judith: "Maybe I could paint another picture of the fire truck."

Teacher: "How would this one be different? [No comment from Judith.] What could the men be doing to the fire truck?"

The teacher asked this question to help Judith see more deeply into the problem, to guide her away from the possibility of repeating the same subject in the same way, and to associate the action and purposes of the men with the truck. Action and movement make pictures more interesting, and knowledge of this principle of art, when understood and applied, helps children to improve their art work. The teacher indirectly pointed this out to Judith, but without undue emphasis, since she knew that good teaching involved many repetitions with a variety of situations.

Judith: "Oh, I know. I could make the men shining it. No, I will make the men fixing it and folding the hose. Or I could make them giving me a ride."

Judith was full of ideas and inspired by the excitement of her subject. She needed no further help from the teacher.

Teacher: "Go right ahead, Judith, and start your painting. But there isn't much time left. Do you want to start it and finish it another time or do something else for a few minutes and save that painting idea for some later day?"

The teacher's reminding Judith that only a few minutes of time remained confronted her with the problem of an unfinished painting. The choice was Judith's. The teacher did not follow the easier course of making the decision for the child.

Judith: "I guess I won't paint my idea now. Could I draw it with my crayons on a little paper? Then I could keep it in my desk and do it in the mornings or something."

Judith made a decision that seemed to serve her best at that time.

Children will and can make intelligent decisions when given an opportunity to do so.

Teacher: "Boys and girls, there are only a few minutes left to complete your painting. Those who have finished can read their library books or get a piece of drawing paper at the end of the table and draw or cut."

The foregoing conversations and comments about guidance give an example of how the teacher functioned with every child in the group. She did not bypass any child. It is not necessary to spend much time with each child, but it is important personally to contact each and to give him some help and inspiration. Personal attention to individual and group problems is the purpose of guidance.

EVALUATION

Much of the teaching of aesthetic qualities, color and form relationships, and of the understanding of individually different approaches to art expression is done through the evaluation of the completed art work. This is the time when the teacher and children discuss together the strong points in the art products and analyze why they are considered successful or what qualities and relationships make them interesting. They talk about the *way* the child has succeeded in creating an emotional reaction to his work. It is important for children to recognize qualities that give a piece of art work its strengths, unity, interest, emotivity, consistency, and appeal. It is also important for the child to understand *why* certain art works are regarded as having one or more of these qualities. *How* the artist has achieved these results is vital if the child is to understand the work and gain knowledge and insights that will help him more adequately to express his own ideas.

In the elementary school the approach to education through the evaluation of the child's art is a *positive* approach. A recognition and analysis of achievements is enough for children of this age. At this age level and for such a personal and individual expression as art work is, the building of self-confidence must be well established. As the child grows and matures through secondary school there is time enough to include an attitude and approach of how weaker areas might be improved.   The child must feel confident that his way is right for him.   He must feel confident in achievements before he can accept a discussion of his shortcomings.   To express himself freely in art the child must feel confident.   The child learns a great deal through the positive approach to his own achievements and to the achievements of others.

With this point of view in mind, the teacher approaches an evaluation of the children's work with a respect and an appreciation for the sensitivities of every child and of his need for approval. The evaluation should be a joint discussion guided by the teacher to:

(a) Keep the discussion moving
(b) Keep the discussion on a positive level
(c) Recognize the work of every child
(d) Add to and fortify the children's learnings

The finished art products need to be seen as they are evaluated. There are different ways of doing this.   They can be hung or held by the children as they are discussed.   In this particular third-grade class all the paintings were hung indiscriminately in a place where each could be seen well by every child.

Teacher: "Your paintings look very attractive.   Let's talk about them a little while before we begin our next art project. What makes them so attractive?"

Sam: "They are all different.   That's why."

Sandra: "You have to look a long time to see each one."

Timothy: "Every time I look at them I see ones I didn't see before or something different."

Alice: "Let's hang them out in the hall so the other rooms can see them.   I want my brother in the fifth grade to see how well I can paint — how well all of us in third grade can paint."

Teacher: "How many would like to have these paintings hung in the hall when we finish talking about them?"

The teacher, following the lead of one child, let the whole class decide whether or not to accept the suggestion.

Teacher: "The paintings as a group are interesting but so is each one by itself.   This first painting is Dominick's.   His two airplanes, shooting at each other, are just about ready to

crash. The two planes fill the whole paper. Nothing
else was needed to make a strong, exciting picture. Because there are not a lot of unrelated things to distract
your attention, and because of the action and position
of the planes, you feel the excitement and disaster that
is about to happen. The bright, intense colors also help
to show this feeling."

In discussing their work with children, the teacher takes the lead in
order to establish a point of view toward recognition of achievements. By the type of statements she makes about the first two or
three paintings she sets the tone for the kind of remarks she hopes
the children will make when she involves them in the discussion.
At the same time she uses this opportunity to teach. She points out
the most successful parts of each child's art and tells why it is interesting or what makes it pleasing. In order to develop their taste,
their appreciation, and their ability to make discriminating judgments of art, children need to be shown *what* is considered successful
and to be told *why*. An important outcome of such a discussion is
the art education that children gain by way of comments skillfully
elicited or contributed by the teacher. The discussion period is
also a time for the re-emphasis of some of the points brought out
during the motivation.

Since the expression of emotion is vital to art, the teacher
in her comments about the airplane picture explained how the
placement of the two planes and the colors helped to communicate
excitement and danger. She indicated *what* emotion had been
expressed and explained *how* the child had shaped and colored
the forms to express it. She also commented upon the directness
of the work by saying that the two planes filled the page and
intimated that the child had been wise in not adding more to his
composition.

Teacher: "I am sure you all notice the beautiful, big, blue lake in
        this picture. It shows up well because Alice has painted
        it a dark color and painted the sandy shore and grass
        around it a very light color. The light yellow sandy
        beach and light green grass make us feel the warmth of
        the day. The fact that she has painted the sun large
        with rays coming out from it also helps us feel the warm
        day. It makes the cold blue of the water more inviting."

Alice: "That's our cabin back by the pine trees. The lake water is cold when we first get in. Then it feels good to get out in the sun."

In Alice's painting, the blue lake was the dominant object. It could be seen from any part of the classroom. The teacher called attention to its strength. Her explanation of its size and dark blue color, which was surrounded by a contrasting light color, helped the children understand *why* it had such a strong appearance. As she mentioned the warm light colors of the grass and beach in addition to the size and shape of the sun, she indicated *what* the feeling of the picture was and *how* Alice had been successful in expressing it. Alice was quick to appreciate her teacher's comments. Her statement about the physical effect that the water and sun had upon her was almost a repetition of what the teacher had said, only interpreted into her own personal experience. Alice wanted to identify herself with the comments of success made by the teacher about her art.

Alice and all of the children learned something about the effect of light and dark colors through the teacher's comments and by seeing how Alice had worked it out. One explanation of an art principle or knowledge will provide only an introduction. Many repetitions are required before most of the children learn and understand it.

Teacher: "What do you find interesting about Jack's picture?"

After setting the example to children of how to approach the discussion of art, the teacher gave the children an opportunity to take an active part in the evaluation.

Doris: "The batter is big and you can see him easily, but the part I like is the way he made the crossing line for wire 'way in the back to protect the people watching. It looks kind of lacy."

Saul: "That red ball suit on the batter looks nice. It makes him show up."

Teacher: "The red does help make it show up because it is such a bright shade. The wire fence helps the picture because the parts are small in size beside the large player. A variety of sizes and shapes makes most art more interesting."

Doris knew what made the picture attractive to her, but she was not able to analyze how the child had accomplished it. To recognize the area of success is a valuable achievement for a third-grade child. The teacher, realizing that it takes much more knowledge and deeper insight to decide why it is interesting, added this information herself.

    To supply new information is part of her role as a teacher. Children's own art provides excellent examples for the teacher to use in teaching. Children hear her talk about it and see an actual illustration of it. Being more interested in their own work than in that of others, children pay more attention to the discussion of it than they otherwise might do. This fortifies learning.

Andrew: "I like that next picture about jumping rope. It looks like a girl jumping rope but I can't tell what the other parts are. They look more like just a design or something. It all looks kind of like an abstract. I thought it was at first. Now I am sure that is a girl jumping rope. Anyhow, I think it looks good."

Andrew's observations and judgments were based upon his appreciation of the total effect of the beauty of the work. He was not coerced by the teacher to say why he liked it. At times this can be a difficult question even for an adult to answer. The teacher knew this. She also knew that children would begin to explore reasons as their knowledge grew. Andrew was beginning to make judgments based upon aesthetic qualities. From other experiences in art, he had learned that it was not important to be able to name the objects in art work.

Teacher: "Judy's painting is an interesting one because it has such a variety of interesting things in it."

Judy: "After I painted the girl jumping rope, I made the door to her house. Then I thought I might paint more houses and people, but I felt I would rather make dots and blocks. I just wanted to. I like them."

Teacher: "Yes. They add an interesting pattern. Everything doesn't have to be real."

The teacher, realizing that it is normal for children to express ideas and feelings both naturalistically and in abstract designs, accepted the fact that Judy had done both in the same picture (47).

Sam: "That next abstract painting makes me feel dreamy if I look at it for a while. I can't help looking at it. I keep looking at it more than some of the others. The lines are all wavy and it makes me feel the same as when I watched the waves at the ocean beach last summer."

Sam could identify himself with Teresa's painting because of a former pleasant experience with waves. More fully to appreciate and enjoy a work of art the observer needs to bring to it his own experiences and a willingness to make some effort to understand it.

Teacher: "Another quality of Teresa's painting that helps you feel that way is the light, bright coloring. These lines in her picture are grouped and the spaces between the others are not even. Variety adds interest — variety of spaces between objects as well as variety of shapes and colors. Grouping helps to hold parts of a composition together and gives it some organization. What do you think is successful about Bob's picture?"

Mike: "Boy, that big bomb is going to bang right into him in bed! He looks scared."

Other children indicated a similar reaction by the nods and sounds that they made.

Patricia: "I saw people getting bombed on television, only this is worse."

Teacher: "What makes you say it is worse?"

Patricia: "Why, the bomb is so big and it is right on him. It can't miss him, and he can't get away."

Teacher: "That's right. Bob has made you feel the helplessness of the person and the terrible thing about to happen because he has made the bomb and person in the bed so close together. He drew all the objects large. This also gives them a more forceful appearance. They fill the entire paper. If Bob had added the other things in the bedroom, like the chair and dresser, they might only have distracted your attention. It probably did not occur to him to add them because they had no meaning as far as depicting this idea of intense fear was concerned. He painted only those things that were important to the action."

The emotional reaction was felt by almost everyone because Bob's picture (48) was so dramatically presented. The children were quick to see that he had emphasized the feeling of fear. They could also understand why the fear was so successfully communicated. The teacher added statements that fortified their thinking and learning.

Joe: "Why did Nancy, in that next picture, make all the trees alike along the road? I think it would have looked better if she had made them different."

Teacher: "Maybe it would, but they look very attractive this way. Nancy has drawn and painted the road almost like a border pattern or a design. We have some famous paintings made with a row of trees along a road. In fact, there is a print of one such painting in our school near the drinking fountain. It is called 'The Flamingos' by the artist Rousseau. Probably you have noticed it. Along the edge of the water Rousseau has painted a row of trees. They are almost identical. Notice them the next time you look at the picture."

47

A child needs the stimulating guidance of a teacher to develop and grow in his ability to express his ideas with art materials. Judy's picture of herself jumping rope resulted from her own idea combined with her teacher's guidance.

Joe's statements were negative. From the beginning, the teacher
had attempted to establish an approach toward recognition of
achievements. To re-establish this point of view she immediately
identified Nancy's intention with successful works of famous artists.
It is the responsibility of the teacher to guide the discussion. When
it begins to move in a direction inconsistent with the best learning
situation, she needs to redirect it.

Dominick: "Well, you said a couple of times that variety was good.
So I thought we should never make things alike."

Children misunderstand at times. They are also sensitive and eager
to do what is expected of them. The examples of work discussed
thus far in the evaluation showed variety as a quality worth mentioning. Therefore, it seemed to Dominick that perhaps it was
always a desirable element in every case. As he and others hear
many such discussions, they will understand that there are various
ways of solving every problem in art and that the qualities of every
piece of art need to be appreciated in relation to the idea or emotion
the artist was trying to express.

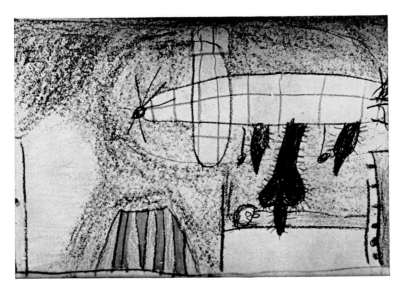

48

*Bob's work, done with crayons, expresses and communicates
a dramatic feeling of the inescapable danger of being bombed
in bed. Children can successfully portray ideas that are both
clear and important to them.*

Teacher: "Variety is important and Nancy has it.   She put in the
             farmhouse, the lane, the barn, and a car.   Sometimes re-
             peating the same object can also add interest in another
             way.   You could remember that we mentioned in Judy's
             picture of a girl jumping rope that the row of dots and
             blocks helped make it look better.   These blocks and dots
             are just another row of objects that present a pleasant rep-
             etition or pattern as Nancy's row of trees do.   Repeating
             an object in a picture can add emphasis.   We have to
             make many decisions as we work to express the ideas and
             feelings for each different picture."

This discussion provided a good chance for the teacher to remind the
children that an art principle did not always hold true in every situation.   What is good in one situation may not be in another, and to
learn this fact in art as in all other aspects of education requires
many reminders in a wide variety of situations and circumstances.

Teacher: "I see that the next painting, Patricia's, has some Indians.
             What impresses you about her work?"

Leroy: "The idea of the Indians around the fire came from our
             reading-class story.   We were reading about how they
             put war paint on and danced around a fire."

Teacher: "We sometimes get ideas for art from things we read and
             Patricia was successful in expressing her ideas.   How
             many of you could recognize the story from her painting?"

Calling upon the group in this way not only varied the approach to
discussion, but also involved all the children in the participation of
recognizing the most evident area of Patricia's success.   Such an approach to the evaluation of children's art frees them from a feeling of
apprehension and fear of what might be said about their work.
The appraisal of art becomes a pleasant experience — a time for giving and receiving recognition and favorable personal attention.
Through many such activities, children begin to see that the type
of comments they make about others' work can influence the kind of
remarks that others may make of their work.   By way of such inter-
changes they see the effect of appreciation upon interpersonal relationships, feel the personal satisfactions and confident feelings that
are developed, and also enjoy the friendly attitude that is promoted
among their classmates.   Such an approach to a discussion of chil-

dren's art has values for the art education of the children.   It also
has deeper values of building understanding among people.

Teacher: "The last painting is Jennie's.   What do you like about
             it?"
Margaret: "It's so plain.   I can see all of the edges.   She didn't
             let the colors run together.   She kept the edges neat.
             You have to work carefully to get it so neat."
Teacher: "Her colors are clear, too.   She kept her brush clean.
             If we don't clean the brush after each color, they get
             mixed.   Of course sometimes we purposely do this in
             order to mix colors.   We can do different things with
             paints.   Colors can be mixed, or they can be kept
             bright by cleaning the brush after each use of color."

After each child's work had been commented upon, a committee of
children was selected to hang the paintings in the hall.

Seeing their art work displayed in a place where many other
children and teachers saw it is stimulating and satisfying to children.
They enjoy the attention of older and younger children to their work.
Children's creative art work improves the appearance of a school.
Its colorful quality brightens a room or hall and makes it look more
cheerful.   The fact that each piece is different makes it interesting.

During the process of working with children in creative art,
the teacher sometimes functions in a general way with the whole
group and on an individual basis with each child.   The teacher
needs to develop enthusiasm as she motivates, guides, evaluates, and
exhibits their art.   Through her questioning, she stimulates their
ideas for art.   By sensitively projecting her thinking into studying
their art, she approaches the guidance of their individual problems.
As she guides and provides comments during the evaluation, the
teacher is educating the children through art.   Appreciation for
the achievements of the children is the foundation upon which the
teacher builds the discussion of the completed work.   Since art is
visual, it needs to be seen to be appreciated.   Sometimes it needs
to be viewed several times to be understood or enjoyed.   Therefore,
every child's work should be exhibited in a place that makes such
study possible.

Suggested activity

Discuss his art with an elementary-school child.   Try to discover:

    (a) His attitude toward art
    (b) His attitude toward his ability in art
    (c) What he likes best about art
    (d) His feelings of inadequacies through what he avoids or feels that he does not want to attempt
    (e) Why he enjoys his art work
    (f) Whether he does any such work at home

See if you can learn any or all of these things through a friendly discussion.   Try to make sure discoveries indirectly, if possible, without pointed questions.

Plan what steps you might takes as a teacher to broaden this child's knowledge or increase his interest in art.   What specific art activities would you provide for him?

CHAPTER *VI*

Teaching assigned topics

IN ASSIGNED topics, regardless of whether the teacher has chosen the subject matter for the art experience or whether the children have decided upon it, the fact remains that the children are working within the scope of one topic.   They have had assigned to them or have assigned to themselves a specific idea or subject upon which they will all work.   Although such a method deprives the individual child of the privilege and responsibility of making a basic choice, it is still a liberal method of teaching. Group projects are one example of assigned topics.

Frequently, when children in the elementary school work with a variety of materials and equipment in developing a three-dimensional art project, they work as a group within the framework of one general theme.   Examples would be the making of mobiles, a construction project that is correlated to another subject, or papier-mâché masks. The concentration on one broad general theme is necessary because children of this age need to build skills and techniques in the use of tools. The teacher needs to concentrate with them on the building of habits of personal safety and of the care of tools. Because of their inexperience, children learn valuable habits, attitudes, and skills best when the group selects one general problem, the solving of which allows each child to select any phase of this general theme, to organize it his own way, and to express it as he chooses. There can and should be broad opportunities for developing each child's originality by letting him set the scope and depth of the task himself, by following his own choices and decisions in every part of the problem as he works on it. Regardless of whether the teacher suggests the topic or the children select it, the fact remains that there are certain art teaching-learning situations in the elementary school in which the children profit from a group focus of attention on one theme, such as the discussion of the works of other artists. When children design and make their own Hallowe'en costumes, they choose a theme that is timely and exciting to them. Within the scope of this one general theme or assigned topic, the children learn sewing, fitting, and other skills as they are needed. Each child is challenged, by the character of Hallowe'en costuming, to design for himself a costume that is different from every other and that expresses some feeling associated with the holiday. The completed costumes should be individualized by each child according to his own tastes, imagination, and emotional reactions. Such topics, common to the group, must give every child a maximum opportunity for making choices from the beginning of the work until it has ended.

A teacher may use assigned topics to focus the attention of the group on some phase of art that she thinks the group needs to learn more about or that will build specific skills or develop a deeper understanding of one of the disciplines of art — or perhaps all three.

In describing the process of teaching art through a topic common to the group, this chapter has two major purposes:

(a) To give insight into the various roles of the teacher as she works with the children by means of an assigned topic in art.

(b) To show the teacher's responsibilities in helping children
to build skills with new materials by teaching these skills
without interfering with the child's right to develop his
work according to his own ideas.

The teacher's role in art education through a three-dimensional art
problem on one general topic or theme for all the children is much
the same as her role in creative expression, as described in the preceding chapter. She leads the motivational discussion, she helps
the children with their problems by guidance, she teaches by means
of the children's accomplishments during the evaluation, and she is
responsible for exhibiting the completed art work.

The example of classroom procedure described in this chapter deals with some of the problems involved as a sixth-grade group
worked through the making of mobiles. The subject of mobiles was
chosen because it is a three-dimensional project utilizing varied
materials. Many of the examples in this book illustrate drawing
and painting because elementary-school children do more drawing
and painting than any other type of art work. Regardless of
whether or not we may feel such experiences deserve priority, they
outnumber other art activities. Children need many art activities
other than flat work. They can easily visualize three-dimensional
forms. Children seem to realize that every object occupies its own
space, and their flat work often shows indication of this reasoning.

All children enjoy making things that can be used. In the
upper elementary grades, children enjoy creating objects that have
form, solidity, and movement and that work, or have some utilitarian
value, as well as those involving group activities. Although mobiles
can be made by young children, such a project is better suited to the
interests and needs of older children. Working out the problems
involved in the delicate balance of movement of mobiles fascinates
children who are older. Such an art project takes time to execute.
Even the introduction of the subject and the discussion of materials
and techniques may take several class periods, but older children
can continue a project for several weeks if there are new and interesting things to learn and to do.

Since the previous chapter dealt with painting and with the
younger age group, this chapter will illustrate how a teacher might
function with a group of older children who are about to begin a

three-dimensional project using materials less frequently used by younger children.

INTRODUCTION OF THE SUBJECT

In spite of the fact that mobiles are sculptural forms that are increasingly used as decoration, many sixth-grade children may be unfamiliar with them. Some of those who have seen them may not entirely understand the principles of movement and balance that are basic to their structure. For this reason, it would seem desirable to preface the work with either actual or pictured examples of mobiles in order to show children the beauty and grace of such moving sculptural objects. The children should have an opportunity to study and to enjoy them by watching them. After this experience, the teacher could call attention to the ever-changing pattern of forms and shadows as the mobiles move and twist and as the light changes. The greater variety of mobiles that children see the better they will understand the many materials that might be used and the limitations and possibilities of materials as they contribute to balance and to free graceful movement. Since such art work depends on movement, at least a part of the visual aids used in the introduction should be motion pictures or a variety of examples of mobiles. As children watch mobiles in action, they get a feeling for the aesthetic movement for the whole idea of this art form. The teacher might then explain the materials used in the examples and why lightweight substances are necessary. Together the teacher and children should talk about balance, its principles, and how it is achieved. They might also study together the suspension materials and the way the artist has formed the joinings.

MATERIALS AND THEIR USES

If the teacher has on hand some interesting and colorful materials from which mobiles might be made, children will be curious about them and will want to work with them. There are also many materials that children may have at home and will want to bring to school to use in their project and to help give to it their personal touch.   To have children depend upon themselves for some of their structural supplies as well as for their ideas will help them develop resourcefulness.   To have them depend entirely upon themselves for all details of materials and equipment may be expecting too much of children of this age.   Children in the elementary grades are still dependent on adults and feel secure when they can see that provision has been made for them.

In showing materials to children it would be helpful if the teacher would relate the materials that she has provided to the examples of mobiles that the children had seen during the introduction of the project.   Showing a sheet of lightweight copper, for example, and pointing to that part of a mobile that had been made from copper, would help children to see the possibilities in that material.

Clark:	"That doesn't look the same as the copper in the mobile you showed us."
George:	"No, the copper in the mobile is shiny. It looks like other copper I have seen. Couldn't it be polished?"
Teacher:	"Yes, but it saves time if we wait until the metal is cut and shaped before we polish it. Why?"
George:	"Because it would only become tarnished again as we handled it. Copper is easy to polish, though. My mother has some good copper polish she used on the bottoms of our cooking pans."
Geraldine:	"If we use that copper, how do we get it cut into the shape we want?"
George:	"Easy. You use metal shears. My Dad has a pair I can bring. He lets me use them."
Teacher:	"I have a pair of metal shears right here. Are these like the ones you use, George?"
George:	"Yes, something like that."

As children begin the study of an art project that utilizes materials and tools, such as the copper and metal shears, they should learn something about their equipment before beginning to work.   When we say in art education that children are free from teacher direction and should carry through their own ideas in a manner personal to them, we do *not* mean that no teaching takes place.   When children are taught to use tools safely, to respect them and to take care of them, they are being taught skills and habits that free them to give concentrated attention to the creative part of the job. When children are shown the unique properties of a material and are shown some of the ways it can be used as well as some of its limitations, they are learning in a short time what it has taken mankind many years to learn. They are also saved the discouragement of learning these things by trial and error. They see a skilled teacher bring beauty into a piece of metal, and they are inspired. The teacher does not cut a piece of metal and have each child cut an identical piece in order to teach such a technique. She shows them and lets

These children are beginning work on stabiles, a type of mobile that stands on a flat surface. Although they solve their problems individually, they frequently assist each other in working out certain processes.

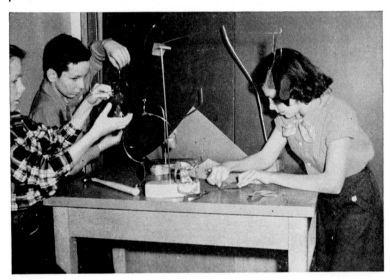

49

one or two try cutting a piece, which is enough to give the others the idea of how it is done. They will have a general idea of how to do it and will be ready to try it themselves. As they work with the metal, she helps the children as their problems occur and teaches additional skills as they are needed.

Teacher: "Would you like to try cutting a piece of the metal, George?"

If the first child called upon to try the new materials and process is one with some experience with it, he is likely to succeed, thus giving the others confidence.

Teacher: "Try it, Mae?"

Mae, being a rather small girl, was chosen next by the teacher to give the idea that it did not require much strength to cut the light-gauge metal.

Teacher: "Both of you cut straight pieces, but it is just as easy to cut a curve.   Try that, Tony."

Although there are other things that the children need to learn about metal, at this point the children were just being introduced to a variety of materials.

Teacher: "I see some of you looking at the rolls of wire.   There are different kinds of wire there.   One of them is copper, the same as the metal.   Which one is it, Jean?"
Jean: "This one."
Teacher: "What has this wire been made from?"
Nick: "Iron."
Teacher: "This one?"
Jean: "Aluminum, and I think it would be the lightest.   Aluminum is not as heavy as other metals."
Teacher: "Some wire is thicker than others."   [She showed the children two different gauges of wire.]

The teacher explained wire gauges and used the word *gauge* repeatedly in her explanation in order to familiarize the children with it and to help them understand how it is used.

Teacher: "What could wire be used for in the making of a mobile?"
Anna: "The horizontals that the pieces are hung from could be made from that heaviest wire.   They have to be stiff enough to hold their shape and they have to be strong enough to hold the pieces hanging from them."
Al: "They can't be heavy, though, or the air won't move them."
Teacher: "Is there anything else that we could use wire for?"
Anna: "Some other parts could be made from it.   I was thinking we could make shapes like we did in wire sculpturing and hang those from our mobiles.   If we made them

from that real thin wire they would still be light enough
to move."

Marvin: "Some of the mobiles had shapes made out of wire, but
it looked like they were soldered together. We couldn't
do that because we have no stove to heat the soldering
iron."

The conversation about the use of the various materials has pro-
gressed so smoothly, with suggestions and ideas coming from the
children, that it might seem as though this group of sixth-grade children are well informed on such matters. Actually, only a few
children in the room had any background at all in using such materials. The teacher brought these informed children into the
conversation and used their knowledge and experiences to help with
the teaching. It served also to give recognition to these children's
achievements. To most of the children in the group the whole
idea of working with these tools and equipment was new. For
most of the children such words as *solder, gauge,* and *mobile* were
new and the processes were unfamiliar.

Sally: "Some of the metal in the mobiles was red. Is there red
metal or was it painted, or was it even metal?"

Teacher: "Yes, it was metal that had been painted. Why did the
artist do that to only one piece of metal among the many
in his mobile?"

The teacher used Sally's question as a cue for calling attention to
an *art* aspect of a mobile.

Francis: "It calls attention to that spot in the mobile. That must
be what he meant as the most important spot in his
mobile."

Ralph: "It keeps it from being too much all the same. You see
that spot first when you look at the mobile. Then you
see the rest of it."

Teacher: "Sometimes an artist uses color spots in just that way —
to carry your eye from one area to another. We have
talked about this in regard to paintings. Mobiles are
art compositions, too. Some of the same principles apply.
Allen asked a question about soldering a minute ago that
we didn't answer. Since we have no heat we will have to
use solder that comes in a tube. It would require a great

deal of expense and work to prepare this room for heating the other kind of solder.   Our fire laws require safety installations before an open flame can be used in a classroom."

Safety is an important part of all teaching.   In the use of any tools and equipment children need to be reminded constantly of safety measures, and they also need frequent explanations of why safety measures are necessary.   The children need to understand the use of the tools before they begin to work.   Since they are about to use them, this is the most effective time to teach the skills, techniques, and processes involved.   When their interest is high, they want to learn.   Such knowledge frees them to create.   They know enough about the use of their materials and equipment to work with them, to see what they will do, and to deal directly with the materials as they create.   It would be both unnecessary and lengthy to describe the procedure for teaching the use of each tool.   Teachers do not need detailed instructions about how to teach such specific skills; they need insight into the teaching processes involved in an assigned topic and in a three-dimensional project in art.   From examples that they can study, teachers will develop their own ways.   Neither would it be desirable to set a pattern for teaching.   A teacher will be most enthusiastic about her own ways.   Enthusiasm is a great asset to teaching.   Teachers do, however, need to study teaching procedures, to evaluate them, and to draw from them whatever help they may find.

Teacher: "There are some other materials here that could be used in making mobiles.   This is balsa wood.   What is one feature of balsa that would make it usable?"

Alden: "It is much lighter than other wood.   Model airplanes are made from it."

Teacher: "I also have a box of pieces of brightly colored glass."

Alden: "The fish mobile we saw had pieces of colored glass inside."

Bruce: "This white stuff is what we use at Christmas to make decorations.   It is certainly not heavy."

Teacher: "It is called Styrofoam, and these are pieces of colored plastic that you may use."

Al: "Those pieces of colored cardboard.   Could we use them, too?"

Teacher: "Yes, and there are many other materials not here that we might think of to use. What might be one?"

Clark: "Corrugated paper."

Thelma: "I was thinking about how we made the heads for our marionettes out of papier-mâché. They were lightweight and we could make it in any kind of shape for our mobile."

Teacher: "In order to help us think of the many things that we might use, let us make a list on the blackboard. We will start the list now, and as you think of something else, write it on the blackboard yourself."

Such a device stimulated thinking and research. It kept changing, growing, and adding interest and knowledge.

Teacher: "I am going to leave these materials on the table for the next couple of days. You can inspect them and think about how you might use them. You can also consider what you might bring from home to use. The things on this table can be used by anyone who wants them."

By giving the children a couple of days to examine the materials and to collect others, she was also allowing time for ideas and thinking to mature. Children of this age like to plan and will do research when interested.

Teacher: "These books I have on mobiles will be on the table, too, for you to look at. I have asked Miss Sands to have whatever materials she has in the library ready for you."

MOTIVATION DISCUSSION

Teacher: "Did you notice in studying the examples of mobiles last week that each one was made with a certain idea in mind? Each had either a theme, a subject that you could identify, or was an abstract. [Showing some of the pictures of mobiles again.] This one is a fish. It is not intended to be an exact form of any particular fish but is a design in wire and colored glass to suggest a fish."

The teacher's statement was the beginning of a discussion about the motifs of mobiles. As the children restudied the examples of

50

Materials need not be expensive or unusual to give a child
experience in creating three-dimensional forms. Newspaper,
string, paste, and paint were used by both children. Jane
added a feather to her bird puppet, and Bill added yarn to
his animal for decoration.

51

mobiles to consider the theme, they mentioned factors about materials and construction not previously noticed.

In spite of the fact that the teacher had shown the children how to use certain materials and tools, they may still be curious about how each artist has achieved particular effects. Since the children, however, are relatively unskilled with tools, they will need help and reminders throughout their work on the project.

Anna: "In magazines I have seen mobiles that were made for a holiday like Christmas."

Teacher: "Those are very often made of shapes and materials suggestive of Christmas. Of course, they can be made for any holiday or special occasion. You could make one for a birthday that would have shapes to suggest the interests and the personality of the person having the birthday."

It is the responsibility of the teacher to add ideas to broaden the thinking on a topic. By doing so once or twice during a discussion, she stimulates the children's imagination.

Barry: "I was talking with my parents about it over the week end. They had some good ideas, too. My Dad is a fisherman, so he was thinking that different fish shapes or even different kinds of trout flies might make good ones. I wouldn't want to do a fish one because one of the mobiles we studied was like that, and it wouldn't seem very original. My mother had an idea I have been thinking about. She said we could hang mine in the stairway because there is a draft there. She said it might be made to go with the living room, and take suggestions from the things in the room — the drapery design and things like that. I was thinking about trying it. We have brass lamps. Maybe I'll use some brass shapes."

Children frequently discuss their school work with their parents. This is part of their independent study before work begins. Barry had several good ideas. The teacher should take advantage of these cues and develop them further without belaboring them, but with just enough comment to stimulate thinking.

Teacher: "If we make any art form for a particular spot, it is a good idea to consider the forms and designs already there, so that our art work will be in harmony with its environment. A stairway is a good spot for a mobile because of the air currents. There are always places in every house where the air moves more than it does in other places. These places are fine for a mobile if it makes an appropriate decoration there. It should be hung where it *looks* well as well as where it functions well. What might be another reason why we want to consider the space where it will hang before we make it?"

Marvin: "The size. In our stairway you would hit your head on it. If we put a mobile in a high place, we can make it to hang down more than if it is in a lower spot. Then how far it reaches out is important, too. It can't bump anything."

Teacher: "Barry mentioned that he might not like to make a fish mobile because one of the examples we looked at had a fish motif. I see no reason why he could not use the same theme as long as he created the mobile very differently. Does anyone have another idea for a mobile?"

Jonas: "I have a little sister. I could make one to hang on the ceiling in her nursery. She likes to watch things that move. I could use toys for ideas for figures or even nursery rhymes or animals."

Arabel: "I was wondering how the artist made the holes in some of the pieces of metal he used?"

Teacher: "You might all like to watch while I do it to see how it is done. Then I can help you individually with it as you work. Why would an artist want to put a hole in a metal form for a mobile?"

Patty: "I think it makes it look better."

Teacher: "Why?"

Al: "The hole is a good shape. It isn't just round."

Teacher: "How can you tell how large to make the hole?"

Sidney: "According to what looks well in the shape of the metal you are using."

Vicky: "That might throw the whole mobile out of balance."

Marvin: "It might be just what you need to bring it into balance. You could do that if you wanted a big piece on your mobile and didn't want the big piece to be heavy."

Sally: "It must look well. It can't be decided just by balance."

Alden: "It has to be decided by balance or the whole thing won't work."

Teacher: "You must consider both. At every step of the way we must consider how well it looks and whether or not what we have done improves its appearance. At every step of the way we must consider balance and movement, too, or the mobile will not function or even look well."

Anna: "If it gets out of balance, you just have to figure out some way of balancing it again. That's all."

Teacher: "There are several things that you might use to suspend your mobile. Think about it in relation to your own problem."

Nick: "The string isn't a very important part of a mobile."

Arabel: "It is so. Without it the mobile wouldn't stay up."

Nick: "Like that, it is important. But not as a part of what you look at. Like a watch, the works are the important part, but they are closed in a case. You don't see them. Some parts, even if they are important to how a thing works, are not important to how it looks. I think the strings of a mobile are like that."

The teacher felt that the children had reached the point where they were ready to leave the discussion and begin to work with the materials. She also felt that there were some things they needed yet to learn. From her experience she knew, also, that some of the processes discussed and demonstrated would be forgotten or only partially remembered. Many of these things would need to be re-taught as the children faced their problems during the working process.

Since many of the materials were relatively expensive, the teacher and children talked about being economical by first planning and cutting trial shapes out of paper.

Teacher: "There is something else, too, that I think would add interest. Among your books and magazines at home may be articles on mobiles and the artists who create them. We would all profit from hearing some of the interesting things you find. Could we start each art work period with a brief report by one or two of you?"

Barry: "My mother gets magazines on interior decoration. They often have pictures of mobiles that I could bring."

Teacher: "Let's use our bulletin board for mobile information f
either pictures or short articles."

As the discussion ended, the children began the exciting and wonderful adventure of trying their own strengths and abilities in a new
field. Each, with plans and ideas of his own, began working them
out. Some were drawing plans, some cutting paper shapes, and
some examining supplies and resource materials. Naturally, each
child would begin in his own particular way.

GUIDANCE

The teacher's role in guiding the progress of such an art
project varies a great deal as the children's individual problems
arise. The differing character of the materials creates challenges
and problems as do the tools, which are new to the children. Sixth
graders attempt complex projects. For these reasons, the problems
arising as they work are apt to be somewhat involved, and the
teacher must be ready for almost any situation. The teacher's responsibility may not be as demanding as it sounds but her job is to
analyze a child's work and, by means of discussion, help him focus
upon one phase of the problem at a time. The teacher's role is to
guide the child toward seeing his problem in a clearer way, to help
him understand it better, and to encourage him to suggest his own
solutions. It is also the teacher's duty to help him evaluate his
solutions in terms of his purpose, materials, taste, and the accomplishments he has made thus far. The teacher does this through
skillful questions and comments. However, the teacher must judge
the extent to which she can follow this course by the reaction of
each individual child to it. If a child seems to have been strug-
gling with a problem to the extent of impatience, it saves him from
further discouragement if the teacher simply points out the problem expediently. Identifying the difficulty is a relief. Discussion
of a solution can follow.

For a while, at the beginning of the work period, the teacher
becomes less the leader and more the adviser as each child becomes engaged in his own creative enterprise. The teacher, following the lead of the child as he meets and faces problems, becomes a
resource. During the work period, which in the case of the making

of mobiles will cover several days or weeks, the teacher's major role is that of giving help, but she must also motivate, evaluate, and exhibit, *always teaching* as she works.

Ina: "Miss Gray, see, I brought two stones from an old brace-let to use in my mobile.   I am going to make mine about my cat and dog.   They are always chasing each other around the house and all over the place.   I thought I would make a shape of my dog out of metal, and all over it I would cut out little triangles and curve them to make it look like her curly hair.   My cat I will make out of wire and stretch grey yarn back and forth over it to make it look woolly.   I might even put a mouse in to balance it if I need to.   The cat and dog could move back and forth and maybe up and down and look like they're chas-ing each other, if I can get it.   I don't know how to get this green stone in for the cat's eye and this blue one in for the dog."

Teacher: "One way would be to wrap thin wire around the stone and fasten it once or twice with that wire to the heavier wire that the cat's form would be made of.   I have some pictures of stones set that way.   You can look at them and then have a better idea of how it looks."

As the teacher explained the operation, she demonstrated it to Ina. In helping Ina with her problem, the teacher proceeded directly toward the solution, because the teacher felt that the setting of a stone was an experience new to the child.   Ina was not ready to deal with the stone-setting and would not be for some time, but she felt it necessary to see the entire scope of her project and to under-stand the solution before she could begin.   The teacher did not in-vite other children to hear the explanation because she felt that few would encounter this particular problem.

Ralph: "When I cut the metal with these shears, it gets curly at the edges.   See?"

Teacher: "The metal can be straightened.   [To the class]   How many of you have had some trouble with the edges of this thin metal curling a bit as you cut?   [Those who did raised their hands.]   You might come up here and watch while I help Ralph straighten his metal.   Anyone else who is planning to cut metal can join us if he wishes."

The problem that Ralph encountered was one that the teacher thought others might meet, so she invited all those interested to watch as she demonstrated. Children who were not facing this problem could continue to work without interruption.

Clark: "I am using some of this balsa wood and I want to make a hole in it.   How can I get it started?"

As the teacher introduced tools and materials, she demonstrated the use of the brace and bit in the boring of wood and had one or two children from the group try it. This procedure was helpful because it gave the children the knowledge that such a thing could be done and an idea of how to do it. However, it was only an introduction to such a technique. Learning takes place best as the actual work is done by the child in relation to his own problem under the guidance of a competent teacher.

Teacher: "Let's go up to the workbench and try it."

The teacher invited those interested in this particular problem to join them, thus involving the children in the teaching process. The specific teaching-learning situation that followed is typical of the many that arise as the teacher guides the children's work through an art project.

Teacher: [To the whole group]   "At the end of each work session, you will want to store your materials in a place where you can easily get them when you want to work on them. If you have free time during the day, you could work on your art if you want to."

Provision for additional work time is good because it: (a) gives the children who work slowly an opportunity to keep up with the others, (b) supplements an enrichment program of education, (c) gives those especially interested in mobiles an opportunity to do more, and (d) gives the children a choice of one more interesting thing to do in their free time.

Teacher: "From one work period to the next, put all of your mobile tools, materials, and plans in a large container and put it on these shelves."

Definite storage and clean-up information can aid the child in his work and will avoid classroom confusion and untidiness.

52

Children are proud of their individuality and want to express it in their art work, but in order to continue to grow and develop, each child needs recognition, from the teacher and others, for his achievements.

Patty: "I can't hold mine and stretch this string at the same time."

Teacher: "Ask someone near you to help. [To the class] It may be that your work will be easier if you help each other. Why don't you work together as you need to?"

As children work on such an art project as mobiles, using tools, metal, and other materials, there is, understandably, a certain amount of noise. The teacher's suggestion that children help each other will occasion some conversation. These sounds are typical of any group of children working in a situation in which they are, to a great extent, on their own. Work noises can be expected. However, the teacher needs frequently to remind the children that handling of tools and materials as quietly as possible will add to good working conditions, as will a minimum of conversation in low tones. Since a responsibility of the teacher is to guard children against interruptions as they work and to protect their right to work without disturbance, she must deal with children who engage in disturbing activities. The fact that art activities involve freedom of decision and of action does not mean that children's behavior breaks down. Courteous, considerate behavior is especially desirable in such a situation.

EVALUATION

In any lengthy art project a great deal of evaluation is done by both the teacher and the children as the work progresses. Much critical judgment goes into each child's choice of theme, materials, shapes, and composition.   As he works, the child makes a value decision about the balance, movement, and aesthetic quality of his work, which in this case is his mobile.   During the working process, the teacher evaluates as she helps each child with his problems.   When she notices an interesting and original piece of work, she often calls it to the attention of the class, explaining why she believes it is interesting.

Teacher: "Ina has finished the cat form for her mobile.   See how the interweaving of the gray yarn has given a fur effect. You fixed the eye in very well, too."

Ina: "I am going to try to make her claws move, too, if I can — and maybe her whiskers."

Whenever she found the opportunity, the teacher praised or called attention to some child's work, explaining *why* it was interesting. Therefore, since evaluation took place to such an extent during the working process, less evaluation of the completed art was needed, lest it be repetitious.   When the work was completed, the teacher and children appraised it, calling attention to those features of the mobiles that had not previously received recognition.

During the evaluation of the completed work the discussion deals with the accomplishments.   The teacher's purpose during guidance of the work is to give help with problems, to recognize less successful areas of the child's work, and to call his attention to such areas in a way that will neither discourage nor embarrass him. The working process is the time for facing and solving problems. It is to be assumed, when the art project is completed, that each child has worked out his ideas to the best of his ability.   The completed product represents his achievement.   Therefore, it should be discussed from this viewpoint.   A project as lengthy and in-

volved as the one used as an example in this chapter requires a
great deal of a child's thought and energy.   He has a lot of himself
in it, is proud of it, and is sensitive to the reactions of other people.
The time for indicating any weak points or less successful areas in
the work is past.   Such remarks about completed art would come
too late to result in any change in the art product, would only bring
about discouragement, causing the child to lose confidence and
pride in his work, which represented the best that he could do at
that time.

EXHIBITION

The final major responsibility of the teacher of art is to display the children's completed art.   Since art is appreciated through
visual activity and emotional sensitivity, exhibiting it is a necessary
part of the cycle of activity involved in any art project.   Children
have enjoyed the creating of an art project and they also enjoy their
completed work.   They want to share with others a part of what is
so vital to them.   Realizing this need and desire for recognition,
the teacher should plan to display the work of the children in whatever way best suits the particular art product.

Most art work can be successfully and attractively displayed
in the children's own classrooms, school halls, assembly rooms, or
cafeterias.   Mobiles, however, present a different problem.   Since
each requires a certain volume of space for its own movement, few
can be shown in the classroom at one time.   In the situation that
has been discussed in this chapter, exhibition outside the classroom
seemed desirable.   The class discussed the problem, making several
suggestions, and finally deciding to place the mobiles in store windows.   The children reasoned that their mobiles would not occupy
much of the merchant's valuable window space if they were sus-
pended from the ceiling.   They also suggested that the movement
of the mobile might call attention to the window display.   The children, acting through a committee of their classmates, found enough
store windows, and each child hung his own mobile.

During the committee's investigation of available shop windows, the children decided to write articles to present to the local
newspaper.   They decided to describe mobiles, explain their uses,

and summarize the educational values inherent in this project. Their writings included the names of the children who had made the mobiles, identifying each with the particular shop window in which it was displayed. Valuable public relations resulted from the newspaper article that appeared. Some of the outcomes were:

(a) Public recognition received by the children for their work
(b) Wider dissemination of information on art education
(c) Better lay understanding of the educational values of an art project such as mobiles
(d) Closer school and community relationships

The teacher has active and changing roles during the teaching of an assigned topic in art. When the teacher introduced the topic of mobiles to her sixth-grade class, she used a variety of visual materials and led the motivational discussion. Since the work period for this complex activity extended over a few weeks, the teacher had many opportunities to help children on an individual basis with their

Children's art work often makes attractive decoration for their classroom. This wall hanging, made with crayons on cloth by a small group, adds interest and color to a wall area.

53

problems as they arose. She evaluated their art with the children
as they worked, often calling the attention of the group to successful and interesting achievements. When the work was completed,
attention was directed toward successful areas of the art that had not
previously been mentioned. Each child became responsible for
exhibiting his own art. Children of this age can and want to assume responsibilities. They want to work independently, to be on
their own, and to be grown up.

Art is not an isolated activity that children do in school as a
recreational relief from their more difficult academic subjects. Art,
as a vital part of children's daily school activities, is related to other
phases of school life as well as to other experiences that the children
have. Art is just as difficult as any other school subject. Having
thought through the mobile project in this chapter, adults can well
understand the complexities and difficulties arising in art work.
Indeed, this challenge combined with the independence, the working freedom, and the individual personal expression made possible
through art is responsible for children's enjoyment of art.

Suggested activity

*Plan an art project suitable for children in the fourth or fifth
grade. Include:*

(a) *Some general art aims or objectives to be gained through
this project*
(b) *A list of the materials needed*
(c) *Ways of introducing the topic*
(d) *A few questions you might use in the motivational discussion*

CHAPTER *VII*

P*roviding* f*or* *growth* *in* *art*

GROWTH in art does not just happen; it is the result of many experiences with a variety of materials in a variety of situations under the guidance and stimulation of a teacher who understands and is sensitive to children and who knows and appreciates art.   In order to provide for growth in art the teacher needs to keep in mind that although she has a very important role in planning for and administrating activities that provide for growth in the child's ability to organize and to express a constantly widening variety of ideas, she must continuously guard the child against activities that interfere with his right to and need for self-expression, for self-development, for independence, and for a stronger individuality.   The teacher needs to keep in mind the long-range goals she has planned in art, study the needs of the children, and provide daily experiences that will help them grow in art expression and knowledge.

THE CHILD'S OWN CREATIVE EFFORT

There are many experiences that provide opportunities for growth in art expression. One of these, which is of inestimable importance in improving the child's art work, is the actual working through of the creative process in art. Through facing the challenges of and solving the problems involved in this type of art work, the child learns by means of his own efforts many important things that help him better express his own ideas with materials. Coming face to face with a new situation, which the child feels must be overcome, presents challenges and makes demands on him. Overcoming the problems involved gives the child a sense of power and achievement. It is, however, difficult to motivate the child to accept another person's choice of such undertakings.

In order to understand more fully the tremendous incentive in self-determined activities and the growth resulting from them, watch a child's behavior in undirected activities with playground equipment. A child will make a free choice of a piece of equipment and then proceed to master the skills involved in using it. He finds his own ways of building these skills and of developing his own needed strengths to function with the parallel bars, slide, jungle gym, or climbing rope.

Each time the child approaches the piece of playground equipment, he not only enjoys what he has already learned to do, but also enjoys proceeding to a new and challenging achievement. He tries to turn himself over in a different way on the parallel bars, or to climb a little higher on the rope, or to balance himself on the top of the jungle gym. The new task that he has set for himself will probably not be easy, but if the desire to do it is strong enough, he will keep working at it until he succeeds. The difficulty of mastery may in itself be a motivating challenge. The rewards are greater and the sense of power more profound when, through his own efforts, the obstacles have been overcome. In working through the physical processes involved in the use of playground equipment the child learns much on his own. Because his efforts are stimulated by his own desire, he becomes more capable and self-confident. The same thing is true of his art work. The child makes the decisions of what he can and wants to do, evaluates the results, sees his own growth, and proceeds at his own rate.

Children have a powerful desire to learn. A child cannot be prevented from learning if he is learning what *he* wants to learn. *No one, not even his teachers or parents, wants the child to learn as much as the child himself wants to learn.* Children have a strong desire to gain new powers and to grow up to do the things that adults can do. The desire to grow and to learn physically, emotionally, and mentally helps a child gain more mastery, learn new skills, and better express himself through his own efforts. The child develops through his own efforts in working through the creative process in art. Through creative expression in art the child learns many new and valuable things and develops skills and judgments.

In addition to the experiences for growth provided in creative expression, some definite learning situations need to be provided if children are to build more fully on their abilities to express themselves with art materials. As the child matures, his ability to use materials creatively and independently should develop in proportion to his other learnings. Each child should feel satisfied that he is making progress in this as in other areas of his growth and development. To do this the child needs the help of a competent teacher. The child needs to accumulate new ideas and deeper insights pertaining to his present information; he needs knowledge about *art* and needs to be taught many things.

How the teaching is done is very important. The *way* the teacher presents information in art can greatly interfere with a child's ability to be creative, or it can greatly facilitate it. The time *when* instruction is given is also important. A child's growth in art cannot be left to chance. Some plans need to be made for activities that will provide for growth. Art educators feel the importance of such experiences:

> There is no value in freeing a person from all restraints. However, he must have guidance in setting up real values. Creative power is not learned in the sense that one memorizes facts. It is developed through experiences for setting up values under sympathetic guidance.[1]

---

[1] Kennedy, D., Bradley, M., Fitzgerald, L., Smith, N., and Joyner, S., "What it means to be creative," *Art Education*, Vol. 8, No. 7, p. 10.

THE COMPLETE ART PROGRAM

Children should not only have many creative experiences
with a wide variety and combination of materials, but they should
also have additional art activities of different but valuable types.
Any type of art work is not acceptable, however, and Chapter III
shows why some kinds of art work are actually harmful to children's present adjustment and development as well as to their future effectiveness as persons and as members of a democratic society.
It is desirable to plan some work in assigned topics, correlated projects, museum visits, and discussion of art work; every lesson does
not have to be done with the materials usually associated with art.
It is advantageous for children in the elementary grades to study
the commercial objects found in stores because they will be con-
sumers of such products.   It is to their advantage, for example, to
be able to select from among many patterns of drapery materials the
best designed pieces.   Children should learn to see and to appreciate
the beauty in nature and in architecture that is functionally appropriate.   Children do not need to be busy every minute making
something with their hands to be studying art.

A teacher needs to develop a program of art so that growth in
ability to express ideas as well as good taste and a love of beauty
can be developed.   The teacher needs to know in a general way
what broad aims and areas of growth she will work for with her
children throughout a year, as well as exactly what materials and
equipment are available to carry out a challenging and interesting
art program.   It is, however, impractical and undesirable to have
a day-by-day or week-by-week program planned in advance for the
entire year because such planning can be rigid and inflexible and
makes no provisions for the unexpected events that inspire art activities, such as unusual happenings in town or in school, worthwhile
exhibitions, a particular weakness of the group, or a special interest
that might advantageously be pursued.   A teacher will have a detailed course of study only after it has been experienced by the children — "This is what the program was" is better than "This is what
it will be."   It is impossible for a teacher to know exactly what the
problems of each particular group of children will be or when these
problems will arise.   Learning is most effective when teaching is

54

Children should have art experiences with a wide variety of materials and processes to provide challenge and stimulation. New processes for using familiar materials can add interest, just as art can be further personalized by bits of attractive materials that children bring from home.

55

done at the time of need for the information or when the children's interests are keenest.

The daily work should be built on the basis of the children's interest, their *need* as determined from a study of previous art work, and on the teacher's knowledge of new materials and ways of using them. If the teacher keeps in mind the over-all purposes of art education and the broad experiences that she believes the children should have, she will form a most effective and complete program of growth in art.

INSTRUCTION AND ASSIGNED TOPICS

Creative art activities should be the core and backbone of every art program. The nature of practically all other art lessons should be derived from the children's needs as diagnosed from their creative art products. This can be the outcome of an evaluation discussion between the children and their teacher about their art work or it can be the result of a teacher's analysis of their work.

After the area of weakness or need has been determined, the teacher should plan an art lesson for the near future, preferably the next art class, during which she will *teach* the children some general principles to help them understand and overcome their problem and to help them better express their ideas. The teaching will take the form of talking and explaining to achieve *understanding*. Understanding is achieved best by broadening and adding to the children's concepts and information, letting each child form his own mental pictures as the teaching proceeds. When teaching is done mainly by showing the children how to draw an object or through the use of illustration, the mental concepts of other people are impressed on the child. Therefore, if illustrations, which do have value, are used at this point, there should be a number of them covering a variety of approaches without too much emphasis placed upon any one other person's way of solving the problem. The over-stressing of illustrations can influence the children's work. If only one or two illustrations are used, the children will tend to build a concept of a fixed form, which will limit their mental scope regarding the directions that can be taken to solve the problem. Not only is it important to teach the child about a particular phase of art, but

it is also important that *at the same time* he should be building a
concept of creativeness about it.   This can be done through using
illustrations that show many different approaches to the problem.
Both naturalistic or representational and design-centered or abstract
approaches should be included in the illustrations.

After the explanation of how the problem might be solved it
would be appropriate to have an art activity that would include a
direct involvement with the problem.   Children profit by such a
concentration on their problem.   This activity should probably take
the form of an assigned topic dealing precisely with the problem that
the teacher and children together had decided needed attention.
For children in the elementary school this much special attention to
one limited subject is probably enough, not because they have mastered the skill or learned all they can about a problem, but because
at this age they need frequent changes of subjects and materials to
hold their interest.   If the teacher feels that more instruction is
needed or that the children need more practice in the subject, she
can reserve it for a later time and attack it from a slightly different
approach.   Children profit from the interval between repetitions
because it gives them time to integrate what they have learned.
Also, by absorbing different experiences and meeting new challenges, the children's thinking and working become more flexible
and they become able to make adjustments from one situation to
another with less mental and emotional disturbance.   This, in itself,
is a desirable educational outcome in our present age of fast-chang-
ing methods of working and of using mechanical and automatic
devices.

A concentration on one thing should be followed by a totally
different kind of art work.   If the work has been lengthy or detailed,
a fast-moving medium would provide welcome excitement and
stimulation.   Finger painting might be an example.   There are
many other such art activities that an ingenious teacher will be able
to suggest.   Certainly, regardless of the medium, the experience
should be creative, with no indication from the teacher that she
hopes to see some improvement in one particular phase of everyone's
work.   When the teacher makes such a suggestion, she is, in effect,
assigning a topic.   Some children will automatically take advantage of their new learning and be interested in and proud of their
achievements, wanting further to show how much they have im-

proved.   Others will have had enough for the present, feeling a need
for some entirely different subject.   The child needs to choose.

The fact that the need for instruction toward growth in one
particular area of art can be determined from children's creative art
products does not mean that the results of every creative art lesson
should be analyzed, weaknesses determined, and remedial instruction and remedial work undertaken.   To do so might very easily

*Such a strong, fluent, and well-organized finger paint-
ing results from a child's freedom to experiment with
forms and with movements of his hands and arms,
as well as from his knowledge and judgment of art.
Children enjoy the physical sensation and the flexibility of this medium.*

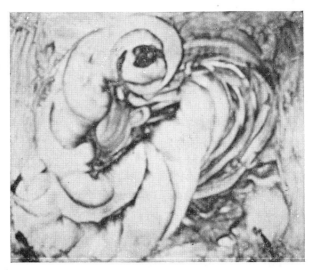

cause children to regard creative art work with apprehension and
to wonder what would be found wrong with their work.   Frequently, creative art work should be undertaken for its own values
and for its own growth potential.   Then, too, at times the teacher
herself makes the examination of the work and plans certain art
experiences according to her opinion of the children's needs.   She
draws her conclusions from watching the children work, studying
their completed art work, and listening to their comments.   Such
diagnoses are made only when there seems to be a general need for

improvement within the group.   Children's art work is always to be considered from a viewpoint consistent with the age of the children.   Their work will not meet adult standards; in no respect should it be expected to do so.   It should be appreciated and enjoyed for its own qualities and accomplishments.   Children build upon their successes in a very positive and encouraging way.

To illustrate how such an educational process takes place, an example of the way one teacher dealt with her fifth-grade group to improve their drawing of people will be described.   This is a very common problem with children of this age.

After a creative expression experience with crayons, all the children's art was exhibited and the class conducted a discussion of it, indicating the achievements and strong points of each piece. When the discussion ended, this conversation took place:

Teacher: "These are very interesting crayon drawings.   You, as a group, have done an especially good job of using light and dark colors to emphasize certain parts of your work. Your coloring is emphatic.   It shows up well from any part of the room.   You have a wide variety of interesting subjects, but I notice only one of you drew any people in his composition.   Gerald drew one boy in his picture. Why have none of the rest of you drawn people?"

Jean: "It is hard to draw people."

Peter: "I can't draw them to look like anything."

Teacher: "Why don't you draw people, Andy?"

Andy: "I can't."

Teacher: "Bill, why don't you?"

Bill: "I can't make them look right."

Teacher: "How many have difficulty drawing people?"

Practically all the children raised their hands.   The children had not, of their own accord, mentioned a need that they knew existed. They were aware of it but tried to conceal it, which is a natural thing that we all do.   The teacher helped them face their problem. She did it gently and without criticism, showing the problem simply as something to accept.

Teacher: "Most of you have difficulty drawing people, or figures as we sometimes call them.   How many would like to know more about drawing people?"

All the children raised their hands again. As has been stated previously, *children want to learn.* They do not want to be handicapped by a lack of ability. They really want some information that will help them better to express their ideas. They want to be successful in drawing people or any other objects and they want to do it freely and skillfully.

Teacher: "Tomorrow in art class we will study some things about how people look that may help you draw them better. Probably proportion is one thing that troubles you."

Proportion seemed to be one of the figure problems that they accepted as troubling them. Their general response to the suggestion had indicated that to the teacher.

Teacher: "Between now and tomorrow, look into a mirror to see if you can find any relationships between parts of your body — arms and legs, for instance — that might help you."

The creative art work had been studied, the diagnosis of need made, and plans made for a teaching-learning situation. The children were encouraged to do a little exploratory work before the next art class. In doing this the teacher indicated to the children that there was much they could learn by studying their own figures. In fact, that is the way she planned to attack the problem on the next day.

The teacher began the discussion on the next day by referring to the suggested activity of studying their figures in the mirror.

Teacher: "What did you discover about the relationships among parts of your body by looking into a mirror?"

George: "I couldn't tell anything except that my body is straighter and not so round as I draw it."

Gretchen: "I could see that my body was larger than I usually draw

---

The three examples of Geraldine's art, on the opposite page, show how a child grows in ability to draw people, through creative art. Illustration 58, drawn in the second grade, shows more detail and knowledge of the human figure than Illustration 57, which was drawn in the first grade. Illustration 59, done in the third grade, shows a relatively well developed concept of a person.

57

58

59

it and that my head is smaller. I have been drawing dancing girls and I think I make their heads too large."

Mark: "I don't know what you mean by relationships to look for."

Teacher: "What are relationships, or what are relations?"

Susan: "We are all the same family. We have the same father and mother, my sister and I."

Teacher: "Yes, it is having something in common, something the same or similar, that makes a relationship between two parts of a thing. In studying about figures we need to look for things that are the same or nearly the same between parts. This helps us remember about sizes."

It was necessary to build an understanding of terms and art vocabulary before the teaching began, since the same word can have different meanings in different situations. *Figure,* for instance, means one thing in arithmetic and another in art.

Teacher: "Stand on the floor far enough apart so that your arms do not touch each other when raised. Drop your hands to your sides. Your hand falls halfway between your hip and knee. A good many of you have been drawing arms too short. No matter in what position the arms are placed in a drawing they should be long enough to reach that far. When you draw an arm raised, judge with your eyes whether or not the arm is long enough to reach halfway to the knee if it is dropped."

The teacher talked about that point because it was a new experience for the children and they needed to learn how to look for and to see relationships of sizes. The teacher takes the lead and then gradually draws the children into the discussion.

Teacher: "Where does your elbow come in relationship to the whole arm?"

Edith: "In the middle."

Shirley: "And it only bends toward the front. But I knew this before."

Teacher: "Yes, we already know many things about our body and how it moves and bends. Press your elbows in toward your sides. Where does the elbow come?"

Gordon: "Right on my belt."

Aileen: "By my waistline."

Teacher: "When you draw arms you have another relationship of sizes to think about. From the shoulder to the elbow is the same as the distance from the shoulder to the waistline. Notice how the body curves in at the waist. Now put the part of your hand that joins the wrist onto your chin. Put your hand over your face."

At this the children laughed and looked at each other in surprise. Many of them tried it again.

Teacher: "You are surprised that your hand is that large. Now you can see how much too small you have been making them. Hands are much larger than you think. When you are trying to draw figures as they look, compare the length of the hands with the length of the face.

"Now locate on both sides of your body the place that indicates halfway from the top of your head to the soles of your feet. [Most children placed their hands on their waistline.] You think your waistline is the center of your body. Many of you placed your hands on your belt. While your hands are still there look around at your friends. Does it seem right or too low or high?"

Alex: "It is too high, I think. It seems that the middle is lower."

Teacher: "Move one leg a little and feel the place on the side of your hip where the leg joins onto the body. There is a ball-and-socket joint there, and that spot is about the middle of the body. Do you think it is exactly the middle for everyone?"

Norman: "Whee-u! Look at Morris! His legs are *long*."

Teacher: "Yes, they are. Morris is tall."

During this time the children are looking around to see their classmates' proportions and to look for differences.

Teacher: "That just proves that not all people are alike and that what we have been saying about the relationships of sizes are only *general* guides. Almost every person varies a little from these general guides. Length of legs varies more than anything else. If you want to draw a tall man, how would you vary the legs from the guide we discussed?"

Mabel: "Make the legs longer.   Is this the same for children?"

Teacher: "Would it be?"

Inez: "No, because children are just smaller than adults.   So I think the middle would still be where the legs join onto the body."

Teacher: "Yes, and there is something else about legs that I would like to call to your attention.   While you are standing you notice that at the tops near the body, the legs touch. Then place your hands on your sides at the place where the legs join the body.   You notice that both legs together are just as wide as your body at the place where they join the body.   The legs get gradually smaller as they go down.   Most of you know this but you forget that the legs are as wide as they really are at the top. There is no sudden change from the body to the legs. You can see that it is a smooth line curving in as the legs go down."

All this time the children were exploring both by touching their own bodies and by looking at their classmates.   The children were learning through three senses at the same time — by *hearing* the teacher's explanation, by *touching and feeling* the parts of their own bodies, and by *seeing* the relationships of sizes in their classmates' bodies.

Teacher: "You were surprised to discover the actual size of your hands.   Put the back of your hand beside the back of the heel of your foot.   You had better sit to do it."

As the children made this comparison, they laughed a little and looked around to see if other children's feet were so much larger than their hands.

Valeria: "Feet are much larger."

Jason: "They would look funny drawn that big."

Teacher: "Most children draw feet much too small.   To look at your drawings I sometimes wonder how the people would balance on such small feet.   Feet have to be strong enough and large enough to carry us around and to support the weight of the entire body.   Think about that sometime, too.

     "There are many more size relationships that we can learn about people's bodies.   We also need to know how people bend when they move. But we will have that for another time."

Mark: "If I can remember this much for a while, I should be able to improve my drawing of people a lot. Are we going to draw people now?"

Teacher: "I think it would be a good idea. You might want to try out some of the things you learned. The relationships of figure parts we discussed will help you if you want to draw people just as they look. Sometimes we don't want to do that, of course. Sometimes we purposely change these actual relationships to show a feeling or emotion. Let me show you briefly the works of some artists who have not drawn people as they actually appear to the eye. Artists are free to shape forms in any way they choose in order to suit their purposes."

The teacher had prepared six or eight illustrations to show different ways that artists formed people, and she commented briefly on each. The emphasis of the explanation had been so pointedly on naturalism that it seemed imperative for the teacher to remind the children that there were other approaches to art and to the way of forming the shapes of people.

Teacher: "Mark suggested a little while ago that we might want to try some of the things we have just learned. There are other ways of doing this in addition to drawing. The illustrations I showed you were not all drawings."

Mabel: "No, some were like statues, like our clay modeling. We could make a person out of clay."

Gordon: "I think that would be good, because then we could see it and do it in three dimensions. It would be more real."

Earl: "We could see better how big certain parts are."

Teacher: "Suppose we plan to model people in clay tomorrow. You can be thinking about what you can make your clay figure be doing."

The teacher motivated the clay lesson as she would any assigned topic. (One way of motivating assigned topics was suggested in Chapter VI.)

After such a concentration of attention on improving the child's knowledge of and expression of the figure, it would be a good idea for the teacher to plan an art experience of a very different nature with materials of a different type. Children enjoy and profit by change. They learn to be more flexible, and are stimulated and excited by a change of materials.

To provide growth in art expression through instruction and creative experience four steps are recommended:

(a) Study of the children's needs
(b) Instruction to provide new knowledge
(c) Assigned topic dealing with the area of need
(d) Creative expression in a different medium

STUDY OF COMPLETED ART WORK

Growth in art can also take place through the study of completed art work. With the guidance of a teacher who knows and understands art, children learn how to make decisions about the quality of art work and how to study and how to enjoy art. They see how certain principles of art operate to improve expression and they learn how different artists have expressed emotion in their work. It is helpful for children to study the work of artists of various maturity levels.

Children's own art work is convenient and highly interesting as a source of discussion. When a group of children examine their own work, the experience becomes intimate and personal. To avoid embarrassment to anyone, the teacher needs to lead the comments in the direction of recognition of achievement. Such emphasis builds confidence. Confidence leads to enthusiasm. Art is not easy. It takes a great deal of drive and perseverance to identify a problem and work it through to a satisfactory conclusion. Injury to a child's feeling of pride and satisfaction in his work can bring about timidity and fear of exposing his ideas and expressions. It can discourage his art. Elementary-school children are extremely sensitive to group disapproval.

Sometimes, however, it is helpful to look at art work and discuss not only its strong points but also ways in which it can be improved. Such an approach can be made more successfully through the consideration of the work of children of the same age and grade level who remain anonymous. When personal feelings are protected the children can approach the art objectively. Children can also be stimulated by the fresh approaches of different people.

Studying the work of children about a year older or younger provides children with further educational opportunities. At a time when children feel discouraged, seeing the less developed work of younger children can provide a sense of achievement. Even without commenting on it, looking at the work of others is a pleasant and enjoyable experience. Looking at the work of older children can help a group set new goals and see possibilities for carrying their own ideas further.

Although the study of the work of other children helps children learn how to improve their own art as well as to appreciate and to appraise other art, if used too frequently it tends to make them feel that their teacher might not be satisfied with their achievements. Then, too, teachers need to keep in mind that children like to work with art materials and are intensely interested in *doing* art work. They tire of discussion.

Children frequently need to see the work of mature, skilled artists from different periods in history. Reproductions of the works of contemporary artists and those of old masters help children to build aesthetic tastes. These pieces of art do not always need to be discussed. Just by exposure to them, children get acquainted with them and form their own reactions and feelings about them. When the teacher makes a point of providing art in the environment, the child begins to feel that art is a part of living and that appropriate, beautiful objects make his life more pleasant and interesting.

UNDERSTANDING THE DISCIPLINES OF ART

Children work spontaneously and vigorously in art. This approach gives their art work a quality that is fresh, stimulating, and interesting. However, children outgrow this stage of their art expression just as they leave behind certain other childish behavior traits. They are eager to learn more mature ways. A ten-year-old child is no longer satisfied with the same art work he did at six or even at nine. He wants to feel that his art work is more developed just as he is more grown up. Children depend on teachers to help them develop their art, just as they rely on teachers for guidance in learning how to behave in a more controlled way. We do not set adult standards of behavior for children in the elementary grades, neither do we set adult standards in art. But we do expect children to learn how to act in a way that is consistent with their age. Children want and need to do this. They also want and need the kind of teaching and guidance that will help them express their ideas in art in a controlled way that is also consistent with their maturity.

Through the ages people have learned some general basic structures that help bring order and discipline into their art expression. These elements are not laws of art, but are broad guides that help artists to evaluate their work, giving them some bases for making judgments and for organizing and controlling the expression of their ideas.

Art knowledge is important in helping children to improve their art products. Art is concerned with the beautiful, the aesthetic, and the appropriate. It is the production or expression of a form of more than ordinary beauty. To achieve beautiful, appropriate, and well organized art work, certain *art* qualities need to be kept in mind.

In mentioning some of the elements or disciplines of art, no attempt is made to educate the reader in how to become an artist. A certain amount of experience in art is, of course, necessary to the teaching of art. You must know a thing before you can teach it. The art disciplines are mentioned merely to remind teachers of the very subtle application of their use with children. A very brief list of basic disciplines follows. It may be that you know and can think of other structural elements of composition — but perhaps these few are enough to introduce to children.

(a) A constant element in every art experience is the *grouping of forms*. Art work can be composed of a number of forms, as in a painting or a mobile, or it can be one form, such as sculpture or pottery. Within the latter, there are planes or parts to be arranged. If, for instance, there are three objects to be grouped, it is generally considered more aesthetic to have unequal distances between the objects than it is to place them all the same distance apart in a straight row. It is also more interesting to have at least one of these forms turned at an angle different from the others. The objects should look as though they belong together. Furniture is grouped,

60

In order to create a pleasing and interesting work of art, such as George has done in this abstract, each child needs a confident, relaxed classroom atmosphere that encourages a free flow of ideas as he works. Children have their own ideas and ways of organizing them. Art work reflects everything a child thinks about, imagines, and feels — everything that has happened to him and how he has reacted. Teachers also need to provide the art knowledge that can come from contacts with and discussions of mature artists' work.

61

62

Three-dimensional animals can have personality and charm, like this one made by Alex, when the child associates his feeling for the idea with the difficult task of constructing and decorating the object.

Holiday activities provide ideas for art. Children especially enjoy making things they can use, such as Hallowe'en masks.

Children reach aesthetic heights in their art expression through freedom to express their ideas, an intense firsthand experience, stimulating discussion, concentration, and judgment.

63

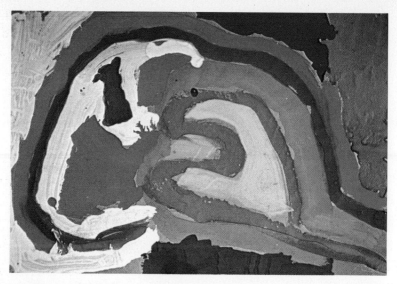

64

Being familiar with some of the elements of art knowledge helps children put their ideas into organized form, but a very strong factor in the success of any piece of art work is the feeling or emotion expressed by the artist.

When a teacher helps a child bring his knowledge and feelings into focus with art materials, she facilitates his ability to create. Peggy expressed how it feels to wait for a bus in cold weather.

65

flowers arranged, and homes are built and landscaped on the *art* knowledge of grouping. When children are occasionally made aware of pleasing groupings and told why these groups are considered to be satisfying, they learn how discipline is brought into the expression of ideas and feelings.

(b) A sense of *unity* is necessary within any piece of art work; something must hold it all together. Two figures facing each other seem more unified than they would if they were the same distance apart and were turned in opposite directions. When forms overlap or seem to go in front of or in back of one another, this helps bring unity into the art work. Forms or lines that suggest fitting around others create a visual bond between them; so does color repetition. The way that unity has been achieved should occasionally be pointed out to children in discussing art. In this way teachers can do a great deal to help children see how to bring a feeling of relatedness among the parts of their art work.

One group of intermediate-grade children were evaluating a three-dimensional farm project that they were building. Since the buildings of a farm are somewhat scattered, they decided to bring more unity into their work by grouping the work and storage buildings, adding rows of trees between spots, and connecting others by paths and roads. They were developing a more aesthetic project because they understood some of the *art* knowledge involved.

(c) *Variety* is another element of art closely related to all others. It has frequently been stated that children need a variety of art materials and a change of kinds of art experiences. Such change brings a fresh outlook and stimulates interest. Within any piece of art work variety of sizes of shapes makes for more interest. Variations within the kind of shapes, within directions of movements, and within colors and shades of colors all add zest. Monotony comes from too much sameness. Most teachers comment on the interesting things that children put into their art.

(d) A vital consideration in almost every art experience is *color*. Color is not a separate thing but is a part of the whole art form. Children think of color as they create their work because it expresses their ideas and feelings about the subject chosen for the art work.

Color is taught, not as a separate study, but according to its appropriateness to the form of which it is a part. Colors suitable for certain fabrics may not serve well for some paintings. Color is judged according to how it relates to its use and to other colors within the composition or within the eye span. Certain colors "go well" with other colors; some do not. Two certain shades of blue may be worn together whereas two other shades would be unpleasant in appearance.

(e) *Balance* brings into equilibrium the forces of forms, movements, and colors within art work. When all the large, heavy objects are on one side of a picture, it seems out of balance. The parts of a mobile do not need to be the same size and shape, but they do need to balance. It may take two or three lighter shapes on one side to balance a heavier shape on the other side. If balance is not achieved, the mobile will not move. Color needs to be balanced by distribution throughout a composition. The colors do not need to be the same shade. Different shades of the same color can still bring balance. The two ends of a piece of weaving do not need to have borders exactly alike, but it would look incomplete if all the colors were on one end.

(f) *Movement* within a piece of art work gives direction to the eye of the observer. Forms and lines make up a piece of art. The subject matter and emotion to be expressed determine the shape and placement of the forms. Forms can be shaped and arranged to lead from one to another like stepping stones. If this kind of discipline is brought into art expression, the shape and direction of each form can carry the eye to the next object. If the forms are placed with no control, chaos results. If there are arrows along the road to show us our way, we enjoy the trip and arrive at our destination; if the way is not marked, we are confused. This is true of art. In discussing art work, the achievement of even a suggestion of movement should be pointed out. Children need to know *how* it has been achieved; teachers must tell them.

(g) Some attention needs to be given to the putting together or the *organization* of the forms, objects, or parts of art work. Organization is closely related to the grouping of objects and to unity. Perhaps the three terms are somewhat synonymous, but, even so, they are so basic to art as to be worth the emphasis of repetition. As the elements of a composition are arranged, organization takes place. Parts can be put together in such a way as to interrelate them. Children determine their own organization for their work.

They are faced with the necessity for deciding where to put different objects in order to express and communicate their ideas. Football players may be placed or organized in a line across the page. This type of organization neither expresses nor communicates the idea of football. If, however, a few players are placed in relationship to a play, the referee added, and some people are watching in the background, then this organization expresses a different idea.

(h) There is one common purpose in each of the preceding seven principles of art. The shared objective and the purpose of each is to contribute to making the art form more pleasing to the eye. *Aesthetic judgment* is basic to art and needs to be developed and built through art experiences. It is an important feature of *every* art activity, including those correlated to other areas of the curriculum. As we work we need to be able to determine which arrangements or forms look better than others. As we look at or purchase art objects or articles of almost any kind, the same kinds of judgments help us.

Some of the art guides mentioned above will help children to bring discipline and control into their work and help them to *improve* their art work.

It would be out of place to emphasize the teaching of such guiding structural elements of art to elementary-school children. Concern with such technicalities can destroy the wonderful spontaneity and freedom that gives to child art much of its charm. Children should have no shackles to their thinking, no set "rules" by which they feel they should be guided — nor should any artist, for that matter. However, a little of this knowledge can be introduced in the elementary grades. Teachers might occasionally use one or two of these terms or their synonyms as they discuss a piece of art work. Children will eventually pick up the meaning by seeing the various examples explained. Such mentioning of the disciplines of art expression is indirect teaching, which is, perhaps, the suitable way of teaching such guides to children of this age. These guides should *not* be taught as an art lesson with the implication that children should henceforth apply them to their art work. They would, then, become a hinderance to the free flow of creative spontaneous expression. These elements of art can be used by the teacher in pointing out to children *why* certain areas of their art are successful.

Art knowledge helps children bring order and control into the expression of their ideas. General principles of art can be introduced to children, but should not be stressed. With emphasis, such guides could become blocks, interfering with the free flow of expression.

Suggested activity

From a set of finished art work of any medium done by children in any one of the elementary grades, study:

(a) *The strong points of the group's work as a whole*
(b) *Any weaknesses of their work*
(c) *The procedures you would follow for helping the children to improve their future art work.*

CHAPTER *VIII*

Art of the young child

THE ART that children create from their own ideas and feelings has charm and quality. The characteristics of children's art are different from those of adults' art. Russell was aware of this in discussing children's thinking:

> Without being sentimental about childhood, it seems fair to say that children's thinking may have a freshness, an imagery, a creativeness, which the adult does not always achieve.[1]

To study and understand these characteristics is very rewarding, for additional areas of appreciation and enjoyment are opened. Children's art is, in fact, a true and meaningful art when it is a sincere expression of the child's own personal ideas and feelings.

---

[1]Russell, David, *Children's Thinking.* Boston: Ginn & Co., 1956, p. 305.

The type of art with which most people are familiar is found in periodicals, billboards, and newspapers, and is different from children's creative art work. This type of art, often naturalistic, is frequently in our line of vision; it looks like real objects, is photographic, and frequently is idealized in style. We become so accustomed to seeing this type of art that the imaginary, creative, design-centered art of children seems "strange." Many people feel that because naturalistic art is so frequently used and because it is what they have learned to accept as art that it is superior. They tend to measure other art expressions by this standard. When we begin measuring children's art against such a background, we are applying a limited kind of adult standard. Children do few things as adults do them. They do art work differently, too. Realizing this difference is the first step toward understanding and appreciating the characteristics of children's art.

The younger the child, the more spontaneous and direct is his art work. His methods of working are direct, and the finished art product that he creates gives the appearance and impression of directness and freshness. The young child quickly becomes stimulated by an idea with which he has had some emotional relationship. Any experience that carries with it an emotional reaction is remembered longer and is apt to be the idea he chooses for his art. The stronger the emotional reaction, the stronger the urge to express it.

In order to assure the child's freedom to create, the teacher needs to maintain in the classroom an atmosphere of understanding. Feelings and emotions do exist and the child's talk about them and his expression of them should be accepted. Feelings and emotions are sensitive, tender spots and, when exposed, must be treated gently. If not, the child tends to hide them and so cannot face his own feelings and emotions. When this happens, his art work suffers because it has to be deeply personal and meaningful to the creator to be expressively done. When the child feels free to discuss his feelings without shame or ridicule, when less socially acceptable emotions are felt, discussed, and expressed in organized form, he feels safe in the adult and sometimes bewildering world in which he finds himself — a world that he is trying so hard to understand. The wise and understanding teacher leads him to express his feelings in art and praises his achievements. In this way the child becomes confident.   He faces his ideas and emotions, going directly to the core of an idea and expressing it.

The young child who is just beginning to paint and to work with art materials works rapidly.   He creates several paintings or drawings while a child of six or seven might be doing one.   The child of nursery-school age is eager to begin.   Preplanning has no meaning for him.   He paints as he goes.   He dips his brush into one color and covers an area of the paper with it.   Then he either makes another form or changes to a different color or both.   The young child is fascinated with the exuberance of painting.   He enjoys the *doing* of it.   This does not mean that the forms, marks, or lines he puts on the paper result entirely from the chance physical movements of his arm and hand.   Watching the young child work and seeing his seriousness of purpose indicate that there are some mental decisions involved in the process.   He seems to decide what color he will use, where he will place his brush on the page next, in which direction he will move it, and when to stop working on each form, as well as eventually deciding that each painting is completed.

There are both physical and mental processes involved in art work.   They are both going on at the same time.   The child must be concerned about each as he works.   For the young child one limitation will, of course, be the extent of his ability.   At three years he has less motor control than a child of seven or eight.   He also has less ability to create an involved composition because he has had a much narrower background of experiences from which to draw.

Children of this age seldom attempt to draw any recognizable forms.   The paintings they create are free in form, abstract, or nonobjective; they are simply shapes, lines, and directional movements. The child continues this form of painting for some time, and maintains an interest in it unless pressure is put on him to paint objects that he can name.

At every age children will want to make these free-form paintings if they feel that the teacher will appreciate them as she does the more objective subject matter.   Sometimes children indirectly are pressured into abandoning this type of art in favor of subject matter simply because of the fact that namable objects are more easily discussed.   Because vocal expression is given to the objective art and because any attempt to describe nonobjective art seems inadequate, children feel that more attention is given to the objective products. The child wants *his* art to receive the same attention and appreciation that his classmates' art receives. To gain attention a child may change his style of expression. Teachers must guard against such subtle and indirect influences.

In an atmosphere where *every* type of expression is accepted and appreciated children of all ages freely paint beautiful abstractions. The child who paints these will paint many other types of art work as well. The child whose interest in many types of expression has been kept alive by teachers will have a well-rounded and balanced appreciation for art and more widely developed ideas. Nonobjective art is a natural way for children of all ages to paint. During the discussion that precedes creative painting, some child will always say: "Can we just paint?" or "I'm going to paint a design" or "We could do abstracts." Welcome the idea; your tone of voice in commenting on the suggestion can be influential.

In order to draw out an expression of the children's thinking about this type of their art, one teacher had a conversation with some of the children in the primary grades. On the following pages are some of their statements:

The work of Susan, age 5½ (66), and Andrew, age 4 (67), is typical of children of every age who enjoy these free-form compositions.

66

Teacher: "Why do you like to paint these abstract pictures?"

Carole: "Whenever you draw an abstract you are drawing something that isn't real. You are thinking, 'I'll just put in some dots or some shapes or something,' so you can do it any way you like, but if you are making some people or dogs you have to make them like they are."

Sara: "Well, I like them because they are not real and you don't have to be real careful to draw it like what it is and worry about staying inside the lines you made, or you don't even have to make lines first. You can change it if you want to. If it is a real picture, it wouldn't look as well when you don't keep in the lines, and you would spoil it."

Patricia: "Sometimes when you have a good idea you get good designs in your picture and then you get a real good picture. I like to do them because you can think your ideas any way you want to."

67

Pamela: "You don't always have to make a design for a picture. You can make whatever you want to."

Bobby: "I think they are fun because they are not real. I like to draw the other kind, too."

Teacher: "How do you feel when you are painting these abstract pictures?"

Carole: "Your hands feel loose and it is different from crayons and real. Crayons you hold something like a pencil, but a brush is softer and you go along smoother. I think it feels looser. Painting the abstracts goes the same way."

Patricia: "It feels better sometimes to do an abstract because you have to keep in and do what it looks like if you are painting something real and if you are not you don't have to worry about anything like that."

Bobby: "It feels just freer because if you smear the paint with your hand or something then it spoils what you drew. But in an abstract you can make it into something maybe even better if you try hard. Just sometimes you can do it with the other kind of pictures. And I think your hands are freer because they don't have to be so tight to try."

Teacher: "How old are you, Bobby?"

Bobby: "Almost eight."

Teacher: "Where do you get your ideas for these paintings? What tells you what to paint?"

David: "Your mind. Only sometimes it doesn't come out as right as you want it to."

Pamela: "As I go along I decide and sometimes I decide my ideas before I start."

Teacher: "How old are you, Pamela?"

Pamela: "Five."

Carole: "When you start maybe you thought it would look pretty in your mind inside, and then you make it that way, and sometimes it is the other way around. It gets different in your painting and then you see it and you like it or you make it so you do. That's how you get ideas for these paintings."

Rickey: "You don't get ideas from anyone else or anything. You are free and you can do what you want to do because you just want to do it."

Ann: "I think in an abstract you can be real easy and you wouldn't have to do it real hard or worry."

Teacher: "When do you paint best — when you worry or when you don't?"

Bobby: "When you don't worry."

Nancy: "Well, I say it would be best if you worry because when you worry you are just thinking about what you want and you would be thinking it so hard it would come out just the way you want it to."

Teacher: "Are thinking and worrying the same?"

Nancy: "No. Whenever you think, you know what you might want to do and you do it. But if you worry you are scared and it does not come out right. You get nervous."

Teacher: "How do you know when your abstract pictures look right?"

Bobby: "Whenever you see them after they are done then you know they look right."

Sara: "Whenever your page is full and you don't want to make more in it."

The above conversation, recorded in a study of the sources of children's ideas for art, was taken from a tape recording of a classroom discussion between a teacher and a group of children.[2]

If children feel that the teacher will accept and appreciate these nonobjective paintings as she does their other work, they will create them just as freely as they do those composed of recognizable forms and ideas. There is a wonderful freedom about these non-representational paintings. The child seems to be guided by his own judgment as he works. He feels a new kind of enjoyment in using form and color as it is needed in the composition or as his personality directs him to use it.

NAMING OBJECTS

Pressure to create the more objective type of paintings can be exerted on the child in subtle and indirect ways by persons who

[2]Jefferson, Blanche W., *Art Experiences in the Primary Grades: A Presentation through Color Transparencies with Accompanying Script.* Project, Ed.D., Teachers College, Columbia University, 1954.

think they are helping him. Adults, anxious to see the child paint or draw something that can be named, frequently ask a child, "What is this?" or "Tell me about your painting." This indicates to the child that he is expected to draw something that he can talk about, or makes him feel that he is, at least, expected to *name* the objects in his picture. This is extremely difficult to do, if, indeed, possible at all with the free, spontaneous, abstract type of art that children do in such abundance. Since the child feels that the parents, whom he loves, and the teacher, whom he respects, want him to name and to discuss his art, he abandons this type of art in favor of forms he can name and discuss. Just through such a seemingly harmless question as "What is this?" the intent, interest, and purposes of the child can be influenced and directed.

Asking the child what he has drawn, even though he may be drawing people, houses, and objective forms, also indicates to the child that his art is so poor as to be completely incomprehensible to us. This causes the child to feel a sense of failure. He tries so hard to be successful and needs encouragement and praise for his work. This is not only true of children, but of adults, too. Put yourself in the child's place. Assume that you have tried hard to make something to the best of your ability. How would you feel if asked "What is it?" Such an insensitive approach can destroy a child's self-confidence and may ultimately discourage him from painting.

On the lighter side, asking the child what he has drawn makes the adult appear stupid to the child. The child is six, and he knows what it is; you are twenty (or so) and you do not know. What he has drawn is very plain to the child. He expects his teacher or parent, whom he credits with more ability and knowledge than he has, to be able to recognize what is so clear to him.

Sometimes a child will create forms or shapes that are abstract or free with no intent to be literal. Perhaps the child was "just painting" or enjoying the exuberance or his freedom to do it in any way he chose. If he is led to feel that adults expect him to talk about his art, he may create a story about it or make up names for some of the objects in it. Children are sensitive and want to please. If they feel that verbalizing about their art is expected, they are much more apt to do it.

There is no reason why art should require or depend on an explanation. Art is a visual area. The enjoyment and appreciation

of art depend on looking, seeing, and reacting. It is through *art*
that we are teaching children. Art has its own powers and can
stand on its own qualities without dependence on another form of
expression.

If a child wants to talk about his art, it is difficult to prevent
him from doing so. He may bring it to you or begin talking about
it when you come near where he is working. Some children have
many interesting things to say about their art; other children have
few, if any, comments about their work. The individual differences
among children make them feel differently about their art and about
explaining it. Sometimes a child may make interesting comments
about his work because he was illustrating a particular action in
which he had taken part; he had thought about the sequence of
activities and the places and people related to it. This narrative
type of art activity lends itself to oral narration, but not all experiences or ideas do — some are based on feelings and reactions. It is
difficult for a child to put such experiences into words. It is even
more difficult to discuss abstract or free-form art. It cannot be
named, it has no story to tell, and so does not lend itself to verbalizing. Abstract art, which children so naturally want to do, is the
type of art found so abundantly in present-day art galleries. Mature artists, sensitive to modern life, express their ideas and reactions in this way — young children and great artists both do this.

When we try to encourage children to draw something we can
name, is it because we, ourselves, lack sufficient understanding of
the beauty of expression found in free-form art? We should be
careful not to deprive or direct children because of the limitations
of our own knowledge of modern art. The more the teacher knows
and the better she appreciates present-day art, the richer experiences and better guidance she can give her students.

Sometimes an adult might be curious about a child's art and
want to understand more about it. Simply give the child an opportunity to talk about it. When talking to the individual child, the
teacher might look at his art and say, "This is a lovely blue area,
John," or "I like what you did here." If the child wants to talk about
his art, he has been given the opening without feeling an obligation.
If he does not, your comments are encouraging and carry no indication of your inability to see for yourself what the picture is.

Some people try to influence a child toward more adult concepts by asking him to draw certain objects before he is ready to do so. Children pass through developmental stages in their art expression just as they do in physical, emotional, and mental growth. Lowenfeld emphasizes the importance of understanding these levels of development and providing art experiences appropriate for each level:

> It is quite clear that motivation which is not keyed to the child's level does not become meaningful to him.
> . . . It is quite obvious that what may be adequate creative expression for an average child of five years can no longer be the art expression of the average eight- or ten-year-old child. As growth progresses the creative expression, a visible manifestation of growth, changes. In order to know the average criteria for purposes of evaluation, the creative development of the child must be studied in its single developmental stages.[3]

The child who is painting lines and forms should be permitted to do so until *he* is ready to make a change. When a child gains control over this type of expression, he will progress to more complex work

---

[3]Lowenfeld, Viktor, *Creative and Mental Growth*, third ed. New York: The Macmillan Co., 1957.

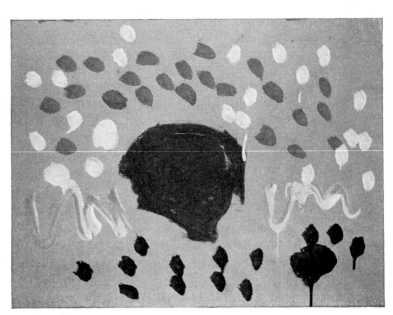

68

A young child's early attempt at representational forms.

of both naturalistic and abstract types.   He frequently will want to alternate between naturalism and abstraction, not to progress from one to the other but simply to change, develop, experiment, and grow.   A child's abstract art is not the result of random physical movement — he selects, thinks, rejects, and shows some degree of organization in his work.

When a child first becomes interested in representational attempts, he gives names to the forms that he creates.   An example of Mike's work, at the age of four years, looks very much like the abstract work he had been doing except that his intention was to create forms that represented objects (68).   This is a change that occurs in the creative development of every child, but does not occur for every child at the same age.   When Mike completed this painting, he said: "This is a storm.   This [the center form] is a big, dark cloud.   It is raining and lightning."   Not all of the forms to which children give names are as easily identifiable as this one.   In some cases a child gives names to forms as he works but a day or two afterward has forgotten the names that he attached to the objects. The act of creating is more important, not the names that children give to the shapes.   Teachers should remember to place more emphasis on encouraging the act of creating than on naming objects or on a conversation about the objects and forms in the art work.

When the young child first begins to name objects in some of his paintings, he should be permitted to name them and draw them as he wishes.   These attempts need to be accepted by his teacher, no matter how incomprehensible they may appear.   The child's first attempts in drawing should be treated like his first attempts in speaking.   When a child first begins to speak the names of objects, he is encouraged and his parents proudly urge him to display his new ability.   They do not mention the obvious fact that this may not sound like "dog" or "water."   Neither do they feel called on to point out that he is just learning and, of course, he will speak plainly when he is eight.   Such procedures, if carried over into the child's art education, would greatly encourage him to build upon his successful achievements, to want to try different ideas, and to be eager to experiment with new materials.   This positive method helps children form an attitude of enjoyment toward art, and helps them grow in their ability to express their ideas.

SPONTANEITY

Children in the primary grades work with a great deal of spontaneity. They approach their work with enthusiasm and vigor and want to get on with it. Each child quickly grasps an idea and goes to work on it. Children of primary-grade age work in much the same way as children of nursery-school or kindergarten age, but because of their maturity they can spend more time on each piece, for the following reasons:

(a) Their concepts and ideas are more fully developed.
(b) They have had more experiences and have richer imaginations.
(c) Their maturity gives them more drive to carry the project further.
(d) Their attention spans are longer.

Most children of this age will spend the duration of the entire art period (usually about 40 minutes) on one piece. They begin to be interested in objective shapes. Their interests are wider, but they enjoy the freedom of abstract art just as do artists of all ages.

The feelings and emotions that inspire the ideas children use for their art are responsible for that quality of spontaneity that makes the art of young children so appealing. Each child will express these feelings differently. Frequently, spontaneity results from the urge to give form to intense emotional experiences.

When the child is free, he approaches his work in a spontaneous way. Since with young children spontaneity is a characteristic of their art, teachers, aware of this quality, will recognize and accept it.

INDIVIDUAL EXPRESSION

Two little first-grade girls, Marjorie and Alice, made the creative crayon compositions about swimming shown in Illustrations 69 and 70. The lesson was motivated by the teacher as creative expression. She tried to draw from each child a different idea. Each time a subject was mentioned she urged the children to think of a different idea. When a radically different idea was expressed, she

69

Marjorie's art shows that she was influenced by her visual impressions of swimming.   How it looked was important to her.

Alice's art shows that she was influenced by the way she felt about wading into the deep water.   The emotional reaction of excitement was what she remembered and expressed.

70

responded enthusiastically. The children were learning to be re-
sourceful, to be imaginative, and to *think*; they were challenged, as
children want to be. Such stimulation inspires and excites each to
be on his own to think for himself. In such an atmosphere each
must feel confident that his idea and his way is best for him.

In such an atmosphere it is likely that two children might
choose the same topic without any intention of copying from someone else but because that idea happened to be the most exciting one
that each could think of. It is unlikely, however, that the products
will be alike. When children are made to feel proud of their independence, they will not want to copy nor want anyone to copy
their ideas. Such "stealing" or "cheating" is shameful.

Marjorie and Alice both chose the same topic. Swimming
had been an exciting experience for them. They remembered it,
and the fun of the swimming motivated their choice of the subject. They chose the same idea but each expressed it *differently*.
Look at the pictures and see how different they look although there
is much of the same content in each. Each has water in the foreground and several swimmers, but it is the *expression* of the two
that makes them so distinctively different. The subject matter is
the same and the general organization is much the same in both.

The shape of the objects or the *way* they are drawn and
formed is one element of expression; the other is the choice of
colors and the *way* they are applied. The particular way the
shaping of the forms was done, the hues selected, and the way the
colors were applied make the expression, which is motivated by
emotions and personal involvement in the idea.

Marjorie's drawing is neater than Alice's and more detailed.
Notice that in Marjorie's picture there are people of different sizes
and ages — men, women, and children. The hair is different and
appropriate for each age and sex, each finger is drawn, and the
bathing suits vary. Alice has no such variety or detail. You
scarcely notice the bathing suits because they are partially covered
by water and because there was no intent to make them in detail.
Something else was more important to Alice. Her swimmers are
all girls of about the same size. You could scarcely say that her
drawing or coloring is neat, although Marjorie's is. There is a
difference in the *way* the drawings were made because there was a
difference in the *way* each child reacted to the experience.

The differences in the two drawings have no relationship to motor control.   In some of her school work, which includes some of her art, Alice is just as neat as Marjorie.   In her personal appearance she is just as well groomed.   The way she colored her composition is not related to habit or general lack of control.   The intelligence quotients of the two girls are above average and almost identical. Therefore, differences in mental capacity do not account for the difference in these two pictures.

It seems evident, then, that the different appearance of the two drawings can be accounted for in the reactions of the two children to their experiences.   Maybe, even though both had swimming experiences, the two children had different experiences in the water. They *felt* differently about it, which, combined with their personalities, would cause differing emotional reactions.   Some children like one thing; some another.   Some children are more timid than others. Personality differences and differences in degrees of the same experience accounted for the drive behind the *ways* that Marjorie and Alice expressed their ideas about swimming.

In Marjorie's picture most of the people are not participating in the activity.   Even the people who are lying on the water are not much involved with the water.   The water is calm, and the people's hair is neatly combed or curled.   It is drawn as though Marjorie's principal concern was in *watching*.   The *way* the people and water are drawn indicates a recording of what was *seen* and how it *looked*.   Marjorie's experience with the water may have been more that of observing others than of having fun splashing and actually getting into the water herself.   Perhaps that was enough for her.   She may not have been ready for more courageous participation.   The detailed way she drew the bathing suits shows her concern for clothes.   It may be that this subject is discussed at home, or perhaps she was simply more concerned with clothes than was Alice.

Alice was excited by the creating of her crayon composition. She worked intently, concentrating so deeply as she worked that the movements of the children around her did not disturb her.   She was more engaged in re-experiencing the feeling connected with her reaction to swimming than she was in the way the children and the water looked.   In her picture the children are *in* the water.   The water is all around them and comes up over them to their faces. The splashes and sprays of the water on their faces are shown, and

their hair looks wet as if they actually had been completely in the
water.   The depth, power, and movement of the water are shown in
a forceful way.   The children have waded out into deep water,
which is an exciting and frightening thing for six-year-olds to do.
The drawing and coloring suggest that the situation is almost out of
control and is on the verge of overcoming the frightened girls.   The
children are holding hands as they do in such a situation; the braver
ones in the group encourage the others.   The expressions on their
faces show their feelings.

One composition is certainly not better than the other.   Each
child has been successful in expressing her own idea in her own way.
If the same standards were required of each child such personal,
highly individual expressions would be impossible.   If Alice had
tried to show the power of the moving water by coloring evenly and
by staying inside the lines, her emotional expression would have been
lost.   If Marjorie had not felt free to work in such a detailed, controlled manner, she would not have been able to show how well she
had observed, how she had enjoyed being there getting a little wet,
doing what she wanted and participating as *she* wanted to do.

The teacher needs to look for and try to understand the differences in the creative expression of children.   Even when the reasons behind certain ways of creating seem hard to understand, the
wise teacher will accept them.   Knowing that children have reasons
for working as they do helps the teacher to accept their works.

PROPORTION

In their urge to express their ideas children shape the forms
they make and determine their relative sizes without much consideration for the visual appearance.   Other factors often determine
the shapes and proportions of the people and objects that children
draw.   Children seem instinctively to realize the importance of the
imaginative and emotional qualities in art and seem to be only
partially concerned with the naturalistic (as objects appear naturally
to the eye).   Since art depends so closely on the imagination, this
quality should be not only recognized and accepted but also encouraged.

Since the invention of the camera, artists have been freed

from slavish representation. Before the camera was used, the artist was greatly limited in what was expected of him. His job was, largely, to reproduce likenesses. Pictures of people, places, and events were necessary for purposes of historical records and for communication. The artist was permitted little opportunity to create; recording was his basic responsibility. In addition to recording likenesses of persons and to making pictorial statements of events, the artist was encouraged to idealize his subject.

The camera can, of course, record much more accurately, in more detail, and quicker than is possible for the artist to do. Just a click of the shutter records the subject in exact likeness. By arrangement of lights and pose the subject can be shown to advantage. The artist is therefore no longer responsible for recording likenesses and is free to create.

The urge to create forms that do not depend on a visual basis seems common to artists of all ages and stages of maturity. We see the wonderfully free abstract and nonobjective paintings and sculpture in the modern art galleries. They dominate current exhibitions. We see this same freedom from naturalistic representation also evident in the work of children.

Visual proportion. One interesting characteristic of children's art is the proportions that they use. The relationships that exist among the objects in their compositions are not always determined on the same basis. Proportion in art, as most adults understand it, means that the relationships shown in the sizes of the forms depend on their naturalistic sizes. The way something appears to the eye is the basis of proportion most frequently understood. The house is taller than the man and the man is taller than the chair. This is visual proportion. Children use visual proportion. In Illustration 71, Ellen, eight years of age, painted this composition of herself and her family on Christmas morning. Ellen's father, still wearing his dotted pajamas, her mother, and Ellen have come downstairs to see the icicle-laden tree. The relation of sizes among the objects is based on visual proportion. The father is just about as tall as the tree, the mother not quite as tall as he, and Ellen is small in proportion to her.

Emotional proportion. In studying children's drawings it becomes evident that other bases are frequently used by them for

determining comparative sizes.   Children sometimes draw the sizes
of objects or parts of objects according to their emotional significance
instead of according to the way they appear to the eye.

   The drawings that children create on the basis of emotional
proportion are not distortions, as some people may think.   Persons
who make such judgments do so on a visual basis, disregarding any
other guiding purpose that the child may have.

   Children often draw largest the object to which they attach
the greatest emotional significance.   The objects or parts of a person or object that they care less about at that moment are drawn
smaller or omitted altogether.[4]

   Illustration 72 is a painting made by seven-year-old Linda.
She has painted herself large and dominant in the center of the page.
Her drawing of herself is the biggest form in the composition.   She
is larger than the house and larger than the tree.   For this drawing

---

[4]*Ibid.*

*Visual proportion shows in the naturalistic relation between sizes
of objects as Ellen has painted them in this picture.   She said, "My
Mother, and Dad, and me came downstairs on Christmas morning to
see our tree.   It was all covered with icicles.   My Dad still had his
pajamas on."*

71

at this time such a relationship among the sizes seemed most real to her. In order to express her feeling about the person and objects it seemed appropriate to draw them in this ratio. She was concerned with herself at this moment and thinking so intently about herself that she painted the form of herself first and made it as large as she could on the page. Then she thought of her house and made it smaller in accordance with the less important status that it held in her thinking *at that moment*. Then she added a tree to complete her composition.

The objects in this composition are not drawn with the same purpose in mind as Ellen's picture of her family Christmas morning. Ellen depicted the scene as it had looked to her. She remembered and expressed her visual impression of it. Because this was the purpose in her mind on which she concentrated as she worked, the proportion of sizes existing among the objects is visual.

Linda's purposes and feelings were different. She was having an emotional experience about herself. She was thinking about herself and feeling excited about being alive and about the good feeling of being herself. She had a sense of well-being and a

Emotional proportion is expressed when the child determines the ratio of sizes according to the way she feels about the objects at the time she is creating.

72

healthy regard for her own importance. These feelings and reactions were filling her mind and emotions as she began to paint. Because this was her emotional state at the moment, it determined the idea for her art. It also influenced the size and shape of the forms that she drew. The girl is big and strong, with sturdy arms and legs, and fills the center of the page with importance. When feelings and emotions are more important than the rational, the relationships of sizes existing among the forms are determined on that basis. Emotional importance determines not only the ratio of sizes but also the parts of an object or person that are exaggerated in size and those that are minimized in size and detail. Children do not consciously reason through the determination of proportion as they work. Had Linda consciously reasoned about the relative sizes of objects, her picture would, no doubt, have been quite different. Linda *knew* that she was not actually taller than her house. She could see this very well and she knew it from moving about inside her house. She has not drawn this composition on the basis of what she has learned from seeing, but rather on the basis of what she has learned from her emotions and feelings. She feels that she is more important than the house or tree. No doubt if you were her parent, you would feel the same way and very well know, too, that she *is* more important. The emotional significance that she attached to herself at this moment and for this painting was the guiding purpose that determined the size of the objects.

Gold tempera was a new addition to the paints that day and Linda, impressed by its novelty and shining color, used it to paint her dress. Not only the largest form but the most impressive color was chosen to express emotional importance. Linda was not wearing a gold dress and very likely did not have one, but this is a painting — this is art. It does not have to be a duplication of what actually exists. Artists are free to determine the size and shape of forms and to color them according to their own desires and feelings. Linda made her judgments on the basis of her feelings of emotional importance.

Functional proportion. The relative sizes of objects are sometimes determined on basis of the work they have to do. The functioning of an object determines its size in proportion to other objects. The child might draw the leg of a football player who is kicking the ball much larger than it naturally is because that is the part of the player doing the job. One arm of a girl picking apples might be considerably longer than the other because it has to be long enough to reach up into the tree to pick the apples (73). Regardless of the fact that this arm might be longer than the girl's total height, to be functional, to do the job, it has to be long enough to reach the apples. This seems logical to a child because if you are going to pick apples, you have to reach them. Another way a child expresses functional proportion is to draw small or omit altogether an object or part of a person not necessary to the action going on in the composition at the moment. In drawing the girl picking apples, Janet greatly exaggerated the size of the arms, in order to make them reach up to the branches and do the work, but she omitted altogether drawing feet and legs because they were not needed to do the work pertinent to that idea at that moment. The child knows, of course, that people have legs. She is well aware of her own legs. It is not a matter of not knowing or of forgetting. Janet was not concentrating on her knowledge but rather on the action. She was thinking about the doing and not about how it might visually appear to an onlooker. She was mentally involved in the business of picking apples; she was not an observer. It takes concentration and imagination to create such personal involvement.

For a teacher to indicate in any way that such exaggeration or omission should be corrected shows her lack of insight into the child's purposes. Children are not the only ones who use nonvisual size relationships. One has only to look at the work of contemporary artists to see many examples of it.

A child is confused by any suggestion from another person implying that he should correct the proportions in his drawing. He realizes that the critic fails completely to understand his meaning and intention. Children are sensitive and such suggestions tend to make them discontinue nonvisual proportions; hence, such suggestions tend to discourage meaningful and personal art expression. The imaginative, the inventive, and the expressive are vital parts of art and to discourage them is to discourage art expression.

Proportion based on the emotional or functional is a genuine art expression that the teacher should accept. She should *not* use other means to try to guide the child toward more naturalistic or visually centered expression. What he is doing *is art*, and it is

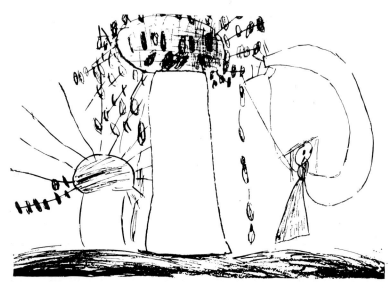

73

*Janet's arms needed to reach the apples in order to pick them.
Feet were not needed to do the job.*

*Proportion based on emotion or function is such a natural
way for children to create that they seem to do it without
conscious effort.*

74

through *art* that we are educating the child. In Illustration 74, Jean, seven years of age, has drawn a picture of herself hanging up clothes on the line. One arm is drawn long enough to reach the clothes on the line; the other is just the right length to reach the pieces still in the basket. The sizes of the arms were determined according to the work they had to do. The relative sizes were determined on a basis of functional proportion.

The child makes no particular effort to draw in this way. It seems logical to a child to draw the arm long enough to reach the line or the whole undertaking would be pointless. People do reach up and grasp the articles on the clothesline. Then, too, it gives the composition greater unity to connect the parts in this way. This is an important art value. The whole undertaking is more meaningful to the child who creates it and to those who see it. Jean took this type of proportion so much for granted that she did not mention it in talking about her picture to her teacher. The achievement that she was proud of and wanted her teacher to see was her drawing of the hair. She said: "When I help my mother hang up the clothes, the wind always blows my hair. See how I drew my hair blowing?"

In other areas of children's expression they are apt to relate function or action to their subject and describe the object or person functionally. Ruth Krauss is sensitive to children's oral expressions. She quotes these definitions that children have given:

> "A hole is to dig."
> "A face is so you can make faces."
> "Snow is to roll in."[5]

These are function-centered instead of description-centered definitions. Children enjoy the doing, the action, the effort, the movement, and the work involved with a subject. Watch a child and you will see how concerned he is with activity. The attempt to keep a child still for a while will be proof enough. No wonder they so readily express function verbally and graphically. Since action is so normally a part of childhood, functionally proportioned art will at times be emphasized, too.

---

[5] Krauss, Ruth, *A Hole Is to Dig*. New York: Harper & Bros., 1952.

SPACE AND DIMENSIONS

Young children seldom draw or paint one object in front of or behind another object. They have difficulty understanding how to represent in two-dimensional art work the three-dimensional concept of one form partly concealed by another that is in front of it. Children can readily see and understand space concepts if they are making a peep-show or a construction project to be displayed on a table top or on the floor, because the three dimensions are immediately apparent. Since a drawing or painting is a two-dimensional art form, the partial concealment of one object by another means that the concealed part of the one form has to be omitted. In drawing one girl standing partly behind another, only a part of the girl in back would be drawn; she would have only part of a form. Such concepts are difficult for young children to accept. They know that no such people exist and feel that such a form is not whole and would not be "right." A great deal of the art work done by children is flat, two-dimensional work. At this young age such a translation from three-dimensional concepts to flat paper is done by children on their own level of understanding. In spite of this problem, children need two-dimensional art experiences. Adults need to try to understand and to enjoy the characteristic way that children solve these particular art problems. Children devise their own ways of representing three-dimensional ideas in two-dimensional art work. Generally, they solve this problem in a way that is harmonious with two-dimensional materials. Realizing that everything exists in its own space, they draw and paint each form in its own space. Frequently, when children paint rain or snow falling, there will be no rain drops or snowflakes falling in front of the people because a child feels that they would be *on* the person. Even the central rod of an umbrella often will be drawn to the side of the umbrella because it must not be *on* the person's face.

The spaces left between objects in a drawing or painting determine the size of other forms that the young child adds. The child has little difficulty placing the first one or two forms in a drawing or painting because the whole space of the paper is fully available to him. With the addition of each form, the remaining bare spaces of the paper become more limited in size and in shape.

Since, to the young child, every form exists fully in its own space
in art work as it does in nature, the child often changes the sizes of
the objects to fit the space remaining after the first forms have been
placed.   According to adult standards, such differences among the
sizes seem distorted.   To the child, such size variations are of little
importance.   The child realizes that the limitations of the space he
has to work in determines the size of the objects he draws.   He also
does not forget that this is art and expects the adults, who are more
mature and better educated, to understand this, too.

75

*Bill's picture shows how a child shapes the forms to fit the
space into which he places them.*

Bill's picture of a covered wagon, inspired by his history lessons, shows how the sizes of the people were determined by the
space left after the central idea had been expressed.   Bill first drew
the pioneer carrying his gun, then the covered wagon beside him.
The size relationship between these two forms is based on visual
proportion because Bill was thinking about how they looked.   He
had seen pictures of them at school and in television.   He conceived
this unity between them and their resulting sizes on a visual basis.
The driver's seat, however, provided a small space, so Bill drew the
driver to fit the space.   An adult artist would have provided a seat
for the driver and kept in mind, as he worked, the size of the other
people.   But Bill is not an adult.   He solved his problems as an
eight-year-old would solve them and he did it in an interesting

manner.   The driver was carefully drawn with clothing details that indicated the approximate historical era.   The woman walking behind the wagon fills the space available in that area.

DISTANCE

As young children work with two-dimensional materials, they conceive their ideas in a manner consistent with the flat surface.   Therefore, the young child disregards, to a great extent, attempts at perspective.   He finds difficulty in understanding that houses that are far away should be drawn smaller than any other houses in his art work.   Although a child can accept the obvious fact that houses vary in size, he finds it difficult to accept the fact that the size of a house should purposely be changed by him because it was built in a location some distance from where another might be.

If a child has a quantity of things to put into his art, he makes provision for all of them by making them smaller in size so that the area will accommodate them.   If he is creating a composition in which he wants to show space between two forms, each about the same distance from him but some distance apart, he draws them small, leaving the distance between them.   He does this on the same basis as he draws small to get many things into his composition — simply in order to get them all in.   Creating an illusion of depth through change of size, however, is too mature a concept for the young child.   One teacher took a child to the window and pointed to a house on the opposite hill, saying, "See, Jimmy, how small the house is away over there."   The child looked at the teacher, with a puzzled expression, possibly wondering if she really thought the house was smaller, and said, "But it isn't smaller."   Space gave the illusion that the child was too immature to see.   Some children in the intermediate grades begin to be interested in perspective, but only a few.

KNOWLEDGE AS A BASIS FOR ART

Have you ever noticed that young children paint or color the sky as a strip at the top of their drawings and paintings?   This is such a universal way for young children to represent the sky in their art that persons at all familiar with children's art notice it. Sometimes they curve the sky or add a cloud or two, but it always stays high overhead, up above the other things in their pictures. The reason for it is very simple: that is exactly where the sky is. Children paint it high up because they *know* that that is where it is. Children frequently draw from their knowledge rather than by their vision.   Later, in the study of geography, children learn about the horizon's being the line where the earth and sky appear to meet. As more mature persons they see it this way when they look at it. One beginning teacher, understanding this concept as an adult, thought that all she had to do was point out to children the very obvious fact that the earth and sky meet, and they would immediately understand and draw this way.   When she saw some of the children put the sky in as a band across the top, she called their attention to it and showed them the sky and the horizon.   One little boy said, "But Miss Miller, if you rode over there in your car the sky would be just like here, way up above.   I know because we were over there once."   He won.   The teacher learned.   There is no place where the sky and earth do touch!   Children know this and they draw from what they know.

Children conceive the colors in their paintings and drawings in relation to the color of the paper they are using.   If a child colors people, houses, and trees with the white paper in mind as he selects and applies the color, one can readily see how it would change the whole color relationship if he colored a blue sky behind the objects he had already completed.   For example, the green trees, looking dark and sharp against the white, would lose some of these qualities if a blue sky were filled in between the objects and down to the ground.

As you have learned from your study of psychology, young children have not enough motor control to do such tedious and precise work skillfully.   The rough edges and the accidental overpainting affect the quality of their work and discourage children. Filling in the background with sky is a job that is wearisome to children and detracts from their enjoyment of art.

As you look at and study children's art, you will find many instances where the child has determined his art work on a basis of his knowledge of the objects and ideas he is using for his art rather than the way these objects may appear to the eye.

76

Although Nellie lived in a row of attached houses, she drew each house separately because that is the way they function.

77

Kenny drew the water snake large in proportion to other objects because of his emotional reaction to it.

In drawing a picture of her house, Nellie, who lived in one of a row of identical attached houses, drew on the basis of her experience with her house rather than how it appeared to the eye. In her picture (76) each house is drawn separately because her experience with the houses in the row has influenced her in this way. Even though Nellie frequently saw that the houses were fastened together and were all red brick, she knew that everybody has a separate house, and that the families live separately. She has heard people talk about the home of each different family. By going into the various homes in the row she learned that they are not alike. In her picture the houses are separate because they function that way. The interior of each house is decorated differently and has furniture different from the others. Nellie expressed this in her painting by giving each house its own individuality and unique colors. Children draw and shape objects from their knowledge about them and their functional relationships with them rather than upon the way they appear to the eye. This is one of the characteristics of child art that makes it so interesting.

EMOTIONAL REACTIONS

The art work of the young child is at times characterized by the impact of an emotional response that the child has had. Sometimes the most impressive thing about an experience is the way the child felt. When the child begins to put such an experience into form, he concentrates on the feeling he had. At the same time he associates this emotion with the object involved. Usually this form is the first to be made, with objects of lesser involvement being included later, if at all. The strength of the emotional reaction determines the subject matter for the child's art. It can also influence the size relationships within the composition, as was explained earlier.

Kenny made a drawing of one event from his summer vacation that shows the effect of such an influence upon his art (77). He had told his teacher about his family's camping by a place in the creek where they could swim. One day Kenny went down to the swimming place and saw a snake in the water. In the region of the camp the water snakes are small, gray, and harmless, but seeing it

in the water surprised and shocked Kenny.   He was still impressed
by it after the vacation was over and school started.   When he drew
it in art class, the snake was almost as big as the pool and was larger
than Kenny and larger than the tree.   He colored it brightly with
black and orange.   It is evident that the factor characterizing that
piece of his art work was his emotional reaction to the snake.

Suggested activity

Study several examples of the art of young children with the
following objectives in mind:

(a) See how many instances you can find of each of the three
types of proportion.

(b) If there are no or very few examples of functional or
emotional proportion, what might be some of the causes?

(c) If there are no abstract pieces among those studied, what
may have caused this situation?

(d) How would you, the teacher, proceed to encourage abstract work?

CHAPTER *IX*

Art of children
in the upper elementary grades

BECAUSE there is a wide range in the maturity of
children in any group, many of the characteristics and qualities of
the art of younger children will still be evident in the art of
children in the upper elementary grades. There is no abrupt
transition from the primary to the intermediate grades.
The change is a gradual one. Although children at
any one age and grade level are more alike than they
are different, mental, physical, emotional, and aesthetic growth takes place at rates that are different
for each. These four growth fields do not develop
at equal rates for a child. A child may grow rapidly
mentally and have little opportunity to grow aesthetically. Therefore, the range of maturity and
ability will be greater for a group of children in the
fourth grade than it was for the same group of chil-

dren in the first grade. Some of the children will still be choosing ideas and expressing and organizing them in ways less mature than those of other children in their group. In a learning situation where individual differences are provided for, as they are in creative art expression, it is normal to find such an ever-widening range. As the teacher works with children in art, she needs to keep this fact in mind to avoid the temptation, which some adults feel, of trying to bring the work of the children in a group to a certain level or standard. It is the standard of *each child* that is important. This emphasis on individuality and on each child's standards as right for him is a continuous thread that runs through the art education of all children in every grade in the elementary school. Children beginning the fourth grade are very little different than they were when leaving the primary grades.

As children become older, more experienced, and better educated, and have greater motor control, certain differences in their art work and in their working habits become evident. Older children have a longer attention span, which enables them to undertake more complex art projects than younger children. This increase in attention span enables them to work through time-consuming group projects and to encompass a broader scope of art activities; they often undertake more than one art problem at a time. An older child might be working with a group on the construction of a large papier-mâché animal, for example, and during the same interval of time be working on an individual problem of embroidery and appliqué. In fact, such an involvement with both group and individual art problems is important for the older child. As an individual, he should be developed to the extent of his ability in directions and ways that are consistent with his uniqueness; as a member of a group, he needs to be provided with opportunities to co-operate with others, tempering and adjusting his ideas to the over-all good of the group.

Older children not only have a lengthened attention span but have a richer foundation of knowledge from which to draw for their art. When an intermediate-grade child chooses the subject of airplanes for his art, he knows a great deal more about the details of various types of planes than his third-grade brother knows. It takes more time and effort for him to put into form the many facts he knows about and wants to put into his art.

As children mature, they set higher standards for themselves. They are no longer satisfied with the art work they did when they were younger, although, at the time, it represented their best efforts and had met their standards and expectations then.   Older children are no longer content to work in the spontaneous, direct way that was characteristic of their work in the primary grades.   The young child puts his ideas into form as they come to his mind.   He develops his art project one step at a time, not always knowing what the very next step will be until the part he is working on is completed.   After the subject is determined, he puts into form the object that he most strongly associates with the subject; after that he forms the second object; then he decides upon the third, evaluating and deciding one step at a time.

Most children in the upper elementary grades plan their work before beginning.   They not only choose the subject for their art, but think about and plan the arrangement of the objects within the composition.   This preplanning does not preclude changes, additions, and deletions during the working process — nor should it. Artists of every age need to feel free to evolve and to develop the expression of their ideas and feelings during the working process according to judgments they make of the aesthetic qualities of the forms and arrangements that develop as they translate mental images into forms made within the limitations of the art materials. However, older children, individually or as a group, feel a need to have a mental concept of the entire project before beginning.   They work more confidently and purposefully if they can visualize and foresee the effects of their decisions and if they understand the total problem and have in mind the general over-all plan.

The extent to which a child plans and the nature of his planning should be left to his decision.   Realizing that older children feel a need to plan, some teachers insist that they make drawings or small models of an art project before undertaking it.   The teachers reason that children can thereby correct any mistakes that they might make, and that they can visually appraise and evaluate their idea before putting it into final form.   This argument may seem logical to adults, but it fails to take into consideration the fact that children become bored by executing the same project twice in succession.   When a child has put his ideas into form once, he has little inspiration to repeat the same thing.   Children want

78

Children of intermediate grade age have varied interests and attention spans long enough to carry them through more complex art problems. A wide variety of materials attract and challenge them: wire sculpture (78), painting (79), clay modeling (80), linoleum block printing (81).

79

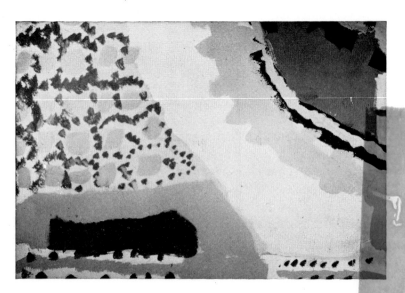

80

*Older children have an interest in creating three-dimen-
sional art forms and art objects that have utilitarian value.
They also set high standards for themselves and want their
art to meet the approval of their peers, parents, and teachers.*

81

change; their play shows how much they need to move from one type of activity into another. This urge to express an idea and then to move on to something different is part of the rich, creative power that all children have.

Preliminary sketches made with one art medium are difficult to compare with the same idea expressed in a different medium. Therefore, the purpose in making the preliminary sketch is lost. Differences in size also affect the results. A design composed and colored on a small surface may lose some of its qualities when enlarged. Children want to and should be encouraged to work directly with their art materials. If a child feels uncertain about how one part of the costume for his puppet will fit, for example, he could try cutting paper shapes until they fit the puppet before he cuts into the textile. The decision to do this should rest with the child, depending on the need he feels.

CONCERN WITH NATURALISM

One characteristic of the art of older children of which all persons who work with children of this age soon become aware is their concern about naturalism. They swing from one extreme to another in their attitude toward wanting to express their ideas in art. Young children are more concerned with emotional or functional expressions of their ideas; older children are concerned with the visual. The fact that this change takes place as children mature and become better educated does not mean that it is a change for the better. It simply means that certain forces in their lives have been operating to condition their thinking in this way.

Pressures of photographic illustrations. The photographic illustrations in the current literature that children are learning to read and have long been exposed to before they could read have a tremendous influence on their thinking. Children see these naturalistic pictures of objects and people, and by the time they have reached the intermediate grades begin to see the difference between what they have been creating in art and pictures they see in newspapers, magazines, and most books. A child measures his art against this type of illustration and decides that the world cannot be wrong and he right. He sees the naturalistic art in the periodicals that adults publish, illustrate, buy, and read and concludes that this is the adult way and his ways then appear childish to him by comparison. Seeing little or no abstract or design-based art in this environment, he concludes that perhaps he should abandon that, too, and turn toward what he considers to be a more mature style of illustration — the naturalistic. Quite often the only imaginative works of artists that a child sees in newspapers and popular magazines are the comic strips and cartoons. A child begins to feel that in the adult world the serious art is naturalistic and the imaginative art ludicrous. Since he wants very much to be grown up and to fit into the adult world, he tries to follow what he judges adult patterns to be. A child works seriously on his art and, since he does not want it to appear ridiculous or amusing, he may avoid the imaginative. The child's growing awareness of his world brings these comparisons sharply to his mind and he is deeply influenced by them. Older children need teachers who understand why they become so anxious about creating art that looks "real" and who know how to help them realize what is happening to their thinking. Children of this age also need teachers who are able to help them solve their art problems and who can give them the verbal guidance and the help that they seek in depicting their ideas naturalistically, but who can *at the same time* keep alive and stimulate their imaginations, emotions, and awareness of design qualities. Wickiser stresses the need for teachers who can help children build strong imaginative qualities in children's art:

> He [the child] especially needs a teacher who understands the difference between the visual world of nature and the world of creative imagination as it emerges in art experiences. . . .
> The sympathetic teacher will, at this age, help the child discover facts and information he desires, but she will also stir his imagination about the untold possibilities these facts hold to express subtle feelings and ideas. Developing imagination is the most serious problem in teaching art activities.[1]

The way in which a teacher helps children to keep in mind the qualities and values that make art exciting and interesting is shown in this example of a teacher working with her fourth-grade group as the children were either painting or working with chalk.

---

[1]Wickiser, Ralph, *An Introduction to Art Education.* Yonkers-on-Hudson, N.Y.: World Book Co., 1957, pp. 269–270.

Following a field trip, which resulted from a science lesson, the children took a trip into the nearby woods to study, more closely, the coloration of the leaves in autumn. They were so impressed by the beauty of the trees and countryside that they suggested using this trip for a topic in their art class. Some wanted to work in colored chalk, feeling that this medium would give them the brilliance they wanted; others wanted to paint. Since the children had previously worked with both chalk and paint, the teacher decided to let each elect whichever medium he wanted. Some children had a great deal of feeling for the subject and worked in an expressive, direct way. Others felt apprehensive about their inability to create a naturalistic or realistic picture of what they had seen. They were confused by the contradiction between their feeling for what they had experienced and by what they thought were more adult ways of expressing an idea. As the teacher worked among the children in his guidance role, he tried to help some of them with this particular problem.

Harvey: "Mr. Patterson, I want to make in my picture the path that went down the hill. Every time I try to draw it, it comes out different from the way it was in the woods. I want to try to get it just like it looked and I can't."

Teacher: "Did it go straight down the hill?"

Harvey: "No, it curved around. It was very pretty. I thought it was the best part of our trip. The path went along the hillside and then it slanted down. Sometimes it went uphill and downhill as it went along. That part I can't draw at all."

Children need help with specific problems that they want to work out in a certain way. This child felt the beauty of the gracefully curving lines of the path and their relationship to the hill, but he needed help from his teacher in expressing his idea and feeling. Learning is effective when it takes place at the time of need.

Teacher: "Think back about the way the path looked as it went uphill and downhill. Did you ever lose sight of any part of it?"

Harvey: "Looking ahead sometimes I couldn't see down to the bottom of some of the dips."

Teacher: "Did the path always look as if it came up out of the dip

exactly opposite the place where it went down, or did it
seem to come up a little to one side or another?"

Harvey: "Almost always a little to one side."

Teacher: "Imagine that you are feeling with your pencil along the
edge of the very section of path you want to draw. Concentrate hard. When the path goes into a dip and you
can't see it, stop drawing and move your pencil to the
place where the path begins again. Feel along the path,
keeping in mind that it goes downhill, so your pencil
should move downward on your paper. Think more
about how it feels and moves than how it looks. Remember, when your drawing is completed, it will have
more of the quality of what you felt about the movement
of the path than actually how it looked to the eye. A
camera can, in just a second, record a picture of what it
looked like. When *you* make the picture, it needs to
show something of *you*; do not expect it to look mechanical or entirely visual. Don't try to think like a camera.
There is more of you than just your eyes to react to the
beauty of the path and trees. I'll come back after a
while to see how you are progressing."

The teacher did not point out the errors in Harvey's previous attempts; neither did he show the child how to draw or show him
pictures of curving paths. He wanted to bring the child's feelings
and awarenesses of his own particular path and idea about it more
clearly into his active thinking.

Rosemary: "I am trying to make the farmhouse and the barn we
passed at the foot of the hill and get some of the trees
and the stream in it just as it was. I put them in just
as they were, but it doesn't look right. I can't get it.
I've tried and tried and I can't make it look as it looked
to me out there. I guess I just can't draw so well any
more, Mr. Patterson. I used to be good at it, but not
in fourth grade."

Teacher: "Don't be discouraged, Rosemary. Everyone has
trouble with what he is doing some time or another.
You are still good in art. I remember many lovely
things you have done this year."

Children can become discouraged in art when they are distracted
from their own purposes. Encouraging as it was, the teacher real-

82

Many sensitive pieces of art work, such as Bobby's two trees, were created as a result of the field trip and the pupil-teacher discussion of the ideas and feelings in terms of an art activity.

ized that simply reminding the child of past successes was no help in solving her current problem.

Teacher: "You are trying to draw the house and barn you saw because you were impressed with their beauty against the hillside of trees and brightly colored leaves. I was impressed by them, too. But when we come to art class we try to remember that the house, barn, stream, and trees, which you have chosen to draw, were only a small part of the broad, wide landscape that could be seen. In your line of vision there were other houses, many mountains, thousands of trees, and a tremendous amount of sky. You chose one part to draw, and in doing so, you have already omitted a great deal. Therefore, it isn't exactly as it really was."

Rosemary: "But it was so beautiful right there."

Teacher: "Yes, it was, but a part of the beauty came from your feeling about it. Not every child chose the house to draw. In fact, no one else did, so none felt as deeply about it as you did. You felt this great beauty and you are disappointed because the drawing you have made doesn't communicate this feeling to others — not even to you. Isn't that it?"

Rosemary: "Yes."

Teacher: "In art we do not always draw a scene exactly as it appears to the eye. We choose a subject and use it as an inspiration in creating. We change its shape or size, rearrange parts, and exaggerate what we want others strongly to feel. We do this in telling a story, too. We tell it dramatically, emphasizing some words, repeating, and exaggerating a little so that people will not only hear what we say but feel the same emotion we felt. We have to do this because the listener was not there when it happened. The people who look at our art in school are not experiencing beauty by walking in the woods, either. In looking at your painting they will not feel the same beauty you felt unless you *make* them feel it through emphasis on how you felt, by exaggerating color and size and by rearranging objects to accomplish it. How could you rearrange the objects in your painting? What could you emphasize or exaggerate?"

Rosemary: "It wouldn't be the way it was."

Teacher: "It might not look exactly as it was, but it would repre-
              sent what you saw and express your feelings about it
              much more emphatically. Remember you weren't
              satisfied with your drawing based on how it looks."

John: "I'm listening too, Mr. Patterson, because I felt the
              same. All pictures show things as they really look, but
              I see now what you mean about drawings being differ-
              ent."

Teacher: "I'm glad you do. Most pictures in the magazines we
              look at, though, are photographs, not paintings or chalk
              pictures made by an artist. Some of the children had
              cameras on our trip that recorded the scene exactly as
              it was. Exactly reproducing a scene is the job for the
              camera and is done fast. This frees the artist to create."

Michael: "I took the idea of some rocks and trees from our trip
              to the woods. I started out with that, then I just made
              it up as I went."

All the children in the group were hearing this discussion and learning something from it by having the emphasis on the imaginative
and emotional in art repeated to them.

Teacher: "That's the idea."

Rosemary: "I am going to start over again."

Rosemary had been disturbed by the conflict between her urge to
express her emotions about the scene and the impact that the bulk of
photographic illustrations in periodicals had had on her thinking.
The teacher knew that it would take more than one explanation before the child could once again create freely and confidently, because education takes place slowly.

This example is representative of the problems that children
encounter in trying to overcome the forceful influence on their art
of the mass of naturalistic and photographic illustrations they see
daily.

Influence of adult values of naturalism. Commercial illustrations are not the only source of naturalistic influence on children's
art. Adults, who base their comments of children's art on naturalism, are a determining force in this direction. A great many adults
understand no other art than the naturalistic and tend to feel that

the more true to life a piece of art appears to be, the better it is. From the time most children begin to express motion and feeling with art materials, the remarks they hear about their art expression are related to subjects that they are expected to name. As a child becomes more skilled, his parents and relatives often encourage him to "make it look more like a house," or say "Don't you know a tree has branches?" When children come to school, all too many teachers ask them to tell about their pictures or ask them what they have drawn, thus making naturalism a valuable, if not the only, asset to art expression. Children are deeply impressed by the values that teachers and parents have and transmit to them. When children are exposed to such influences until they reach the inter- mediate grades, they find them difficult to overcome.

The intermediate grades are crucial for children. Because they are becoming more sharply aware of the world around them and especially of adult ways and values, children tend to reject for themselves things that they feel are "babyish." They tend to dis- card, as immature, their former art expression. If these children are not cautiously guided by a teacher who understands children of this age and who understands art, they cast aside art qualities that they should retain, build on, and improve. Of course, there should be evidence of growth in art from the primary to intermediate grades, but imagination, design, exaggeration, and emotion in the children's art should not be sacrificed. The social pressures in the direction of naturalism in art are persuasive, and these influences should be pointed out to children so that they better understand how to deal with them. Teachers need constantly to emphasize the *art* values in art activities.

Correlation with other school subjects. Frequently, children of this age get their ideas for art from other school subjects. Many of these correlated activities are group projects. The educational purposes of other subjects are, for the most part, different from the values to be derived from creative art activities. History, for ex- ample, has sequence and facts to be learned as well as inspirational achievements to be felt. Other elementary-school subjects are based on facts that children are encouraged to learn. When these sub- jects are correlated with art, to a certain extent their factual nature is carried over into the art activity. In part, the implications for accuracy in naturalistic or factual art forms are felt by the children because of this association. Teachers need constantly to remind children that art activities are based on art values regardless of the source of these ideas. This can be achieved while respect for the other subject is still maintained.

Illustration 83 is one example of the way in which a group of intermediate-grade children solved a problem of correlation. The decision to make a large painting to fit a particular wall space in their classroom was made by the children after the study of the history of Pennsylvania. They discussed together topics that would be appropriate from dual viewpoints of exciting events, and opportunity for interesting, expressive art work. The resulting group painting, of William Penn receiving the charter for Pennsylvania from his king, has strength and is well composed. This is an example of art values being considered simultaneously with a respect for the subject.

The art class should not be usurped by another subject for the teaching of subject's content material. Art has values of its own.

Lack of contact with contemporary art. Children have little contact with art products that are not naturalistic in form. This, too, helps direct their thinking and their art toward realism. Not

Intermediate grade children enjoy group art projects related to other school subjects. Art values need to be kept in mind, however, as the work progresses.

83

many illustrations in periodicals and books are abstractions or are centered in design, gesture, or movement. The photographic images of television and motion pictures are part of the cultural influence toward naturalistic art form. Children have little opportunity to see and to experience abstract or other modern art forms. Many children in the upper elementary grades have never seen an art exhibition. Few parents do sculpture, pottery, or painting as a hobby; many know too little about it to be able to comment on it in a way that is helpful to their children. Other parents, feeling revolted because it is not true to life in form, cannot accept it, and their disparaging comments influence children to feel the same way. If left to develop without these interfering influences, children would more freely experiment with many types of art expression. Since such influences are not always the most desirable educationally, teachers need to keep before children examples of contemporary art of good quality. Whenever possible children should be taken to the art galleries to see the original works of art — to be able to walk around them and examine them from different angles. Reproductions are a good substitute for actual trips to art galleries, but should not replace gallery visits when it is possible for children to attend the exhibits. The viewing of a reproduction cannot supplant a view of the original. Even the change of size between the original and a reproduction alters the effect which that particular art form communicates and expresses. Some schools, however, are so far from art galleries that visits are impractical. When this is the case, teachers should use an abundance of color reproductions of art and discuss some of them with children. Intermediate-grade children enjoy such activity; their interest in adult ways and their longer attention span makes this more suited to them than to younger children.

NEWLY DEVELOPING CONSCIOUSNESS OF OTHERS

Friends and family are always important to children of every age, but an awareness of group associations develops strongly at this age. Art teachers frequently take advantage of children's new urge for co-operation with their peers by planning art activities that can be worked at in pairs or in small groups. Older children

84

*Older children develop a sharp awareness of others
and enjoy working in groups of their peers.*

enjoy the fellowship of discussing a project with classmates, working it out together, and evaluating it as a group.   A child of intermediate-grade age is willing to compromise, and this is a quality
that facilitates group work.   A child also likes to have a part in the
achievement of a product of a depth and scope that he could not
possibly achieve alone.   To do so gives him both pride in his work
and security in having others work with him and for him.

USEFUL AND MORE LASTING ART PRODUCTS

The utilitarian value of art appeals to children in the intermediate grades.   Children of this age like to create art that works,
can be given as a gift, or can be put to some practical use.   They
will spend a great deal of time working out intricate locks or open-
ings for a valentine, for example.   They want to create art products
that they can operate, manipulate, bend, or change in some way.
They are apt to spend a great deal of time making wheels that will
turn for a wagon that will stand still in a specific place in a construction project.   In spite of the fact that movable wheels are of no
importance to the wagon for this project, they may spend as much

time on this feature of the wagon as they do on the rest of the
wagon. They want to know that it works and that they can make
it go; they are fascinated by this kind of challenge.

Older children enjoy art problems that include somewhat intricate steps in the process of working. Linoleum printing is an
example of an activity characteristically enjoyed by children of this
age. If they decide to print their own Christmas greeting cards,
for example, the children's motivation is heightened. Printing on
textiles, because it can be used and seems permanent, is more interesting to them than printing the same design on paper, unless the
printed paper has a specific use. They are often so impatient to
begin cutting the block and printing, however, that they disregard
design quality. A teacher, recognizing this impatience, needs to
make children aware of the fact that art work *always* needs to have
quality and be expressive and that eagerness to proceed with cutting
is no justification for a poorly designed block. Teachers have a
responsibility not to underrate the ability of children but to expect
each to work up to *his own* best standards.

An intricate art problem, such as linoleum printing or the
making of creative string marionettes, gives intermediate-grade
children an opportunity to learn new processes and skills and to put
into use the skills they have already learned. When children know
that the art products will be enjoyed by others, their more strongly
developing need to function with and for others provides an incentive for work of high quality.

ORGANIZED EXPRESSION OF EMOTION

The accompanying examples of the art expression of three
intermediate-grade children are evidence of the well-organized expression of emotions of which children of this age are capable.

Marie's crayon composition (85) of a haunted house shows
how well she has organized the floating ghosts around the unhinged
door. Their white color stands out sharply against the dark, cob-
webbed interior of the house. She was skillful in expressing the
unnatural transparent character of the ghosts by drawing the ghosts
and the objects behind them as though one could look right through
the shadowy figures. Other objects in the room add to the seasonal
suggestion of Hallowe'en.

85

*An older child has more knowledge to include in his work
and also has a longer attention span than the younger child.*

Kenny calls his tempera painting (86) "Trouble." He said:
"I am in trouble with my mother. She wouldn't let me go out and
play in the ball game. I came downstairs dressed in my uniform to
go and had to sit and watch out the window while the other boys
went." The entire feeling of Kenny's picture communicates a
feeling of dejection that the child must have felt at being disappointed. The elongated forms in the picture help convey this
emotion. Feeling an emotion deeply and concentrating on it as
he worked has helped him express it so successfully. The design of
the back of the chair against the deeply colored wall is beautiful
and is emphasized and repeated in the design of the arm rest.

Stanley's crayon composition (87), an unusual subject of a
mother whale with her baby, is another example of good organization and successfully expressed emotions. There is a tender feeling between the mother and her baby. The small one looks frightened and huddles beside his mother, and she looks pleased and
confident as she watches him. The baby whale is blowing a small
spout; his mother blows a large one. Stanley must have experienced
the strong, gentle emotion of a parent-child relationship to have
chosen this subject and to have expressed it so tenderly.

RESPONSIBILITIES OF THE TEACHER

A great many children choose not to elect to study art in the secondary school because they have either lost interest in it or have become discouraged in art during the crucial intermediate grades. A skillful, enthusiastic teacher can do a great deal to build the interests and abilities of children.

86

The art knowledge children have gained plus a strong emotional feeling aid in bringing about expressive art.

Throughout this book emphasis has been placed on the responsibility of the elementary-school art teacher. As children's art
was discussed, her duties and responsibilities were indicated in relation to each discussion. The intermediate-grade art teacher has
much the same responsibilities as the art teacher of children of any
age. However, children of different age levels have unique characteristics. These characteristics affect their art, and teachers cogni-
zant of these distinguishing features can be especially helpful in
guiding art activities.

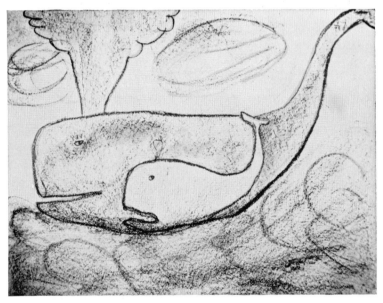

87

*A tender feeling for relationships inspired Stanley's
crayon drawing.*

The following brief summary is intended only to point out
and to remind teachers of qualities that they can develop and build
on that will make their art instruction more effective.

(a) To be able to make discriminating judgments of a wide
variety of types of art work is of inestimable value to a teacher and
to the children she teaches. Children's attention should constantly
be called to the qualities of many different kinds of art products.
Art products change, and our viewpoints toward color, design, and
style also change. Artists constantly search for new ways of ex-

pressing beauty. Teachers need to keep their art knowledge up to date by frequent visits to art exhibitions and by studying ever-changing commercial products.

(b) Teachers should be able to enjoy a variety of contemporary art forms on the professional level. Persons who teach in the elementary school sometimes have a tendency to feel that they need only to become acquainted with art projects suitable for children. To improve her professional ability every teacher needs to build her own mature knowledge and *at the same time* build her knowledge of activities suitable for children. Enjoying art makes teachers feel more secure in dealing with the problems of older children.

(c) Adaptability to the individual intentions and purposes of each child is a quality that every successful teacher needs to develop and to use daily. In art the teacher tries to study the work of each child as it develops, making an effort to understand what each is trying to express, and associating her own feelings and interests with his. Only then can the teacher help and guide children in the manner that they each feel they need. As children progress through the upper elementary grades, their range in abilities and interests becomes wider.

(d) As the teacher works with the group or with individual children, she helps build their imaginations, creativity, and resourcefulness when she suggests different ways of solving a problem and calls to their attention a variety of art styles and forms. Giving children frequent changes of art materials and combinations of media also serves this purpose. Older children are eager for such diversity.

(e) Indirectly through discussions of children's own art work and the products of professional artists, teachers need to transmit to children art values and knowledge that help them better to understand art and help them improve their own art products. Keeping alive the *art* qualities of art activities is especially important at this age when the older child becomes overly influenced toward naturalistic art.

(f) Enthusiasm for art and for teaching art is one of the most valuable assets a teacher can possess. Her lively interest in art and her warm zeal for teaching it are contagious at a time when children sometimes become discouraged by their inability to produce adult, naturalistic art.

Suggested activity

Read from the following references:

(a) Lowenfeld, Viktor, "Pseudorealistic Stage," Creative and Mental Growth, *third ed.* *New York: The Macmillan Co., 1957, Ch. 7.*

(b) Wickiser, Ralph L., "The Art Experience in the Upper Elementary School," An Introduction to Art Education. *Yonkers-on-Hudson, N.Y.: World Book Co., Ch. 8.*

(c) de Francesco, Italo L., "Art Education in the Elementary School," Art Education: Its Means and Ends. *New York: Harper & Bros., 1958, Ch. 8.*

CHAPTER *X*

Importance of the child's individuality and experiences

EVERY child is different from every other. These individual differences, developing from heredity, environment, and experiences, influence and determine the child's art products. The individuality or uniqueness of the child is shown in his personality as qualities that distinguish him from others. Experiences of the child are simply the things that have happened to him, such as the things he has done, seen, read, heard, imagined, felt, or dreamed. The personality of the child and his experiences interact in a way to influence each other. Because each child is different, widely varying reactions to activities occur. Because experiences affect each child differently, each develops in a way that makes him unique. This uniqueness determines the child's art work. Since the child himself decides upon the subject matter for his art, he draws upon his personal resources for ideas.

Even though several children are exposed to the same activity at the same time, each is impressed differently by it. Each is attracted to that aspect of it that personally interests him. Therefore, he does not actually have quite the same experience as the others.

It is the purpose of this chapter to show how some of the factors that make up the personality and background of a child determine his art. Some of the areas to be included will be the way in which the child's reactions to an experience affect his art product, and also the way his background, as well as cultural differences, determines what he selects for his art and how he expresses it. Emotional blocks influence the child's art. This chapter is not an extensive inventory of factors that determine the child's art, but includes samples to represent broad and complex areas that are influential factors in the child's art expression.

REACTION TO AN EXPERIENCE

Involvement in an activity brings to the person physical participation, mental stimulation, and emotional reaction. The child's emotional response to the event depends on his individual personality and on the effect that similar or related experiences have had on him. The way he feels influences the way he expresses his ideas. Differences in the ways children react to the same experience are shown in the examples of the art work of two boys (Illustrations 88 and 89).

One day the second grade went outdoors to have the art class. No instructions were given to the children about what they were to draw or how they were to do it. Before the children left their classroom, the teacher motivated the work as she would have for any creative art work. Some of the children drew the buildings and trees; others developed abstracts. Excavation for a new building caught the attention of some of the boys, and they drew it. As Andrew gave his picture (88) to his teacher after it was finished, he said: "I like to do that. Let's do it again tomorrow." Although he chose the excavation as the topic for his art, his picture has a pleasant look. Birds are flying overhead. The picture is brightly

88

The unique personalities of different children cause
them to react in different ways to the same experience,
and these reactions affect their art.

89

and smoothly colored. It communicates the feeling he had about his experience.

Christopher drew the steam shovel and the excavation — a subject almost identical to Andrew's. His art (89) shows that the same experience had a different effect on him. When he gave his picture to his teacher he said, "Boy, they're sure tearin' it up out there."

The rough way his composition was colored and the absence of gay objects show that he was much more sensitive to the destruction of the lawn and trees that was taking place than Andrew was. The different personalities of the two boys influenced their reactions, and each plainly showed in his art work the effect that the experience had on him.

BACKGROUND OF EXPERIENCES

Through examples of their work and through statements about some of their experiences, insight is given into the ways in which background determines children's art. Background is considered to mean the broad experiences that make up the children's home, school, community life, and relationships with others, particularly family relationships. These experiences help to build the knowledge and reactions that provide sources of ideas for art.

The two accompanying illustrations (90 and 91) are the work of one child and dramatically show the way in which her family relationships, home life, and school life have affected her art products.

In second grade Florence painted the picture of herself by her house (90). Most of her drawings and paintings showed the same subject repeated over and over again, and this one, like the others, is depressing. She has painted the girl with brown and black, looking unkempt and dejected. The sun, which is usually bright and important in children's paintings, is dull and dim, with little color. There seems to be a lack of orderliness even in the arrangement of the windows. Florence always depicted herself alone.

Florence was withdrawn in school. She repeated the first grade and this painting was done in her second year in second grade.

90

*Children's out-of-school life affects their ideas and
emotions and helps determine their art.   A change in
these conditions can often be detected by a change
in the child's art expression.*

91

In class or on the playground she very rarely communicated with anyone.   None of the children wanted to play with her.   At recess she always stood against the side of the school or in some obscure spot.   None of her teachers could remember her approaching them to tell about little incidents that had happened, as children so often do.   Being two years older, she was, of course, larger than the other children in her group.   She sat slouched down in her seat most of the time.   Even when called on in class, she just sat still.

Florence seldom wore a dress that was ironed and none of her clothes looked as though they originally had been bought for her. Her hair was seldom combed.   It is not difficult to imagine the effect that these things had on her.   Children are sensitive and find it difficult to understand why they cannot have what others have or are not as well cared for as their classmates.

Florence was, no doubt, feeling the effect that frequent illnesses of both her parents had upon their family life and upon their economic status.   Her father was unable to work regularly, thus reducing the family income and the advantages that Florence might have had, and her mother's limited strength was used for only the most essential jobs in caring for her family of four children, of which Florence was the youngest.

Florence made the second picture (91), of two children picking flowers, several weeks after the first one was painted.   The effect of this picture is quite different from her other one.   It looks gay and pleasant.   For the first time she has shown another person with her.   Every leaf on the trees and every flower is meticulously placed and colored.   The arm of one child is long enough to reach down to the flowers, showing functional proportion, which is a normal way for children to solve such a problem.   Florence's art work showed a sudden and dramatic change.   A certain change in her life at home had brought about a change in her emotional outlook.

An older sister, Mary, had gotten a job and from her first pay had bought Florence a new pink coat with gold buttons.   The first time that Florence wore it to school, she went right up to her teacher and showed it to her, telling her about Mary's taking her to the store and getting the coat; this was the first time she had sought out a teacher to talk to her.   After recess she told the teacher that she had lost a button from the new coat that meant so much to her, and

Vincent's close and happy relationship with his father made him feel pride and interest in his work as a coal miner.

92

naturally she was upset. The teacher, who had encouraged the child on every possible occasion, took advantage of the opportunity that she saw to call the attention of the group to Florence in a personal and happy way. She showed the coat and its remaining buttons to the class and asked all the children to help find the lost button. The teacher was wise enough to know that the few minutes required to find it was time well spent in building a relationship between Florence and the rest of the group. This was an unusual experience for the child, one in which she felt that people were working for her and with her.

The next illustration (92) shows how the particular relationships that a boy had with his father affected his art.

Vincent was a happy, well adjusted child, pleasant to work with. He had a great many friends in school. He was proud of his father and talked about him to his third-grade teacher and to his friends. The father was a coal miner who spent a great deal of time with his son, talking to him about many things, including his work in the mines. About this picture, Vincent said: "Last night my daddy was telling me about the mines. That's where he works.

The coal is all around.   See, I made it like that.   It's dark in there.
The men have to wear lights on their caps.   He eats in there.   My
mother packs him a bucket.   They dig the coal, then put it on the
cars like this, and the mules pull it out to the motors.   My dad often
tells me about the mines."   Vincent's interest in the information
about his father's work is evident in this piece of his art.   Children's
art shows the influence of their experiences and their relationships
with others, the most important of which is their relationship with
their parents.

CULTURAL DIFFERENCES

Differences in cultural background cause differences in the
art of children.   Maria, a Hopi Indian girl, drew this picture of her
mother and her house (93).   The way of life determines the kind
of house, and Maria's many experiences with her house have taught
her how it looks and how it functions.   The approach to her house,
above the ground floor, is also typical of her culture.   She has drawn
her mother walking up the ladder in an upright position, as Hopis
do.   Food is hanging to dry on the outside wall.   The row of
candles on the edge of the roof are lighted and placed there in celebration of Christmas.

The other illustration (94) shows Eagle Katchinas dancing to
the music of two Hopi drummers; many Indians sit or stand on top
of the pueblos to watch the dance.   The white sand and the violent
red mountain help convey the feeling of the heat of the day and the
excitement of the dance.   The traditional style of painting, as done
by the people of this fourth-grade child, has become a part of her
experiences and shows in the way she expresses her art.   The cultural background of the Hopis and the influence of their environment have made their creative art distinctly different in content
from that of another culture.

Children from other cultural backgrounds create art that reflects their own particular life.   In a town in which steel production
is the major industry much of the life is influenced by the mill.
Most of the children's fathers work there.   In Emily's picture of the
mill (95) she has shown some of the buildings, piles of coal, and the
small train that transports materials from one place to another

93

*Maria's art shows the influence of her home environ-
ment and her way of life in a Hopi Indian village.*

*The activity of the dance, the heat of the day, and the
traditional style of Indian painting are aspects of her
life that have affected this child's art.*

94

within the mill. She has also included a workman. A great deal of smoke comes from the stacks all the time; some of it is brightly colored, as Emily has shown in her picture. She has learned many things about the mill from her close contact with it. A child who lives near a mill gets acquainted with it through all his senses. He smells the smoke and hears the noise night and day. He feels soot on his skin. He sees many workmen on the streets at specific times as they change shifts. He sees raw materials go in and finished products taken out, and he must watch out for the big

95

In a town in which steel production is the major industry, the life of the people and sometimes the art of the children is influenced.

trucks transporting steel. It is necessary for a child to have such first-hand acquaintance with something in order to use it so freely in his creative art.

Every culture has its own peculiarities, and these affect the thinking and behavior of children. A fourth-grade child in New Zealand painted the composition of milking activities on a farm (96). He has shown two cows in stalls and two standing outside. The farmer is carrying the milk buckets on a yoke, which is a method of transportation seldom used in America. A child of another culture,

unfamiliar with this method of carrying pails, would not likely put
it into his art.

The culture of the people of Hawaii is not as different from
that in the continental United States as the American Southwest
Indian culture is, but some of the existing differences are evident in
the art of children.   A fifth-grade Hawaiian child painted the row
of bamboo trees shown in Illustration 97.   This type of tree is not
found in the other illustrations of this group because a bamboo tree
is not found in the environment of the other children.   The intense
Hawaiian sunlight is shown by the warm colors in the sand.   In a
warm land the shadows seem cool and inviting and make a sharp
contrast to the sunny areas, as this child has shown.   The child is
also familiar with the structure of the trees and with their quickly
moving, long, thin leaves.   Cultural differences give the child different concepts, ideas, and experiences that help to determine his
creative concepts as well as other factors in his art.

EMOTIONAL PROBLEMS

Emotional problems affect a child's art, and the art products
change as the emotional problems are solved.   Change sometimes
comes about slowly, however, as it did in the case of Winifred whose
mother died when she was born.   Her maternal grandparents reared
her, giving her many material advantages.   The economic level
provided for her was above average.   Perhaps because the grandmother associated the death of her daughter with the baby, she
often cried when she picked Winifred up.   This kind of relationship
undoubtedly failed to provide Winifred with happy contacts early
in life.

To try to protect Winifred and to prevent her from being in-
jured, the grandparents restricted her play.   In order to protect her
from cold, she was required to wear clothing unlike that worn by
other girls of her age.   She was the only girl in her group who wore
long stockings and long-sleeved dresses.   Winifred's father thought
that the grandparents were overstrict and, when he visited, there
was often quarreling.   On one such occasion, without forewarning,
he picked up his daughter and took her to the new home he had
established since his remarriage.   At this time Winifred entered the

A child in New Zealand used an idea familiar to him for his painting.

96

97

Hawaiian children are familiar with trees typical to their environment and put these familiar forms into their art.

third grade.   She had always been shy and somewhat withdrawn in school and seldom smiled.   After any new experience, she merely dabbled in the art medium.   She usually had clay or finger paint all over her or she painted mixed-up puddles.   Sometimes she used so much paint that it ran off her paper onto the table and the teacher would have to gather up her paper and pour her painting into the sink.   It was not possible to save any samples of this stage of her work.   In the first illustration of her work (98) she has made a design.   She offered no explanation for the forms that look like two pairs of eyes.

As Winifred was completing the next painting (99), the teacher said: "That's you, isn't it?"   Winifred merely nodded her head.   The colors are dark and the whole feeling is morbid; the dark eyes, alert and watching, add to this effect.

In a cut-paper composition (100) Winifred made the figure of herself in her house.   She is as large as the house, and again the piercing effect of the large eyes is felt.   The strip of red paper below the center of the girl is her skirt.

The swimming picture (101) was made by Winifred in the last part of her third-grade year.   About this time she began to choose gay colors and subjects.   Her work has lost most of its morbid quality, although some confusion is still evident.   This picture is better organized than her earlier ones.   The body of water fits around the interesting variety of shapes at the bottom of the page, and the children are having fun together.   By this time much of Winifred's art incorporated many interesting things that probably reflected her own broader scope of interest.   She seldom painted puddles any more but continued to be slow to complete her art and hesitant about beginning another problem.   All three of her primary-grade teachers helped her by accepting whatever art work she did and encouraging her.   Her stepmother helped her by frequently visiting school and discussing with the teacher ways of helping the child.   She immediately purchased for Winifred some brightly colored dresses with socks to match.

These typical examples of Winifred's work were selected to show how home and school experiences affect a child's art.   The experiences make up a long series of incidents and relationships with her family.   The illustrations show the changes that occurred in her art as her home life and her relationships with her family changed.

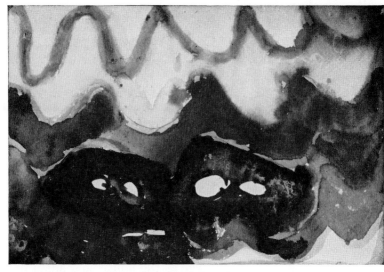

98

Emotional problems help determine a child's art. When Winifred's problem was most acute, her art was indefinite in form and morbid in feeling.

The forms became more distinct as she began to work out her emotional problem.

99

Frequently her art showed pre-occupation with herself and little control of the medium.

100

As her problem became resolved, her art work showed in-clusion of other people, more complex organization, bright colors, and better control of the medium.

101

102

*Much of the child's life and feelings are expressed in her art.   Donna,
who has a congenital ear disorder and an unhappy home life, said of
this Thanksgiving picture: "This is a turkey and these are her eggs.
She doesn't have any feathers or sisters.   She has two feathers and
a rug.   This is her house.   She doesn't got any moon and no one
likes her.   They don't like her because she only has two feathers.
She doesn't have any children.   Sometimes there isn't anyone to
have fun with her, and she broke her leg.   She has to sit on the rug
and take a rest and she will be all right."*

In working with children it is wise for a teacher to disregard
an occasional deviation in a child's art.   For instance, if a child is
usually interested in and does interesting art of a variety of types, a
teacher is wise to ignore the time he does not do well, the day he
paints all over his work, or the moment of discouragement that
prompts him to destroy his work.   We all have days and moments
when we are emotionally upset.   It is only when such deviational
behavior becomes a habit or a pattern of action that the teacher
should feel that the child needs help.   As she sees such a pattern
developing, the teacher, of course, should encourage the child and
build his confidence in himself.   When she sees him repeating an
idea or form one time after another, she should encourage (but not
pressure) him to try other ideas or variations of the favored idea.
When this fails, she should seek help from someone whose specialty

is work with problem children, such as the school psychiatrist or psychologist. Teachers do not have the knowledge to diagnose and prescribe for children's emotional problems. There are many things a teacher can do, however, to help such children. She can be gentle, understanding, and sympathetic, accepting the child and his art and refraining from harsh criticism or using a sharp, cutting tone of voice. It is helpful if the teacher encourages the children whenever she can, without making the encouragement appear false or artificial. Although a teacher can do helpful things, she is limited by the pressure of the needs of many other children who deserve as much of her attention as the problem child. *Every* child is important, deserving, and needing some special personal attention from the teacher every day.

OTHER INFLUENCES

The methods used in the teaching of art are also among the school experiences that determine a child's art. They can directly determine the art produced by teacher-dictated processes, copy work, prepared outlines, and patterns. Methods used by teachers can have a long-range effect on the art of children, as shown by John's work in Chapter III.

Experiences from other areas of the curriculum affect and determine children's art. Workbooks are frequently used in the elementary school and many contain pictures that children copy or color. Such experiences are the same as copy work or prepared outlines that are sometimes used in the time scheduled for art by teachers who do not understand the values of creative art.

Emphasis on naturalistic representation without regard for the intent of the child or without concern for the other bases for expression are other school experiences that influence art.

Suggested activity

Study a few samples of one child's art. Parallel this with a study of his personality, work habits, home life, school life, and relationships with his friends and family. Find out all you can about him. Try to see how these things have determined his art. Discuss how you, as the teacher, might best help him.

CHAPTER *XI*

Relation of art to other
areas of the curriculum

ART is related to every human experience and emotion. There is an existing connection between the activities and feelings of the artist and the art work that he creates. Art is inspired by life situations and by the imagination that finds its basis in an experience. A very important part of the experiences and activities of children in the elementary school is their curriculum of studies. Art is a part of this curriculum. Relationships exist between art and the other areas of the curriculum. Some of these areas are direct influences and associations; others are less direct in their relationships.

It is important for teachers to understand that such relationships exist and that learnings from the one re-enforce, intensify, and magnify the learnings and understandings from the other areas. It is just

as important, however, for a teacher to realize that every a
curriculum has its own merits and qualities and that the
has a responsibility not to let one subject become subordin.
the other or to encroach on the other.

QUALITIES OF ART

Art has inherent qualities of its own that are different from
those of other school subjects.   The values of art have been known
to mankind from the beginning of recorded history.   Some of the
very earliest records that we have are art forms — for instance, the
drawings on the walls of prehistoric cave dwellings.   Throughout
the ages people of every culture and era have found satisfactions and
values in art expressions.   At different times and in different places
art forms have expressed the spirit of the times and the needs of the
people.   During the Middle Ages architectural forms dominated.
In present-day America industrial design for mass-produced articles
seems to fulfill a need and express the spirit of our time.   For every
person of every age individual creative expression in some form has
been and is important and essential.   In Chapter II of this book are
described specifically the values that are inherent in creative art
work.   These values explain the deep implications of creative expression in solving the immediate needs of the child and in preparing him for adult life, such as learning how to make his own choices
and acquiring discriminating judgment.   These are personal values
to the child as well as art values.   They are important for the individual and for the society of which he is a part.   A society can be
no better than the people who comprise it.

In addition to the values of creative art expression there is
knowledge about art that is necessary to growth in art expression.
Some of this knowledge is detailed in Chapter VII.   Understanding
unity, for example, and gaining some insight into how it is achieved
helps children better to express their ideas in an organized way.
Knowledge helps children to gain control over the media with which
they work.   It helps children in art when it is used merely as guiding principles which they may recall and use or reject as they choose.
Children will be richer for having some information about *art*
called to their attention, explained to them, and discussed in rela-

tion to art work.   It can be a tool that they may or may not use in any way that serves them.

CORRELATION

Relationships between one subject and another or among several subjects mean that there are particular ways in which these areas extend into each other.   In teaching art it is wise to be aware of the close connection between it and other areas of the curriculum and between art and life experiences out of school.   Art depends for much of its subject-matter content on these activities. Learnings from other areas of the curriculum are frequently transferred to art.   In poster-making, for example, it might be interesting to list the skills and knowledges involved that were acquired in the study of other things — such as spelling, for one.   All learning depends on integration of the new experience with past learnings; art education does, too.   The more extensive the integration, the more easily the new knowledge is learned and remembered.

Without any particular intent to frame such a juncture between two areas of the curriculum, children often choose such relationships because of their interest and values to them.   The example explained in the discussion between Janice and her teacher in Chapter V (pages 106–107) shows that the child's interest in her reading story became the subject matter for her art.   In the early part of Chapter VII (pages 165–172), the children and teacher discuss the ratio of sizes existing among the various parts of their own bodies. A direct dependence on the knowledge gained in this way was used by the children to improve their art expression.   Such relationships between art and other areas of study occur every day.   They are so common that, frequently, we take little notice of them.   Realizing the advantages to be gained in such relationships, teachers sometimes plan with children for direct correlation between art and other subjects.

Putting together two or more school subjects for the purposes of promoting learning through the common grounds of these subjects is not a new educational procedure.   Educators have long recognized the values of building on interests and knowledges in one subject to bring about a better integration of learning with another.

One of the most common forms of correlation is the climaxing of the study of some unit of work in social studies or reading, for example, with the inclusion of a project in art built around the subject matter of the other area of study.   Frequently music, writing, or story-telling are brought into the correlation.   For the purposes of this text, however, the values and activities as they relate to *art* will be stressed.

A child's appreciation of and abilities in art can grow from such a correlation.   Interests and knowledges already established can be utilized.   Time saved in building background information for the art work can be used to teach some of the art knowledge that will enhance the child's abilities to express his ideas in art and will, in turn, improve his art products.   Skills and information are learned more quickly and remembered longer if related to a strong interest.

The art expression can be used to fortify the area to which it is correlated.   Recall is required of the child in the planning of the art project.   The use of this review of the material in another situation and in other ways makes an effective learning procedure. This is *not* an art aim, but it is one of the valuable outcomes of cor-

103

Jim's interest in history motivated his drawing of a stagecoach robbery while an airplane flies overhead.   What children draw and associate is based on their interest regardless of historical accuracy.

relation. The necessity for putting some of his ideas into form is a visual, concrete way for the child to determine whether he needs to know more about a particular phase of the subject. He has to know a great deal about an object before he can model it out of clay or draw it. More research may thus be an outcome of correlation and may thus lead to additional learning.

There are also some possible limitations to the values of correlation. One such limitation, and one that teachers need to guard against, is that art becomes merely a tool for further study of the other area. The demands of the other subject encroach on and supplant the type of learnings and judgments that are unique to art. When this happens, there are little or no *art* values in the correlation; therefore, it is difficult if at all possible to call it an *art* experience. The use of materials usually associated with art does not assure that the activity is an art experience for the children. Some teachers, in developing with children the art activity that will be correlated with the study of another subject, insist that every detail of the art project be factual, to agree with the content of the subject matter. In planning and discussing such an activity, emphasis is frequently placed on the accuracy of visual representation. Guidance and suggestions during the working process are based on what is "right" from the standpoint of the actual appearance, arrangements, and facts as they apply to the subject matter studied. When facts that are accurate from this viewpoint become the dominant purpose of the group, art values are lost. The art-class time used for such a project becomes, to a great extent, an extension of the time devoted to the other area of learning. The "art" work becomes, in effect, a two-dimensional or a three-dimensional social-studies (or other) project. True, the children may be learning to be more facile with the art materials, but art materials are only a means by which an idea is expressed. The same skills can be gained when the art work is based on design structure, when it deals with emotional reactions and is guided by aesthetic judgments as well as by the forms and knowledge of the subject that inspired the project.

The development of creativeness, inventiveness, and originality is a vital purpose of art education. When this is discouraged or forbidden, the child loses the type of experiences that were meant for him when art was included in his school life.

There is, basically, one factor that determines whether the child is provided with opportunities for his *art* growth or whether the time allotted to art is being used to teach and to emphasize other learnings. This factor is the *basis on which judgments are made* throughout the working process. The basis for judgments in art should be *art qualities*. To be an art experience the activity must be centered in *art* purposes, *art* judgments, and *art* education.

The domination of art by another area of the curriculum during a correlation of the two need not occur. It is the purpose of this chapter to show how art can be and is correlated with other areas of the curriculum and yet retain its own particular nature. From your reading in the earlier chapters of this book, you have noted many examples of this relationship. In Chapter IV, mention was made of how the interesting things that children had learned about the Pilgrims and the first Thanksgiving provided the subject matter for their art, forming a very direct relationship between the two subjects. Studying the art work reproduced in this book will give you many other examples.

An incident that happened to an elementary-school art teacher illustrates an infringement on art. Miss Stein was new to the school. In her previous position she had helped children develop many interesting group projects that were correlated with other areas of the curriculum, which she developed as art problems. The children enjoyed them and profited by them, and their teachers co-operated. The teachers in her new school had heard about these projects. One of the first to suggest a correlation to Miss Stein was Mrs. Hale, the sixth-grade teacher. She said, "Miss Stein, I have been looking forward to working with you. I have heard about your excellent work in developing units including art. I wonder if we can develop one with my group?" Eager to establish co-operative relationships in her new school, Miss Stein said, "Yes, of course. What are you studying? What have you in mind?" Mrs. Hale said, "We are just beginning our study of Beowulf. When we complete it I would like to have you plan a group project or have the children do large individual compositions about the subject. Then give them to me, and I will correct them for accuracy. By doing that I can judge how much they have learned about it. Miss Johnson, your predecessor, was always very co-operative in doing this for me. I am sure you will be, too." Miss Stein was interestingly following Mrs. Hale until she mentioned correcting the compositions for accuracy. She could sense immediately that Mrs. Hale wanted her to teach about Beowulf and *not art*. This is an example of how art had been used to teach the factual material of a subject without regard for the art values that might accrue.

An example of how a correlation worked to the mutual advantage of both art and social studies is shown in the following description. Mr. Clark, the teacher of a self-contained fourth grade, provided quite a different correlation experience for the children. They had been studying about Pennsylvania, their own state. In discussing how they might relate their art work to a unit that they found interesting, the children and their teacher decided to divide into four groups and develop four phases of their study. They selected:

(a) A group painting of William Penn buying the land from the Indians
(b) A three-dimensional construction of the industries in western Pennsylvania
(c) A large Indian tepee big enough for three or four children to be inside
(d) A study of Pennsylvania Dutch hex designs (These were to be all about the same size and large enough for the whole class to see.)

As each group proceeded with its chosen art project they made decisions that dealt with the phase of Pennsylvania that they had chosen, as well as decisions and judgments that dealt with art.

The group that decided on the industries of western Pennsylvania listed the industries that they would include. Then they decided to divide their group into committees, each of which was to construct a certain part. Two boys agreed to build a small oil derrick to represent Drake's first oil well; two other children worked on a steel mill; two more undertook a coal mine; and the remaining two chose lumbering. They worked together, trading comments and comparing ideas. They measured their constructions against each other and to fit the table on which they would be displayed together. From the first they gave little consideration to naturalistic relationships of sizes or distances. This would have required that their work be made very small, and they wanted it to show up.

104

Susan's gay, warm personality is reflected by her choice of objects and colors. Details, such as the bricks, show her personal concern and feeling for the subject. She left space between the earth and sky for freedom of movement.

In this group painting of William Penn buying land, the children retained the historical essence of the subject while pursuing and expressing aesthetic qualities as well.

105

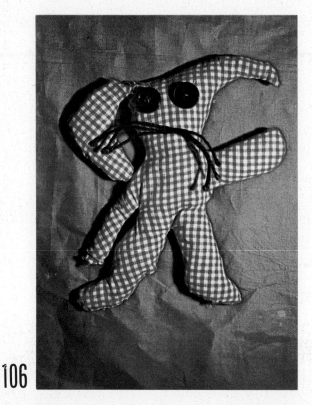

106

Children like to make things that can be used, such
as this imaginative stuffed toy, and they find a change
of materials stimulating.

Children enjoy creating imaginative forms in
their three-dimensional art. Clark has made
his clay animal with strength and character,
adding interesting texture, as did others in his
sixth-grade group.

Although children in the primary grades usually like to work independently, they occasionally want to share an art problem with a friend. Such voluntary cooperative activities are the beginnings of group activities.

109

Carl's spaceman and rocket were inspired by his interest in science. Many areas of the curriculum provide children with fascinating ideas that they may use in their art.

Milton created this attractive abstract design because the idea was appealing and urgent to him at the time. A child's imagination is a great asset to his art expression.

110

Their major interest and purpose was in the industries, so they were built large in relation to their importance to the children at that time. To a limited degree the ratio of sizes was based on emotional proportion, as explained in Chapter VIII. After the major industries were represented by their cardboard and wood structures, the children discussed what they might do next. The two boys who had built a small oil derrick felt that their one small oil well looked too small when placed among the other work. The group agreed with the boys that the oil well did not show up to advantage in comparison to the large steel mill and the coal mine. They felt that it looked isolated in the large space provided for it. At this point they were dissatisfied with the *art* aspect of the project. It did not *look* well. This decision was based on an *art* judgment. The children discussed it further.

Marilyn: "Why don't you make more oil wells?"
Joe: "We could. Only we were trying to show Drake's first one, but it looks lost in all that space."
Mitchell: "Yes, let's make more. They did drill more oil wells, lots of them after Drake started it. We could still have Drake's and show how more followed."

Although the children's reasoning followed factual lines, their decision to change their original intent was based on their judgment that this one part of the project looked inadequate and was out of balance. It was based upon an *art* judgment. Several more oil wells were added and grouped. The decision as to number and placement was made on the basis of where they looked well and how many were needed to bring the whole art enterprise into better balance.

After the four industries were completed and placed, the children appraised their partially completed project and made several additional decisions based on the visual appearance. They wanted their work to be attractive, so they placed groups of trees where they felt they were needed to make the buildings show up well; this was another art decision. A section of railroad and some bright red cars were placed near the coal mine to add color to the dark piles of coal and the gray buildings. Roads of different kinds were added to help connect the parts and give the project unity. Color contrast and a unified organization gave greater aesthetic qualities to their work. From the beginning to the end of the work, the children were using *art* knowledge and making *art* decisions.

This art project that was correlated with another area of the curriculum provided the children with many art experiences. The knowledge gained from the other subject provided the subject matter, their interest in it provided the motivation, and their own feeling for balance fortified by their knowledge about *art* guided the development of the work. Such planned projects built on the relationship of art to other areas of the curriculum offer strong educational opportunities for children.

It can be just as beneficial to children when interest arising from an art problem inspires the correlation of other school subjects. Outgrowths of the art project can result in the writing of stories or poetry, study and research, creative drama or dance, correlated units of study in other subjects, or a number of other valuable learning situations.

Frequently, the relationship of art to other areas of the curriculum is brought about by unit planning. In this case, areas of the curriculum should be planned and related studies, including art, begun together. There are many ways in which art is related to other areas of the curriculum. Some of these associations are more direct than others. Some are planned and some are spontaneous.

WORKBOOKS

In the elementary grades, workbooks are frequently used as one of several aids to promote learning in some of the school subjects. Realizing the advantages to be gained by relating art experiences to another area of the curriculum, many of these workbooks contain pictures that may illustrate the work of another subject, by providing opportunities for children to color inside outlines or even to copy pictures. In fact, many of the workbooks contain specific instructions for children to copy a certain figure and to color it with a particular hue. This is particularly true of many workbooks used in the primary grades. The intent and purpose of preparing such workbooks is to relate the textual material to the drawing and coloring activity in order to promote learning through more than one type of experience. In doing this, emphasis has been placed on the desired effect on the subject-matter learning and little regard has been given to the effect that such workbook copy experiences may have on the children's art.

Art educators have long been aware of the possible effects on children's art of these copy activities as well as those requiring the children to color within prescribed lines. As explained in Chapter III, such activities have very little or no value for children. In fact, they may often have detrimental effects on the child's confidence in his own ideas and on his creative art concepts. Interfering with the child's ideas and displacing his own concepts of form with prepared shapes can cause mental and emotional confusion and affect his creative work.

The effect of workbook copy experiences on the creative concepts of children were measured in an experience with 28 first-grade children.[1] Early in the term, before the children had been exposed to workbooks, they were each asked to make several individual drawings of objects that were later presented to them on reading and arithmetic workbook sheets. The workbook sheets each involved a copy experience. Following this, they were again asked to make individual drawings of the same forms on 9 by 12-inch drawing paper.

Comparing the second drawings against the first showed that few children were able to withstand the influence of the workbook forms given them to copy; their second drawings show various degrees of resemblance to the workbook forms. The quality of the art work in their second drawings had deteriorated, and many were noticeably smaller in size after the copy exposure. Many of the second drawings were more difficult to recognize because of the conflict between the child's idea and that imposed upon him by the workbook.

The accompanying examples of two children's work (pages 258–259) show how workbook copy experiences affected their art. Three drawings are shown with each example. The first shows the child's creative concept of the form before the workbook experience, the second is a line drawing enlarged many times from the very small one used in the workbook, and the third is the same

---

[1] Russel, Irene, and Waugaman, Blanche, "The Effect of Workbook Copy Experiences on the Creative Concepts of Children," *Research Bulletin*, Eastern Arts Association, Kutztown, Pa., Vol. 3, No. 1 (April, 1952).

111

house

Curtis drew the top picture before he colored the workbook form (center). The bottom drawing, made afterwards, shows the barren effect of the workbook form.

Girl

Lucille's art expression shows marked deterioration as a result of her workbook copy experiences. 112

child's drawing of the same subject following the workbook copy experience.

The first example of Curtis' work shows a well developed concept of a house. The side view is shown, with a porch. There are chairs on the porch, curtains on the windows, and other details that Curtis associated with living in a house. The center line drawing is the enlarged workbook form. The last drawing of a house is one made by Curtis following the workbook experience of copying the form of the house. The second drawing greatly resembles the workbook form; many of the meaningful details are lost, and it lacks the interesting art qualities of the first.

Lucille's work is another example of the deterioration that took place following a workbook copy experience. In the first example, done before the workbook experience, the girl in the picture looks happy and is holding her doll, an activity common to little girls and one that they all seem to enjoy. Her arms are bent to hold the doll (not an easy thing for a six-year-old to attempt to draw). The body, arms, and legs of the girl have solidity. The girl is drawn in a front view, which most small children use in their drawings. Lucille has included a doll carriage to complete her picture.

The enlarged workbook image in the center is a grotesque drawing of a girl. Children, themselves, know better. Study details of this figure, compare it with Lucille's first drawing, and you will see how much more interesting and well developed her drawing is.

In looking at Lucille's second drawing, you can see the deterioration in aesthetic quality and in the concept of the figure that has taken place. Lucille still wanted the girl to hold her doll, but she found it difficult with a side view. The girl is holding the doll by the hair with one hand, which is not only an unnatural position, but also causes the picture to lose much of its warm, human, emotional appeal. The only item in both Lucille's drawings that did not appear in the workbook copy experience was the doll carriage. Nothing interfered with her concept of the carriage, so it remained the same.

Since areas of the curriculum are related, and since transfers of learning take place from one to the other, teachers need constantly to appraise the experiences that they provide for children. Teachers who believe in creative art and who would not consider using copy work or prepared outlines in art often are proud of the numerous workbooks that they use with children. Often teachers use the workbooks without having regarded the possible consequences of the copy experiences that many of them contain. Coloring inside a form is actually a copy activity because it forces the child to follow the form.

Just looking at the very small size of the spaces that are provided for children to color should be evidence to teachers of the inappropriateness of such work for small children, who have not yet developed enough manual dexterity to control their work in such small areas.

A few teachers may try to justify workbook experiences on the basis of the importance of such work to reading or any subject. It seems questionable whether the emphases of activity in some workbooks are those connected with the subject the exercises are intended to develop. Sometimes the matching of a word is the only subject-matter activity — the emphasis of the child's time being given to the drawing or coloring activity.

Teachers need to be discriminating in their selection and use of materials in every area of the curriculum because subjects are related and learnings from one affect learnings and expression in another.

Suggested activity

(a) *Study a set of children's individual creative art work. Study each piece and decide whether or not the whole or any part of it might have been related to another area of the curriculum.*

(b) *Study a completed group project in which art has been correlated to another area of the curriculum. Try to discover whether sufficient emphasis has been placed on the art qualities in the development of the art project. Has it been an* art *experience?*

CHAPTER *XII*

Competition, contests,

and grading in children's art

THROUGHOUT this book, the emphasis has been placed
on methods of teaching art to children in the classroom and in
situations involving direct relationships between the teacher and
the child. There are other practices associated with the teaching
of art to children to which teachers need to give thoughtful
attention, even though these practices may involve
less direct relationships. Some, associated with the
children's daily art experiences, can affect the processes in the art work, the art products, and the way
the children feel about the art experiences. Others
may come into play only occasionally but can have
immediate as well as lasting effects upon the children's art and their attitudes toward it. By calling
attention, in this chapter, to some of these practices
— particularly competition, art contests, and grad-

ing — it is hoped that teachers will come to understand some of their influences. Through evaluation and discussion of these practices, teachers may gain some criteria by which they can make critical judgments of other practices that have some relationship to art. It is important for teachers of art to understand and evaluate any practices or factors in classroom or community life that may have effects on the art experiences of children. Anything that affects the child's art also affects the child, and anything that affects the child will also affect his art products.

ART CONTESTS

A contest is a competition for some advantage over some other person or group. It involves a struggle to win over adversaries or a fight to gain superiority over other contestants. Each contender in a contest is deeply concerned with establishing his own excellence above that of all others. A contestant is not only trying to do the best he can but also to do better than anyone else. In order to accomplish this victory, a contestant must be, from the beginning, deeply concerned with an accomplishment that is closely related to the purposes of defeating others as well as to developing his own interests and purposes.

Conflict arises from the contestant's struggle between what he may feel is right and what he feels is necessary in order to gain the advantage over others. The contestant may feel an urge to express himself in a certain manner, or he may be drawn toward the selection of ideas that attract him, but neither of these factors can be the final basis of his choice. He must also consider the chances that his choices will have of winning and make a decision with this in mind. Conflict arises also in his feelings toward other contestants. He loses his feeling of co-operation in favor of a competitive one. If he helps another contestant, the other may win, and he may lose. He therefore cannot afford to be helpful in ways that might endanger his chance to gain the winning advantage.

Purposes and problems of art contests. Because art products are tangible, have form, and can be seen and handled, those who propose contests seem to regard art as a field well suited to competition.

The purposes of contests vary. Sometimes a contest is associated with an exhibition of art. Each exhibitor selects his "best" work for the display. From among these pieces so selected, one "best" is chosen to receive a prize. In this way, an exhibition also becomes a contest for the superiority of one or a few pieces. This selected work then receives a great deal of attention and publicity. In many cases the amount of emphasis placed on the prize-winner is out of ratio to the difference in quality between it and other pieces of art work in the exhibition.

Some contests grow out of the desire of some organization or association to promote their own objectives. By having people work on an art project related to a theme chosen by the organization, it can acquaint these persons with its aims and purposes. Contestants need enough information about the organization and its purposes to express their ideas with the conviction and enthusiasm necessary for communication.

Sponsors of contests often feel that competitions are beneficial because of the prizes awarded. Since only a few children can win, the rejection of their serious attempts to solve the problem is difficult for the others to understand.

Sponsors feel they are of service by giving children a topic for their art. Teachers and children do not need to be given topics to study and to develop in school; children have many ideas for their art work. Teachers realize that there is much to be taught and to be learned, and their problem is not one of finding additional things for children to do but of finding time to teach the many things that they know are essential.

Children in school are a captive audience and have time assigned for art activities. Persons in favor of contests feel that these conditions are excellent for establishing a contest. These school conditions are, of course, excellent for establishing any learning opportunities.

Since rewards are given to a select few from among those entering a contest, some method of determining the winners must be decided. Usually, one person or a panel of a few persons is appointed to make the final decision. If there are many entries, some selection and elimination usually takes place before the judges face the task of making a final decision. Therefore, the works of some children have no chance of even being viewed by the judges.

Judges are usually selected from among those persons who have little or no involvement with the sponsors, the contestants, or the processes of preparing the entries. The aim is to find an "impartial" jury, who cannot know the personal struggles, hopes, dreams, and emotions that have gone into the making of each entry. Yet, this personal involvement of the artist is the very essence of creating art. Every judge necessarily approaches the selection with his own prejudices, special interests, reactions, tastes, and experiences.

Since contest judges differ in personality, background, and value judgments, it is evident that they will not all make the same decisions. Sometimes each judge has selected, as his choice for a

113

"Cinerama makes you feel that the planes are right over you," said Ed about his picture. No contest was necessary to stimulate this expressive drawing.

prize, a different piece.   When this happens, a compromise must be made.   There have been instances of a prize being awarded to a piece of art that no judge had selected as his first choice; it was simply one on which they could all agree.

Many contests are directed toward one particular form of art, such as posters.   When this is the case, the sponsors may often determine not only the subject but also the size, number of words, and other guides for the contestant.   They frequently give, as one example, slogans intended to suggest themes or topics and to give some ideas of what the sponsor would find acceptable.   Some contests have percentage or numerical-value scoring for various aspects of the work, which are intended to guide contestants' work and the judges' selections.   Such a rating, intended to be a helpful guide, can become a deterrent.   A piece of art work that is successful and outstanding but does not conform to the stated value ratings could be eliminated.   If a piece of art work, on the other hand, is chosen for its quality regardless of its score on the rating scale, an unfair situation arises for children who have complied.   These same contestants might have produced work of higher quality had they also freed themselves from the restricting rules.

The most difficult problem of all, of course, is the selection of one piece of art work above all others.   One composition appeals because of a certain quality; another, not having this quality, attracts because of a different reason.   The difficulty is not so much finding attractive and interesting art work to choose as it is having to reject work of quality.   A judge, sensitive to various distinguishing factors in art, regrets having to withhold prizes from excellent pieces.   He is confronted with a job that is extremely difficult to do in a completely satisfactory way.

Some persons, faced with making a final choice of one among several excellent pieces of art work, feel that they cannot make a mistake because whichever work is selected will be a proper choice. They feel that someone will be pleased by having won.   Yes, some *one* will be, but the others will find it difficult to understand why this certain piece was selected above their work or over that of some other person.   At times, the judge has difficulty justifying his choice.

Effects of contests.   What happens to the *winner* of a contest?   To be elevated above many others because of the quality of his work is most certainly an intoxicating success for a child and greatly builds his morale. He is strongly motivated by the reward and recognition, which can fortify his interest in art and in education. It is a triumph that he can remember and can point to with pride. It can encourage him to do more art work, but it can also impede his art progress. Some winners repeat the successful art form in later art experiences in order to continue to receive recognition. They become afraid to try new or different ideas and materials lest the result fail to be as successful as the prize-winning one. Winning an art contest can also cause the winner to have an exaggerated opinion of the quality of his work. Such a success may cause him to think that he is more capable in art than the other contestants, whereas another judge possibly might have chosen another child's work. Whether a child's art was selected or not, the quality of it remains unchanged, but the child will be either elated or discouraged by the value judgment that someone else places on it.

The winner is also sometimes affected by his parents, relatives, or friends, who are justifiably proud of the successful child and praise him and boast about him to other people. Praise is a rich incentive, but when carried too far, it creates a reputation for the child that he may not be able to maintain, thus causing him to become discouraged. He may lose interest in art or turn from it rather than reveal his inability always to produce art of such a high standard. He may be equally interested in many things; or he may not want the stress that such a reputation can put on him to do more art work.

The *loser* is deeply affected by defeat. Children in the elementary school are too young to understand why their work was not chosen. Each takes the promises of the contest personally and expects to win. Children typically react in this way and should not be expected to behave as adults. Even adults are disappointed by not winning a contest, but children are more sensitive, more tender, and more expectant and so are hurt more deeply. At such an impressionable age, these deep failures and frustrations can cause lasting damage and can cause the child to associate art with failure.

Children who lose an art contest tend to be influenced in subsequent attempts by the pieces of art that won the award. The

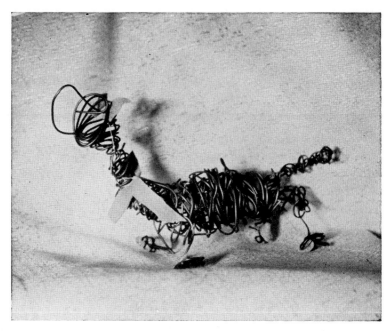

114

*Competitive experiences bring pressures and fear of failure
that complicate a child's art problems. This creative wire
sculpture resulted from a non-competitive atmosphere.*

awarding of prizes showed the children what the judges liked, and
even if the children do not repeat the same idea that won the prize,
they are often greatly influenced by it.

Although the sponsors maintain that one of the aims of the
contest is to increase the children's interest in art, the opposite
effect happens after the contest is over and the entries judged.
Since most children are disappointed, they are reluctant to try such
activities again.   Contest sponsors find it difficult to understand
why children's participation in an annual contest wanes and why
prizes are no longer the inducement they once were.

Each year more children have their expectations shattered,
with the result that fewer children have anticipations of winning,
and therefore fewer children enter.   An annual hobby contest held
by an organization for children in the intermediate grades is an example of this point.   Most children entered the contest the first year
it was held.   The display was interesting and varied, and the first

prize was awarded to a doll collection. In replying to the presentation of the award, the little girl said: "I thank you very much for this award. My doll collection was started for me before I was born and has been added to every year by my relatives." This doll collection could scarcely be said to be *her* hobby. She had no choice in its existence, nor had she selected the dolls that went into it; she was simply the recipient of someone else's ideas and choices. Yet she won the prize. The doll collection was large, varied, expensive, and showy, but the choices and sacrifices that went into it were another person's. The doll collection was selected in preference to a notebook of childish poems created by a fifth-grade girl. Most of her poems had been written in school about the personalities in the room and about daily school activities. The poems were charming, fresh, and wholly hers. She added to the notebook frequently. It was a personal and creative hobby, but it won her no prize.

In the next year the same contest was repeated and extended to other schools. The number of entries from the school that had participated in the previous year dropped. Doll collections, however, appeared in every participating school. After four years of repeating this contest, so few children entered that the sponsor discontinued it. They found it difficult to understand why the children lost interest. Increasing the amount of the awards neither stopped nor slowed down the withdrawal of the children from the annual contest.

To motivate children to engage in a hobby is a worthwhile undertaking. To encourage each child to follow a hobby that he selects, enjoys, and benefits by is consistent with the philosophy of modern art education. *To encourage every child* is the key to growth in worthy use of leisure time but does not happen in a contest. Instead of giving prizes to a few, some recognition should have come to every child who had a hobby and entered it in the display.

The kind of structured competition that pits one child against many others in a struggle to gain victory for only one is inappropriate for children. Children have their own private challenges. They compete with themselves by successively trying to do better work. A child will secretly compete against another, as, for example, in trying to ride a bicycle faster. Children will often compete without a spoken word between them. These personal strivings for a better place or for achievement are normal. The child feels these for himself and can control them as he wants. In that respect they are very different from imposed contests that the child did not initiate and cannot control.

Some persons think that children should be exposed to the practices of competition in order to give them experiences that prepare them for adult life, and the earlier they begin the better. Some persons think that children who compete in contests become adjusted to this practice and learn how to cope with it. Children profit by early experiences with many things, but not with all things. There are some things that are right and logical for adult life, but not for children. Many experiences are reserved for adults because they can best be dealt with by mature persons.

Contests and the general aims of education. The two major purposes of education are to prepare children for life in our culture and to make this a better world.

Although competition is a major factor in the private-enterprise system upon which American economics are based, structured competitive art experiences for elementary-school children do little to prepare them for life in our culture. Before an individual can compete, he must be prepared to do so by feeling confident in both the skills that he has mastered and is able to use to his advantage, and in the broad knowledge that he has acquired and can draw on and manipulate to serve him best. Children in the elementary school are still in the process of the development of skills. Some areas of education have not yet been presented to them in school. Children of this age lack sufficient background for structured competitive experiences in art.

Children are also emotionally unready for such activities because in elementary school they are more ego-centered than older persons. When a contest is presented, they regard it and the winning of the prize in reference to themselves.

Teachers and others who work with children should carefully consider the effect that losing has on the children. Since so very few win in proportion to the much greater number who do not, attention should be given to the greatest good for the greatest number — the many should not be exploited in favor of the few. Our democratic ideal is based on the dignity and worth of every human being. Activities in which children participate should help

115

*When the teacher is warm and friendly and treats each child as an
individual, competitive feelings are lost, and the child feels confident.   Individual expression in art flourishes in such a climate.*

them put this noble objective into practice; contests for children are
not among these activities.

The American free-enterprise system, based on competition,
has given us a high standard of living.   It also provides opportunities for creative, enterprising people.   Business, industry, and, to a
great extent, the professions are built and developed on initiative.
Personnel who have courage, are confident, and are creative are
constantly sought.   If we want to maintain and advance our high
standard of living, we must educate children with the needs of our
culture in mind.   In elementary school children are better prepared
for life in our culture if the concentration is on the developing of
fundamental skills and knowledges and every child is given the
opportunity to educate himself to the extent of his ability.   Contests
and competitions should be avoided until the individual is ready,
feels ready, and determines for *himself* when he should compete.

The other major purpose of education is to make this a better
world and constantly to improve conditions and opportunities for
all persons.   Both aims of education must be accomplished con-
currently and considered in life situations.   No individual can ignore
one aim and concentrate on the other without harming himself and

others in the process. Life in the classroom must be consistent with living conditions out of school. School life is life. A child is out in life from the moment he is born. He takes his place as a responsible person in public life on the day he enters school.

To make the world a better place entails co-operation, and appreciation of other peoples and other ways makes co-operation easier. People need to work together, to help each other, and act in ways that are beneficial to others if living conditions are going to be improved. People need to learn to have a respect for the welfare of others and to learn how to advance a high standard of living for the rest of the world, and these values are learned by application to their own lives, among their own friends, and in their own class-rooms. If started in childhood, the helping of others and co-operation become fixed attitudes and habits that carry over into a variety of situations and, being part of the person, they go with him and represent him. These habits and attitudes are unselfish and pertain more to co-operation and to peace than to disagreements and war.

Contests and art education. In reading this chapter, up to this point, it should have become obvious that art contests are contradictory to modern methods of teaching art. Some of the reasons for the contradictions follow:

(a) *Contests emphasize the importance of the finished art product.* The quality of the completed art work *is* important to both the child and his teacher. Both must feel a pride in the child's achievement as evidenced by his art work. *Educationally*, however, it is *what happens to the child during the creative process* that is significant. When such emphasis is placed on the clay piece, the painting, or the poster, children tend to do what they already know how to do and feel certain they can do reasonably well. They hesitate to experiment lest it not compare well with the work of their classmates. They are reluctant to try new ideas and new ways. Learning is affected. To ensure an acceptable result, a child may be tempted to copy a picture or shape instead of creating his own. The detrimental and injurious effects of copy experiences on a child's creative art are made clear from the research study discussed in the previous chapter.

Some teachers, too, are influenced by the stress placed on the completed art product.   When prizes are given, teachers are anxious for their children to win.   When a child wins, recognition comes to him and, indirectly, to his teacher.   Teachers want to receive this focus of favorable attention on themselves and their students and to have their work honored.   For these reasons, some teachers are tempted to pick out those few children most likely to win and spend most of their time with them.   In other instances, teachers might actually pick up the materials and work on the children's art, changing it and making it conform more nearly to adult standards.   If adults are tempted to cheat in order to gain indirect recognition for themselves, it must be obvious that children, who are directly involved, are much more likely to feel enticed to do so.   It is unfair to elementary-school children, who are still building character, to place before them such temptation.

The finished art work and the process of creating and working are important and should be emphasized because they are interrelated.   There should be a balance between them.   When the finished art product is overemphasized, this interferes with a child's feeling of freedom to experiment.   By placing value on the end result, the child may be made to feel that any means to achieve this end is desirable.   "The end justifies the means" can be an attitude resulting from contest emphasis.   The end does not justify the means; it is a product of the means.   The attitudes formed and the facts acquired are learned during the means or process of producing art.   In the long run, these outcomes are the ones most likely to affect the child's behavior now and as an adult.

(b) In a great many contests the topic or *theme* for the art *is determined by someone other than the child.*   Other restrictions and limitations are sometimes placed on the contestant as well. Creative expression in art gives to the *child the opportunity to choose his own subject matter for his art.*   In a contest, the child is often not free to choose, from the many ideas that come to him, one that excites and arouses his urges to create and to work his idea through to completion.   The first, basic choice is not his.

(c) The strength of modern art education lies in the value and worth it places on every child.   By *recognizing* the successful areas in the art work of *every child*, every child is dignified.   Each is encouraged to build on his successes.   Such educational processes are consistent with democratic American ideals.   These processes will build into the child value standards and behavior patterns that will make him a more confident person and a more appreciative world citizen.

The basic characteristic of a contest is that *recognition is not given to the achievements of every child.* This fundamental principle is in opposition to the foundation on which modern art education is built. The opposing values and practices of competitions are apt to carry over into art activities that are not associated with contests and affect the way a child works, thinks, and evaluates. This carry-over effect of contests should be well considered by a teacher before she encourages her children to enter a contest or before she makes an agreement for the children to compete.

(d) Sponsors of contests are right when they say that *competitions strongly motivate children.* They certainly do, but the driving motivational force is the desire to win and to gain special personal recognition. When contests or competitions are advertised or presented, the opportunity for one or a few children to win an award or a coveted prize is described and stressed; no mention is made of what will happen for the majority. Children of elementary-

The children created their own ornaments and decorated this beautiful Christmas tree in a cooperative way. Each child had a part in the decisions, and each child's ornament was attractively displayed.

116

school age are too immature to foresee that most of them will not
win.   They are so dazzled by the prizes offered and by the power
of the motivation that they concentrate on the awards, and each feels
that he will win if he tries.   Usually being the only one of his age at
home, the child is accustomed to recognition for his achievements.
If a reward or praise is to be the outcome of the accomplishment of
a task, he receives it.   At school the child's successes are emphasized, and, therefore, the motivational pressure of contest prizes for
a few builds false hopes.   It would be much more honest to state to
children that no matter how hard they tried, most of them would be
defeated.   If this factual feature of a contest were made clear and
stressed equally with the rewards for the few winners, much of the
motivational force would be dimmed.

 (e) In a contest, most children are defeated regardless of
the fact that they have followed the prescribed rules and have done
their best work.   They often *lose confidence* in themselves and in
their abilities in art.   Children tend to lose confidence in their
teacher, too (or whoever presents the contest to them), because she
made promises to them of awards for winning, but because of the
nature of contests was forced to withhold prizes from most of them.

 (f) A child *cannot understand why he does not win*.   The
reasons for his not winning are very difficult for the contest judge
or sponsor to explain and much more difficult for the child to accept.
Since the child cannot understand why he lost, he becomes confused.
He is not concerned with the fact that many other children besides
himself also lost but thinks of it only in relation to himself.

 (g) Contests are also inconsistent with the purposes of elementary education.   Elementary-school teachers are anxious to
have every child learn all subjects and to make progress and to feel
successful.   Teachers realize that every child will not learn to the
same extent, make the same progress, or experience the same measure of success.   Neither teachers nor children expect uniformity, yet
teachers strive to have *every child* feel the satisfaction of even a
small amount of success, and they praise each child for his achievements.   For example, Sam has difficulty with reading and cannot
seem to remember words.   Therefore, on the day that he reads with
more fluency and comprehension than he previously has done, the
teacher is pleased and praises him.   She thus gives him recognition
for his achievement even though he is still a slow reader.   His class-

mates are pleased, too.   Children are accustomed to this practice, but are not equipped to deal with the mass failures brought about by contests.

GRADING OF CHILDREN'S ART

A grade, as it applies to art in school, is a symbol used in rating the attainment of a child in that particular art problem or to indicate the quality of his work over a certain period of time.   A grade is usually a number or a letter indicating which one among several degrees of quality or achievement the child has attained.

Grading systems that indicate varying degrees or classifications of excellence separate the work of children into categories or divisions.   This practice suggests that every piece of work within each of the different steps on the rating scale is of the same rank or standard of quality.   This exact categorizing of art is extremely difficult to do.   Since each child was motivated toward originality and individuality in his art, each resulting art product should be different in subject and feeling from the others.   There is, then, no standard or uniformity by which the children's work can be measured.

In art, the work of the child is closely tied up with his feelings, emotions, reactions, ideas, and personal experiences.   The art work that each child creates represents a part of himself.   When children's art is graded, it almost suggests that the personal characteristics of each child are rated, too.   When children begin to feel that their backgrounds, ideas, and feelings are going to be evaluated, compared, and graded, they tend to withdraw from exposing these intimate things.   Such individually distinguishing features are the essence of what makes art interesting, exciting, and expressive. Therefore, whatever discourages children from expressing feelings and emotions in art should be avoided.

Grading of children's art is inconsistent with the use of creative expression as a way of working in art or as a method of teaching art.   Since creative expression gives to every child the opportunity to choose the subject matter for his art, to organize, and to express it in his own way, it implies that the work of each child will be accepted.   The art product that results from every child's serious at-

tempt to solve his art problem should be received by his teacher
with the same warm approval that is given to every other child's
work. The acceptance of every piece of art work emphasizes the
worth and value of *every* child, and if this emphasis is interfered
with, the warm, mutual exchange of confidence between children
and teacher is affected.

Influences of grading. Elementary-school children need to
build their self-confidence, skills, and motor co-ordination before
they are ready to be subjected to such competitive practices as
grading. A feeling of success and confidence is necessary to the
child in order to sustain him through the sensitive years when he is
most actively learning. He does not yet have a resource of power,
which comes from education and skills, to draw on. He needs to
have the support of confidence in order to know his strengths and
limitations and to understand why certain gradings or ratings are

117

*Children come to school with widely varying backgrounds and
abilities, as shown by these selected samples of drawings of people
taken from the work of one group of children during the first week
of school. This is an example of the difficulty of establishing any
basis for grading.*

right for him, requiring much more maturity than children have.

Children, being sensitive, are hurt by a practice that puts them in a position of being rated lower than others. Many things can happen to a child and to his art as a result of grading. The child may form a dislike for art when he receives grades lower than those of some of his classmates and friends. He may copy the approved art work, thus abandoning his own ideas in favor of someone else's. In rejecting his own ideas in favor of another's, he forfeits his chance for developing his inventiveness, creativity, and imagination, as well as for developing his ability to make decisions based on discriminating judgments. In their formative years children should be indoctrinated with ways and means of working and living together and of developing viewpoints and attitudes that contribute to the maintenance and further development of our American way of life.

Grades given in art, as in any school subject, are based on the finished product, thus placing an undue amount of emphasis on the finished art work. The completed work has importance, of course, because it represents the child's ideas, feelings, and per-

118

Hallowe'en inspired this sensitive self-portrait made by a first-grade boy. For someone else to place a grade on it would interfere with Danny's own personal relationship to it.

severance and the process through which it was created.   What happens to the child during the process of creation of art is of primary educational significance because it is during the working process that most of the learning takes place.   Both the end product and the working process are interdependent and important, but grading emphasizes the end product, and when this happens, children are apt to become more concerned with the visual appearance of their art than with the experimenting, the learning of new skills, and the free approach to art.

Parents, too, are influenced by the grading of their children's art.   Parents tend to regard the grade as the total statement of their child's ability in art, his interest in it, the quality of his work according to his ability, and the quality of his work in comparison to his classmates' work.   Actually, what may also enter into the grading are the teacher's personal likes and dislikes in the children's art expression.

Some bases for grading.   Some school systems require teachers to determine grades for each child in the various school subjects at stated intervals during the school term.   They include art among the subjects to be graded, in spite of its special nature.   Creative art does not lend itself to being measured, categorized, or graded. Teachers, faced with this requirement, realize that they will need to devise some standard that can be applied to all children's work. Such a basis is extremely difficult, if at all possible to find, because of the contradiction between creative art and grading.

One standard sometimes used is the amount of improvement shown within a stated period of time.   If samples of a child's art show growth and improvement over a six-week period, he receives a higher grade than a child whose art showed less of an advance. One objection to this viewpoint is that children's art often does not show such a regular chronological pattern of growth.   Because of intense interest in a topic, a high pitch of emotional involvement with it, or other reasons, a child may create a composition of a higher than usual quality of excellence.   Even though he may consistently work hard in art class, his work will probably vary in complexity and art qualities.   Over a long period, a child's work should show general growth in a number of aspects, but it is difficult to measure growth by day-to-day achievements.

Another difficulty with improvement as a standard of measurement is that very often only the flat work is kept for the grading. Three-dimensional work is difficult to store and therefore is seldom kept for long periods. Memories being what they are, scarcely any teacher is able to recall the work of each of her children over a period of time, so that if the three-dimensional work is omitted, the grade is then a partial one.

Children of greater mental capacity will make more progress than their less fortunately endowed classmates. Mental power, then, is being rated, and since children find it difficult to understand or to accept this basis for grading, they can become confused and emotionally upset by it.

Quality in children's art is such a difficult thing to measure that various persons arrive at different grades when attempting to measure it. Any measurement of quality is difficult for children to understand because of their level of maturity. Therefore, adult judgments are imposed on the products of children's thinking and feeling.

Effort is sometimes used as a basis for grading children's art. Teachers, realizing the difficulties in making quality judgments of children's art, rely on the apparent amount of work the child has put forth during the art class. One difficulty with this basis is that so much art work is mental. How can the amount of mental effort be measured or judged? When effort is determined by the child's degree of busyness, time spent in the making of decisions and in contemplation is ignored or negatively evaluated.

Art grades determined by effort alone are misleading. A child whose mental capacity is relatively low will work harder and achieve less than a child whose mental capacity is greater. This means that the slow child, working hard all period and achieving less, may actually receive a higher art grade than the child who achieves more with less effort. The less complex or lesser-quality art may receive the higher grade. When the art grade is based on effort, it is quite possible that a child may receive a high grade in art and low grades in other subjects. The child and his parents may form the false impression that he has art ability, if nothing else. People also get the false impression that children who cannot do the more academic work are successful in art or that artists have less general intelligence than persons in other fields. The opposite, however, is true; art ability is related to general ability. Students who do high-level work in other subjects will probably do so in art.

When grades are given in art, children, wanting to make a good impression, to be successful, and to compare favorably with their classmates, will substitute for their own motives and purposes the basis on which the grades are determined.

Since grading of the art work of elementary-school children is such a difficult thing to do, and since it is incompatible with creative expression as a method of teaching art, it seems evident that children would be freer to grow in art if no grades were given. When grades are given in art, children develop a fear of failure. This fear restricts their freedom.

One school system, where discriminatory grading in art had prevailed for several years, changed the art grading to a nondiscriminatory reporting symbol that indicated that each child had made some achievements in art. Several of the teachers affected by this change felt that when children were no longer motivated by grading, they would no longer put forth their maximum effort in art. The teachers regarded grades as motivation, feeling that children needed the threat of low grades to stimulate their work. The children were happy about the change and worked at least as diligently as and much more freely than before. The quality of their art work actually improved when the fear of failure was removed. Teacher time previously spent in grading art work could be spent on instruction and motivation, which were other reasons for the improvement of the children's work.

The words "satisfactory" and "unsatisfactory" are used to some extent in reporting children's progress in art. In this case, children whose art products appear to have some acceptable quality are rated as satisfactory, the others as unsatisfactory. The word "satisfactory" conveys the impression of work that is mediocre or merely acceptable. When a child receives the highest grades in his other work, the "satisfactory" rating that he receives in art seems not to measure to other grades. The word "successful" would have a better effect upon children. The use of the opposite of these words is closely connected with failure, which is of no encouragement or help to children.

119

The time and apparent effort a child puts into his art
are poor bases for grading.   One child paints a tree
quickly, another works slowly; both trees have quality.

120

Suggested activity

To see for yourself how difficult it is accurately to categorize the art work of children and to see how inconsistent the judgments of different adults become when faced with the task of grading art, separate the creative art products made by a group of children into four levels of excellence. Record the results of your selections. Put this first listing out of sight. Mix the art work so that you leave it in no particular sequence. A week later reclassify the work and record your selections in each level of grading. Compare your two listings to see if you may have changed your decisions about any of the work.

Ask one or two other adults whose tastes or points of view may be different from yours to rate the art work. Compare their findings with your own to see if they made any decisions about the grading of any of the art work that are different from yours.

Bibliography

Alschuler, Rose H., and LaBerta W. Hattwick, *A Study of Painting and Personality of Young Children.* Chicago: University of Chicago Press, 1947, 2 vols.

Bannon, Laura, *Mind Your Child's Art.* New York: Pelligrini and Cudahy, 1952.

Barkan, Manuel, *A Foundation for Art Education.* New York: The Ronald Press Company, 1955.

Bartlett, Francis G., and Claude C. Crawford, *Art for All.* New York: Harper & Brothers, 1942.

Browne, Sybil, "Beginning Art Teachers Appraise Themselves," *Art Education*, November 1954.

Cane, Florence, *The Artist in Each of Us.* New York: Pantheon Books, Inc., 1951.

Cizek, Franz, *Children's Colored Paper Work.* New York: G. E. Stechert & Co., 1927.

Clannon, Edward, *Making Your Own Materials.* New York: Museum of Modern Art, Committee on Art in American Education, 1943.

Cole, Natalie Robinson, *The Arts in the Classroom.* New York: The John Day Co., 1940.

Cox, Doris, and Barbara W. Weisman, *Creative Hands.* New York: John Wiley & Sons, Inc., 1945.

D'Amico, Victor, *Creative Teaching in Art.* Scranton, Pa.: International Textbook Co., 1953.

D'Amico, Victor, and Frances Wilson, *Art for the Family.* New York: Museum of Modern Art, 1956.

de Francesco, Italo L., *Art Education — Its Means and Ends.* New York: Harper & Brothers, 1958.

Department of Fine and Industrial Arts, Teachers College, *Art Education Today* (1948 edition). New York: Bureau of Publications, Teachers College, Columbia University, annual publication.

Dewey, John, *Art as Experience.* New York: Minton, Balco & Co., 1934.

———, "Foreword," in *The Unfolding of Artistic Activity,* by Henry Schaefer-Simmern. Berkeley: University of California Press, 1948.

Duncan, Hamlin J., and Victor D'Amico, *How to Make Pottery and Ceramic Sculpture.* New York: Museum of Modern Art, 1949.

Eastern Arts Association, *Art: The Balance Wheel in Education,* 1948 Yearbook. Kutztown, Pa.: State Teachers College, 1948.

———, *Art in General Education,* 1949 Yearbook. Kutztown, Pa.: State Teachers College, 1949.

———, *Integrative Function of Art Education,* 1950 Yearbook. Kutztown, Pa.: State Teachers College, 1949.

———, *Sources and Resources for Art Education,* 1954 Yearbook. Kutztown, Pa.: State Teachers College, 1954.

Emerson, Sybil, *Design, A Creative Approach.* Scranton, Pa.: International Textbook Co., 1953.

Erdt, Margaret, *Teaching Art in the Elementary School.* New York: Rinehart & Company, Inc., 1953.

Faulkner, Ray, Edwin Ziegfeld, and Gerald Hill, *Art Today.* New York: Henry Holt & Co., Inc., 1941.

Gaitskell, Charles, *Art Education for Slow Learners.* Peoria, Ill.: Chas. A. Bennett Co., Inc., 1953.

———, *Children and Their Pictures.* Toronto: Ryerson Press, 1951.

Gaitskell, Charles, and Margaret Gaitskell, *Art Education in the Kindergarten.* Toronto: Ryerson Press, 1952.

Gesell, Arnold L., and Frances L. Ilg, *The Infant and Child in the Culture of Today.* New York: Harper & Brothers, 1943.

Ghiselin, Brewster, *The Creative Process.* Berkeley: University of California Press, 1952.

Goodenough, F. L., "Children's Drawings," *A Handbook of Child Psychology.* Worcester, Mass.: Clark University Press, 1931.

———, "Studies in the Psychology of Children's Drawings," *Psychol. Bul.,* May 1928.

Gotshalk, D. W., *Art and the Social Order.* Chicago: University of Chicago Press, 1947, Chapters IX and X.

Gregg, Harold, *Art for the Schools of America.* Scranton, Pa.: International Textbook Co., 1941.

Haggerty, Melvin E., *Art — A Way of Life.* Minneapolis: University of Minnesota Press, 1935.

Harrison, Elizabeth, *Self Expression through Art.* Scarborough, Ont.: W. J. Gage, Ltd., 1951.

Hartman, B., and A. Shumaker, eds., *Creative Expression: The Development of Children in Art, Music, Literature, and Dramatics.* New York: The John Day Co., 1932.

Hayakawa, Samuel I., "The Revision of Vision," in *Language of Vision,* by Gyorgy Kepes. Chicago: Paul Theobald, 1944.

Holy Bible, I Corinthians, 13th Chapter, 11th verse, Rev. Stand. Ed. New York: Thomas Nelson & Sons, 1953.

Hoover, F. Louis, "Improving the Education of Art Teachers," *Art Education,* April 1950.

———, "Who Are the Teachers of Art?" *Art Education,* February 1949.

Hopkins, L. Thomas, *Integration, Its Meaning and Application.* New York: Appleton-Century-Crofts, Inc., 1937.

Hurlock, E. B., and J. L. Thomson, "Children's Drawings: An Experimental Study of Perception," *Child Development,* June 1934.

Jefferson, Blanche W., *Art Experiences in the Primary Grades: A Presentation through Color Transparencies with Accompanying Script.* Project, Ed.D., Teachers College, Columbia University, 1954.

Kainz, Louise, and Olive Riley, *Exploring Art.* New York: Harcourt, Brace & Co., 1951, Chapter I.

Keiler, Manfred L., *Art in the Classroom.* Lincoln, Neb.: University of Nebraska Press, 1951.

Kennedy, D., M. Bradley, L. Fitzgerald, N. Smith, and S. Joyner, "What It Means to Be Creative," *Art Education,* Vol. 8, No. 7.

Kepes, Gyorgy, *Language of Vision.* Chicago: Paul Theobald, 1944.

Krauss, Ruth, *A Hole Is to Dig.* New York: Harper & Brothers, 1952.

Kundis, Lawrence E., "Teacher Training Programs in Art Education," *Art Education,* November 1954.

Landis, Mildred M., *Meaningful Art Education*. Peoria, Ill.: Chas. A. Bennett Co., Inc., 1951.

Larkin, Oliver W., *Art and Life in America*. New York: Rinehart & Company, Inc., 1949.

Little, Sidney W., "No Grade," *Art Education*, October 1949.

Logan, Frederick M., *Growth of Art in American Schools*. New York: Harper & Brothers, 1954, Chapter VIII.

Lowenfeld, Viktor, *The Nature of Creative Activity*. London: Kegan Paul, Trench, Trubner & Co., Ltd., 1952.

———, *Your Child and His Art*. New York: The Macmillan Co., 1954.

———, *Creative and Mental Growth* (third edition). New York: The Macmillan Co., 1957.

Lynch, John, *How to Make Mobiles*. New York and London: Studio Publications in association with Thomas Y. Crowell Company, 1953.

Maul, Ray C., "Art Teachers for the Future," *Art Education*, May 1954.

McVittey, Lawrence, "An Experimental Study on Various Methods in Art Motivation at the Fifth-Grade Level." Doctoral dissertation, Pennsylvania State University, 1954.

Mendelowitz, Daniel M., *Children Are Artists*. Stanford, Cal.: Stanford University Press, 1954, Chapter I.

Moholy-Nagy, Laszlo, *The New Vision*. New York: George Wittenborn, Inc., 1947.

———, *Vision in Motion*. Chicago: Paul Theobald, 1947.

Mumford, Lewis, *Art and Technics*. New York: Columbia University Press, 1952.

Munro, Thomas, "Franz Cizek and the Free Expression Method" and "A Constructive Program for Teaching Art," *Art and Education*. Merion, Pa.: Barnes Foundation Press, 1929.

National Society for the Study of Education, *Art in American Life and Education, Fortieth Yearbook*. Bloomington, Ill.: Public School Publishing Co., 1941.

Nicholas, F. W., D. Mayhood, and B. Trilling, *Art Activities in the Modern School*. New York: The Macmillan Co., 1937.

Parkhurst, Helen, "Creating with One's Hands" (a recording). New London, Conn.: Alpark Records, distributed by Arthur C. Croft Publications.

Pearson, Ralph, *The New Art Education*. New York: Harper & Brothers, 1953.

Poore, H. R., *Art's Place in Education*. New York: G. P. Putnam's Sons, 1937.

Purcell, Virginia, "Art Is a Personal Matter," *Art Education*, February 1957.

Read, Herbert, *Education Through Art* (second edition). New York: Pantheon Books, Inc., 1945, Chapters I and II.

———, "Education Through Art — A Revolutionary Policy," *Art Education*, November 1955.

———, *Grass Roots of Art.* New York: George Wittenborn, Inc., 1947.

Robertson, Seonaid, *Creative Crafts in Education.* Cambridge, Mass.: Robert Bentley, Inc., 1953.

Rugg, Harold, and Marian Brooks, *The Teacher in School and Society.* New York: World Book Co., 1953, Chapters I, III, XV, XVII.

Russel, Irene, and Blanche Waugaman, "A Study of the Effect of Workbook Copy Experiences on the Creative Concepts of Children," *Research Bulletin.* Kutztown, Pa.: Eastern Arts Association, Vol. 3, No. 1, April 1952.

Russell, David, *Children's Thinking.* Boston: Ginn & Company, 1956.

Schaefer-Simmern, H., *The Unfolding of Artistic Activity.* Berkeley: University of California Press, 1948.

Shultz, Harold, and Arlan Shores, *Art in the Elementary School.* Urbana: University of Illinois Press, 1948, Chapter II.

Strang, Ruth, *The Role of the Teacher in Personnel Work.* New York: Bureau of Publications, Teachers College, Columbia University, 1946.

Sweeney, James Johnson, *Alexander Calder.* New York: Museum of Modern Art, 1941.

Viola, Wilhelm, *Child Art and Frank Cizek.* New York: Reynal & Company, Inc., 1936.

Wankelman, Willard, Karl Richard, and Maretta Wigg, *Arts and Crafts for Teachers.* Dubuque, Ia.: William C. Brown Company, 1954.

Wickiser, Ralph L., *An Introduction to Art Activities.* New York: Henry Holt & Co., Inc., 1947.

Winslow, Leon L., *The Integrated School Art Program.* New York: McGraw-Hill Book Co., 1949, Chapter I.

Ziegfeld, Edwin, ed., *Education and Art: A Symposium.* Paris: UNESCO, 1953, Section I.

Ziegfeld, Ernest, ed., "Human Values in a Democracy," in *Art and Human Values*, 1953 Yearbook. Kutztown, Pa.: National Art Education Association, 1953, Chapters I and IV.

Index